No 199

£1

D1492528

WALKS IN AND AROUND JERUSALEM

WALKS IN AND AROUND JERUSALEM.

BY THE REV.

J. E. HANAUER,

Honorary Canon of St. George's Cathedral, Jerusalem.
Author of " Tales told in Palestine," " Folk-lore of the
Holy Land," etc., etc.

" That ye may tell it to the generation following."
Psalm xlviii. 18.

Second and Revised Edition.

CHURCH MISSIONS TO JEWS.
London Society for Promoting Christianity amongst the Jews.

PUBLISHED AT THE SOCIETY'S HOUSE,
16, LINCOLN'S INN FIELDS, LONDON, W.C., ENGLAND.
A.D. 1926.

Printed in the City of London by
M. LOWNDS & SON, Printers and Stationers,
Heneage Lane, Leadenhall Street, E.C. 3.

ERRATA.

Title Page.—Text. Psalm xlviii. *18* should be 13.

Page 49.—Line 2 from top. *Golnbooricz* should read
"Golubowicz."

„ 55.—Line 9. Illustration [*36*] should be [35].

„ 56.—Illustration [36] is printed upside down.

„ 209.—Illustration [125]. *Exterior* should read "West
end of crypt."

„ 237.—Line 9 from bottom of page. [*139*] should
be [138].

„ 297.—Illustration [167]. *With El Kas in foreground*
should be omitted.

„ 340.—Paragraph 2. *Tantoor Pharaoh* should read
"Tantoor Pharaon."

„ 342.—Line 2 from top. *Locali* should read "loculi."

INTRODUCTION.

N OT without a sense of temerity, do I accede to the
request of my good friend, the Rev. Canon Hanauer,
that I should write a preface to this new edition of
his work on Jerusalem. Few men can know Jerusalem
better than Canon Hanauer ; in comparison with his
knowledge, my own is but scanty and superficial, as I have
had occasion to realise times without number during the
years in which I have been privileged to hold personal
intercourse with him. He has accumulated a vast store of
information regarding the buildings of the city and their
multifarious traditions. He has lived on terms of familiarity
with members of all classes of its complex community, and
he has stored in the treasures of his memory a wealth of
lore, garnered from every available source.

To walk around Jerusalem in the company of Canon
Hanauer is an inspiration, though at the same time the
disciple cannot but feel discouraged by the unattainable
standard set by the master. Those who read this book will
catch something of the inspiration, and rather less of the
discouragement. It would have been impossible for
Canon Hanauer to include everything that he would tell a
companion on one of these walks ; the book would have
grown almost to the size of an Encyclopædia ! In an
actual walk in the company of Canon Hanauer, almost
every stone that possesses any individuality at all becomes
the centre of an interesting story.

In his youth Canon Hanauer assisted General Sir Charles, then Lieutenant, Warren, when he made the first serious attempt to open out the secrets of underground Jerusalem. Nearly sixty years later, he followed with close attention the excavations carried out at the Holy City by the Palestine Exploration Fund. Between these two widely separated dates, he has been in close touch with all the explorers who have worked in the city from time to time, and he has taken every opportunity of making himself familiar with their results. The recovery of ancient Jerusalem, so far as it has been carried down to the present time, has thus taken place under his eyes. At the same time he has followed the development of modern Jerusalem. In the book before the reader he tells of the city of his earliest recollections, confined within walls whose gates were closed inexorably every day at sunset. He has lived to see it bursting those boundaries, and spreading tentacles far and wide over the neighbouring hills.

Even in my own short experience of Jerusalem, I have seen many changes, not always for the best. I arrived in the city just in time to see the Jaffa Gate as it was, before the great breach was made in the wall at its side in order that the German Emperor might enter in a manner befitting his dignity. I was just in time to see the graceful balustrades in the Haram, and the impressive façade of the Aksa Mosque, before painted decorations of nightmare hideousness had been added to them, to make them the more acceptable in the same Imperial eyes. The breaching of the wall was a symbol and a portent, little though we suspected it at the time. It typified the opening up of the city to western influences which have been pressing upon it ever since, with an intensity and with visible consequences that increase every year. All wheeled traffic now enters the city through the breached wall : when I entered it first, in the autumn of 1898, my carriage was obliged to make use of the narrow and dangerous right-angled passage through the Jaffa Gate itself.

When last I walked through the gate, in the spring of 1924, a huckster had established his stall under its shelter. Among the goods which he was offering for sale I noticed an Arabic translation of *Tarzan of the Apes*. Thus is Europe holding out a helping hand to the East, and sharing with her the blessings that she herself enjoys!

There are many interesting facts set forth in this book which it would be difficult to find elsewhere in a convenient form. As an example, I see on an early page a notice of the mud shower of 1857, and of its permanent effect on the appearance of the city. Though I have read a considerable number of books on Jerusalem, I do not recall having found a record of this event anywhere else.

I may add that it is a pleasure to find for once a book on Jerusalem that avoids controversial subjects. The reader may feel the unwonted security of solid ground under his feet practically all the time. If I qualify the absoluteness of this statement by the word " practically," it is because no two people can possibly agree upon *every* detail of Jerusalem history and topography, and there are one or two points upon which theories, that differ to some extent from those held by Canon Hanauer, make a greater appeal to myself. But such friendly divergencies— of which there are very few indeed—have been but the spice that have added to the enjoyment with which I have re-perused the book, and to the unqualified pleasure with which I now pen this, very superfluous, commendation.

R. A. S. MACALISTER.

Dublin,
    20th November, 1926.

NOTE BY THE AUTHOR.

I DESIRE to express my gratitude first of all, to the numerous friends who, verbally and in writing, have expressed their kind appreciation of the first edition of "Walks about Jerusalem," and thus encouraged me to put forth the present revised and enlarged Second Edition of the book.

I also wish to acknowledge my indebtedness to Miss Blyth, Messrs. F. Vester & Co., of the American Colony, C. Raad, Esq., C. A. Hornstein, Esq., the White Fathers at St. Anne's, and others who have kindly allowed the use of their photographs as illustrations. And lastly, but by no means least, I am deeply grateful to Mr. H. J. Bentall, at Headquarters of the Society in London, who, with infinite patience and care, has not only seen the work through the press, but has also given invaluable help with the classified Indexes to the book.

J. E. HANAUER.

JERUSALEM,
November, 1926.

NOTE—For the sake of brevity and easy reference, the *London Society for Promoting Christianity amongst the Jews* has always been known and referred to in Palestine as the *London Jews Society*. Therefore this shortened title is used throughout the work when mentioning the Society.

Index of Illustrations.

INDEX OF ILLUSTRATIONS.

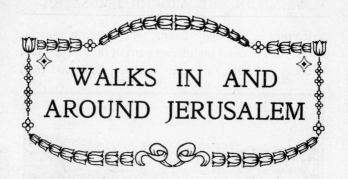

WALKS IN AND AROUND JERUSALEM

THIS book is intended as a guide to those who desire to learn something about the sites and scenes of Jerusalem, but have no chance of beholding them except in pictures.

Let us therefore suppose that—under the wing of one of the Tourist Agencies, which in modern times practically do the work, *minus* fighting the Saracens, for which the famous monastic and military order of Knights Templars was established in *A.D.* 1118—we have safely reached the little railway station, after a journey from Jaffa taking three and a half hours as against ten to twelve hours in past days. The station is south-west of the old city, and close to the neat colony occupied by the members of the *German Temple*. This is not a monkish brotherhood, but an ultra-Protestant sect, which made Palestine its Headquarters about the middle of the Nineteenth century and professed as its object a desire to build up the Kingdom of God by introducing trade and improving agriculture in the Holy Land. There are, at present, several such colonies in different parts of the country and, speaking generally, they have done so much good that,

[1] First glimpse of Jerusalem, showing Jewish settlements in Upper Valley of Hinnom. [Photo—American Colony]

although the colonists were interned in Egypt during the Great War, yet, when peace had been established, the British authorities considered it expedient to allow them to return to their homes and work.

As we leave the station and reach the great road to Bethlehem, there suddenly spreads out before us a wide panorama. Beginning with the Hill of Evil Counsel on our right, the eye ranges, as it gradually turns toward the left, over the Moab hills, Olivet and Scopus, with Gethsemane and Siloam nestling at their feet, to the great dark greyish blue domes of the buildings inside the Temple-Area, and further Westwards, the stately pile of the Dormition Church, with Bishop Gobat's School on the summit and slope of Mount Zion, *outside* the long line of tawny wall and towers that form the southern limit of the city.

[2] Approach to City.   [*Photo—Edelstein*]

Here it may be as well to call attention to the fact that all the exposed Southern and Eastern faces of the fortifications and older buildings are of a dull ochre colour, which was caused by a remarkable shower of yellow mud that fell early in February, 1857 "plastering the houses from top to bottom " (*Jewish Intelligence, July* 1857, *p.* 221), the traces of which the rains of seventy winters have not yet washed away. The eminent naturalist, Professor Roth, of Munich, who was in Jerusalem at the time, examined this mud and found it to consist in part of minute shells peculiar to the peninsula of Sinai. The deposit remains on the " *Kakouli*," or soft lower limestone, but not on the hard reddish and grey "*Mizzie*" or upper Hippurite limestone.

The northern and western faces of buildings become blackish-grey wherever exposed to rain and damp.

Descending into the Valley of Hinnom the carriage road crosses to its eastern side and runs along the length of the large and ancient pool, called by the natives, "Birket Es Sultan," but known traditionally, though erroneously, as the lower Pool of Gihon. High above us, against the sky line runs the western city wall, the two towers of which are called for reasons unknown, the "Ghazza Towers," and just ahead, the imposing Western and Southern towers of the Citadel with a minaret on their highest point [3].

In the valley bed just north of the great pool, and also on the slope of the hill to the west of it, are Jewish

[3] Western Tower of Citadel.   [*Photo—Edelstein*

settlements which have sprung into existence since 1856 [1]. Before that date the valley bed contained an olive grove and prickly pear hedges, and the hillside was bare and waste.

As we approach the Jaffa Gate [4], which is the principal entrance to the City, it may be of interest to recall the most remarkable change which has taken place in the immediate surroundings since I first knew it over Seventy years ago. It was a time of general trouble and unrest throughout the World—the time of the Crimean war and the Indian Mutiny, and the massacres in the Lebanon. There were then no houses outside the City walls, except the " Neby Daoud " block outside the Zion Gate and Bishop Gobat's School, then in building, and a small house on Consul Finn's plantation. The desert country reached on every side right up to the town walls. One was in the open country as soon as one emerged from the gates, which were closed at Sunset, and also on Fridays, from Eleven o'clock in the forenoon till One in the afternoon, during the time that the garrison were at their weekly prayers in the mosque. During that time no one could either enter or leave the City unless provided with a special permit, not always obtainable, from the Pasha.

On several occasions about 1867, when serving on the staff of the excavations and exploration party led by Sir Charles Warren I was compelled to have myself lowered by a rope over the City wall close to the Haram, in order to be at my appointed post outside. At this time there was no traffic of any kind at the various Gates. A Turkish soldier, armed with a Minié rifle and sword bayonet, stood there on guard, and in the deep alcoves, now used as stalls for the sale of soda water, iced drinks and fruit, cooked food, etc., there stood racks on which rows of rifles were ranged. The roadway was unpaved. In the rainy season there was a " slough of despond " just outside the gateway, and in the open space just within the City, a pond about a foot deep in the centre, but which might be passed, if you used the small and slippery stepping stones which a Municipality regardful of public comfort, had placed for a couple of yards or so along the northern edge ! In Summer, the bed of the little lake became a receptacle for all sorts of filth, and not infrequently the rotting carcases of dogs, cats and smaller animals.

A change for the better came soon after the accession of Sultan Abdul Aziz, in whose time the roadway was paved by gangs of prisoners brought from the common gaol, and made to work in chains. This was in the year 1864, about the same time that the first line of telegraph was laid, and the first petroleum oil and lamps for its use were imported, as well as the first steam engine set up in the Holy City. Clocks were first introduced in 1846. Since then other European innovations, not in every case improvements, have gradually come in and especially so during more recent years, until to-day Jerusalem has developed almost into what is known as a "modern" city.

Up till 1898 the Jaffa Gate [4] was connected with the Citadel by a low crenellated wall crossing the ditch surrounding the latter. When, however, preparations were made for the reception of the then German Emperor, William II., this part of the great trench was

[4] The Jaffa Gate. [*Photo—Edelstein*]

filled up, and the wall lowered. There is now an imposing entrance to the City between the Jaffa Gate Tower and the north-western tower of the citadel and the " Grand New Hotel," just inside the Jaffa Gate [6]. The latter is the only gate in the western wall of Jerusalem and that which has most traffic. Though fairly modern, having been built at the time the present walls were erected by Suleiman the Magnificent, it doubtless stands on the site of an ancient city gate, in all probability on that by which, in our Lord's days, an aqueduct conveyed water into Herod's great Citadel

Palace close by. Though called the " Jaffa Gate " by Europeans, its present name amongst the natives is " Bab ul Khalil," or " the Gate of the Friend," *i.e.,* Abraham, the reason being that the road to Hebron starts from here. An ornamental Arabic inscription facing us as we enter, reminds us that "There is no God but Allah, and that Ibrahim is his friend." Three other inscriptions record Suleiman's name and titles and the actual date of the building *A.H.* 945—*A.D.* 1538-9. The clock tower [5] now removed from the gate tower, was put up in honour of the jubilee of the late infamous Turkish Sultan Abdul Hamid.

[5] Clock Tower at entrance between City and Jaffa Gate. [*Photo—Edelstein*

By Arab writers before the Sixteenth century, the gate at this spot is sometimes called " Bab el Mihrab," from the " Mihrab Daoud," or " Oratory of David," shown

in the adjacent castle, and sometimes "Bab Lydd,"
i.e., "the Gate of Lydda." This is because the road
to that place starts from this point, and also because
some Moslem theologians believe that the Gate of
Lydda, where, according to the eschatology of Islam,
the Messih el Dejjal, or Antichrist, will be defeated
and slain by our Lord, is the western gate of Jerusalem.
Others, learned in the faith of Mohammed, assert that
the great event will take place at Lydda itself, and
mention, as the actual spot, the famous Bir es Zaybac,
or "Quicksilver Well," inside the little building, under
the great sycamore, half-way between Ramleh and Lydda.

[6] Entrance between Jaffa Gate tower and Citadel—Clock tower
removed. *[Photo—Edelstein*

CHAPTER II.

MONGST the scores of traditional or doubtfully historical sites pointed out within the walls of Jerusalem, there are at any rate three, which are really interesting, even though in the case of only two of them, viz., the Citadel and the Temple area, Archaeologists are agreed that they really occupy the historic ground they represent. I propose on this occasion to speak of the first of these two, leaving the Haram and the famed Church of the Holy Sepulchre to be described in later chapters.

The Citadel, also called the Tower of David [7] though that name is often used in a restricted manner to designate the remarkable and ancient structure at its present north-east corner, is situated south of the Jaffa Gate from which it was, before the visit of the German Emperor in 1898, separated by a deep fosse. This was purposely filled up at this point, in order to furnish a more imposing approach to the interior of the City, than that through the Jaffa Gate. The Citadel, known in Crusading times as the Castle of the Pisans, consists of three principal towers connected by a massive crenellated wall. Just below the crenellations there are quadrangular holes or sockets, evidently intended to bear the supports of an exterior scaffold, or balcony, from which missiles, boiling oil, etc., might be poured on assailants. Similar holes are to be seen in other fortifications of the

[7] Tower of David.   [*Photo—American Colony*

same period in Europe, for example, at Carcassone in the Pyrenees. The walls of the Citadel are loopholed for musketry. Since the British occupation of Jerusalem several of the loop holes have been enlarged so as to form proper windows to apartments which, after repairs, are utilised as a Museum of Palestinian crafts and industries.

At different points, especially on the eastern and western fronts, the castle wall is strengthened with a glacis or sloping work rising from the bottom of the trench, part of which is undoubtedly ancient Roman masonry, dating back to New Testament times. All authorities are agreed that this fortress, the interior of which is in ruins, occupies the site of the palace castle of Herod the Great, or at any rate, part of that site.

Just inside the gateway passage a beautifully carved sarcophagus of the Roman period [8] and found at Turmus Aya, arrests the attention of visitors. The sculpture shows a group of pagan deities, etc.

Herod's palace-fortress was remarkable for its three great towers named Phasaelus, Hippicus and Mariamne, and it is believed that the two towers standing one at the North-west, and the other at the North-east corner of the Citadel [9] mark the exact position of the two first-named. Though the tower at the north-east angle is popularly called Hippicus by local guides, it corresponds in its general plan-measurements with the description given by Josephus of the Phasaelus. It would follow that the tower just south of the Jaffa Gate, stands on the site of Hippicus, it having been found by the English Royal Engineers who had charge of the first Ordnance Survey in 1841, that its plan-measurements tally with those that belonged to Hippicus. Connected with Herod's great structures in this part of Jerusalem as it was in the time of our Lord, there were extensive pleasure grounds, which spread over the tract now occupied by Christ Church and various mission premises of the London Jews Society and the present Armenian quarter. As a matter of fact, it is not at all unlikely

[8] Entrance-passage to Citadel showing Sarcophagus.   [*Photo by Author*

that the stately pine trees which are scattered about over the open plots of ground we meet with here and there in this neighbourhood, may be the direct descendants of seedlings from the gardens of Herod. The depth of debris hereabouts is very considerable.

Good views over the City eastward and its surroundings southward and westward can be obtained from the gallery or balcony of the minaret on the southern tower of the castle.

[9] Tower of David and entrance to Citadel.

[*Photo—C. Raad, Jerusalem*

When the foundations of Christ Church were laid, the workmen were obliged to dig to the depth of forty feet before they struck rock.   When they did at last find

14

it, they came across a very remarkable underground passage, probably intended as a conduit for water. Some authorities have suggested that this may be the aqueduct in which, according to Josephus (*B. J. ii.* 17 § 9) Ananias, the high priest, the same man who, whilst presiding at the trial of St. Paul by the Sanhedrin (*Acts xxiii.,* 2), illegally ordered the Apostle to be scourged—hid himself from the robbers, who, however, eventually found and murdered him.

At the entrance to Christ Church premises are the shafts of two large granite columns which were dug up during these excavations and must originally have been brought from Egypt in order to adorn Herod's buildings hereabouts. Another column, and also a large catapult-ball, are preserved in the Mission buildings close by, whilst, during excavations in the Mohammedan premises just south of these, the remains of a beautiful chamber, constructed altogether of marble, were found at a considerable depth below the present surface. A very beautiful mosaic pavement was also recently discovered.

The lower part of the traditional Hippicus is constructed of great blocks of drafted stone, and has been ascertained to be quite solid right through. On the top of this there is a large chamber of mediaeval times, which is provided with a Mihrab or Mohammedan prayer-niche in its southern wall, showing that the apartment was at one time a mosque. This niche indicates the direction in which Mecca lies, and towards this Moslems must turn their faces when at prayer.

Immediately opposite the eastern front of the Castle are situated, counting from the north southwards, Cook's office, various other places of business, and Christ Church premises.   Christ Church, consecrated in 1849, boasts of being the first Anglican Church building erected in the Turkish Empire [10-12].   It

[10] Christ Church and L.J.S. Mission premises in 1860.
[Photo from old print.

is a Gothic structure capable of seating some three hundred worshippers, and is much frequented by English Church people who appreciate the quiet and reverent services held there.   It is the centre of the work of the London Jews Society, and connected with it are a Boys' Boarding School, a Girls' Day School, Workshops and a fine Hospital. The latter institution is, like the Boys' School, situated outside, and about a mile distant to the North-west of the City. Patients of all religions and nationalities are thankful to avail themselves of the advantages it offers, and, as its Registers show, many thousands of out-patients are prescribed for annually.

[11] Christ Church and surroundings to-day. *[Photo by Author*

South of the Christ Church premises and reaching as far as the city wall, are various buildings connected chiefly with the great Armenian convent of St. James, the son of Zebedee, the first Apostolic martyr, the burial place of whose head is shown in a shrine, the doors of which are richly inlaid with tortoiseshell and nacre. The very chair used by the Apostle is also shown ; and as a great favour, and to specially distinguished visitors, some of the interesting objects, preserved in the treasury of the convent, and consisting of ancient vestments, mitres and valuable copies of the Armenian liturgies and gospels, and the amber sceptre of the Armenian king Hetum, &c., are exhibited by special permission of the Patriarch.

[12] Interior of Christ Church.
[*Photo by Author*

In the central hall of the college there is also an interesting collection of objects from various countries, whilst on the wall of the great reception room of the Patriarch there hang good pictures of various European monarchs and also replicas made by one of his predecessors, of the beautiful "Shield of Hamza" [13] which, a quarter of a century ago, was still to be seen in the Dome of the Rock, but has now mysteriously disappeared from there. Hamza was the uncle of Mohammed (*Sale's " Koran " footnotes to pp. 45, 206. Chandos' Classic edition*). The beautiful object traditionally called his Shield was in reality an ancient Chinese mirror and is interesting as a proof of the varied and extensive commercial traffic between Palestine and Eastern Asia during the Middle Ages. This, at any rate, is what Sir Charles Wilson says of it on the authority of the British Museum. I must, however, confess that, with all due respect for these high authorities, I am rather inclined to think it Persian art.

[13] Shield of Hamza. *[Photo by Author*

The convent, originally founded by the Georgians in the Eleventh century, was sold by them to the Armenians Four hundred years later. It can, it is said, accommodate from three to four thousand pilgrims, and contains a printing press. At the time of writing, the convent shelters several hundred Armenian children orphaned during the Great War and after. These orphans are being supported by the American " Near East Relief Society " and the " Armenian Benevolent Association."

CHAPTER III.

THE church of the Armenian Convent contains the traditional grave of St. James, and over the grave, what is pointed out to be his episcopal chair. Just beside it, on the right, is the episcopal chair of the Armenian Patriarch, and a few paces distant from these two chairs, there is to be seen in the north wall of the church, the shrine of St. James with doors richly inlaid with mother-of-pearl and tortoise-shell, where the head of St. James is said to have been buried [15].

On the walls there hang quaint and grim old fresco-paintings representing the sufferings of martyrs, the last judgment, and also pictures of various saints.

In the porch of this church are two curious and interesting gongs hanging in the South-eastern corner [14], one of them is a plank of some hard wood suspended by ropes at either end, the other a long and thick plate of iron hung in the same way at the end of chains. Similar gongs are to be found in other Eastern monasteries. They are called " nakus " (*plural* " *nawakis* ") and serve to call to mind one of the terms of the treaty made with the Christians, when, in *A.D.* 637, Jerusalem surrendered to the Khalifeh Omar bin El Khattab (*see footnote*). The stipulation in question was that the Christians were not to be allowed the use of bells on their churches, but might use these gongs. This regulation was strictly re-in-forced when the Crusaders were expelled by Salah-ud-din in 1187. In 1823 the only bell in Jerusalem is said to have been a hand-bell in the Franciscan convent. Since the fall of Acre, in 1840, how-ever, Christians have had more freedom, and it is probable that the old bell of Christ Church was one of the first amongst the many introduced in modern times.

[14] Gongs in porch of Convent of St. James.
[*Photo—C. Raad, Jerusalem*

Before leaving the porch we notice a number of grotesque little faces painted here and there in the colouring on the walls.

The Moslem tradition is that God commanded Noah to use such a gong in order to call together the workmen building the ark, therefore gongs are permissible.

'At the entrance to the convent is the drinking-fountain erected to commemorate the 25th anniversary of the accession to the throne of Turkey of the late Sultan Abd ul Hamid. Closely connected with the convent of St. James is the Armenian nunnery of Ez Zeituny, or

[15] Shrine of St. James in Church of the Armenian Convent.
[*Photo—American Colony*

" the olive-tree," so called because a tree in the court-yard is said to be the very plant to which our Lord was tied whilst His persecutors were deliberating as to His fate ! The mediæval church in this nunnery, which is said by tradition to stand on the site of the house of the high-priest Annas, contains the usual ornamentation of encaustic tiles and paintings. These encaustic tiles as well as those in the large Church of St. James are said to have been brought from Spain (*P. Barnabas' Meistermann's Guide, page* 119). It is remarkable for the number of crosses—over thirty have been noted—of different shapes, to be seen on the walls. Close to the olive-tree a stone forming part of the corner of a building is pointed out to the visitor, who must, for politeness sake, control his features and forbear from laughing whilst the abbess gravely relates that, when the high priest found fault with the Saviour for not silencing the children in the Temple crying " Hosanna," and He told them that if the little ones held their peace the stones would cry out, this miracle really happened. The stone here shewn, " burst into a melodious ' Hosanna ' as soon as the children were silent." Another stone, " which would have cried out," is to be seen in a different part of the city, in a side-lane opening into the Via Dolorosa. It is quite black and greasy with the kisses of pilgrims.

We retrace our steps and leave the great convent of St. James by its western portal, which opens into a large clear square [16 and 17], much over-shadowed by some of the ancient and magnificent pine-trees descended from ancestors in the gardens of the palace of Herod.

Turning northward we follow the first lane to the right. After passing the ruin of the mediæval Syrian Church of St. Thomas, a tortuous route, leading in a general north-easterly direction, brings us first to the Syrian convent, recently rebuilt, because of the damage it sustained as a result of a severe earthquake some years ago.

[16]   Square in front of Armenian Convent of St. James.
[Photo—C. A. Hornstein

This convent is believed to stand on the site of the house of Mary the mother of Mark (*Acts xii.* 1, 15). The church or chapel is mediæval, resembling in plan that of St. James the son of Alphæus, close to Christ Church, and that of " the prison of Christ " in the traditional

" house of Caiaphas," just outside the Zion Gate. With it are connected a number of traditionary relics, such as a picture of the Virgin Mary, painted by St. Luke, the font in which the Virgin was baptized, and the door at

[17] Entrance to the Armenian Convent of St. James.

[*Photo—American Colony*

which St. Peter knocked after the angel had delivered him from prison. It is pitiful to see how pilgrims believe that all these things are genuine. Just opposite the entrance to this convent which is the only one belonging to the Jacobite Syrians in Jerusalem, are the old houses which used to be occupied by the Hospital of the London Jews Society before it was removed to its magnificent new quarters outside the town.

Here it may be as well to remark that the part of the town which we have been passing through, now occupied by the Citadel, Christ Church compound, the Armenian and Syrian convents, the old hospital premises and house of the Rev. J. Nicolayson—now tenanted by Jews—the Jewish " Bikur Holim " Hospital, and the present Maronite convent, in our Lord's time was covered by the fortified residence of Herod the Great, as already related. After the destruction of Jerusalem by Titus (*A.D.* 70), it became the fortified camp of the 10th Roman legion which was left by the conqueror to guard the ruins. It occupied the summit of the south-western hill, which is generally known as the traditional Zion. The long and fairly straight street called on the Ordnance Survey Plan of Jerusalem, " Harat al Jawany " and " Tarik Bab Neby Daud," and running southwards, at not quite a right angle, to " Suweikut Allun " and " Suk al Bizar," which forms the western part of " David Street," may be considered as marking the Eastern boundary of the legionary camp. In the time of Our Lord the market street in the present Jewish quarter was known as "the Upper Market." It is mentioned by Josephus.

The Harat al Jawany and the Tarik Bab Neby Daud, which form the westernmost of the three parallel streets that run southward, and are intersected by various smaller lanes and alleys, constitute the present Jewish quarter. The descent is steep to the middle street; called the " Harat al Yahud " [18]. This street, which runs along the bottom of a marked depression, perhaps occupies the fosse or trench which formed part of the defences of the legion camp between *A.D.* 70 and 135. The surface-levels shown on the Ordnance Survey Plan (1864-5) in this part of the city make it clear that the old Jewish quarter, or Ghetto, which reaches Eastward as far as the brink of the precipices overhanging the Tyropœon Valley, is built on the lower eastern slope or terrace of the hill. The third and easternmost of the three parallel streets

[18] Street Scene—Haret el Yahud.
[*Photo—C. Raad, Jerusalem*

running through this district, is called, together with a

side-street opening into it from the west, " Harat al Meidan," that is, " Theatre Street."

" Theatre Street" is a most significant name and very valuable, as it perpetuates the memory and points to the situation of the Roman theatre, of which, as I was informed by the late Dr. Merrill, remains were discovered a few years ago, at the time I was stationed at Jaffa, and, therefore, I had not the opportunity of seeing. They were situated just outside the city, a little south-east of the great tower called " Burj al Kibryt " at the semi-circular recess shewn on the Ordnance Survey between the levels marked respectively B.M. 2376.2 and 2.322. Through the Harat al Meidan, then, we may, without any great stretch of fancy, be justified in imagining the pagan population of pre-Hadrianic Roman Jerusalem, and later on that of Aelia Capitolina coming, the legion-aries from the west, and the traders and others with their families from the north, to behold gladiatorial and other exhibitions, perhaps the death of Christian martyrs in the theatre.

CHAPTER IV.

DURING the Crusading period the Harat al Meidan was the quarter allotted to the Germans. The great Convent of the Teutonic Knights and another Church of St. Thomas, were situated here, whilst the Church of St. Martin, with the various buildings therewith connected, stood where the Khurveh, or synagogue, and school of the Ashkenazi Perushim now stand.

[19] Perushim Synagogue—Interior.
[Photo—Anon

In New Testament times the palace of Herod Agrippa stood somewhere on the line of the Harat al Meidan, on the edge of the cliffs overlooking the Xystus and the Temple courts, and not far south of the point where the present Harat al Meidan opens into the " Tarik Bab es Silsileh," as the eastern part of David's Street is now called (*Josephus, Wars. Bk. ii. ch.* 16 § 3). The palace of the high priest probably stood at some distance to the south-west, perhaps somewhere not far from where the great synagogue of the Chassidim [20] now stands. We give a view of the exterior taken from a house-top in Der Deutsche Platz, shewing the entrance to the right from the Harat al Meidan.

[20] Exterior of the Great Synagogue of the Chassidim.

[*Photo by Author*

The Jewish population of Jerusalem is of a compara-tively modern date. The soldiers of the first Crusade massacred every Jew or Jewess they could find in the Holy City, and as their successors barely tolerated the presence of Jews in Jerusalem, there was little that would encourage the latter to settle there. When Rabbi Benjamin of Tudela visited Jerusalem he found only 200 Jews there. That was about *A.D.* 1130. The successes of the Moslem arms, combined with the brutal treatment which was experienced by the Jews in

[21] Interior of the Great Synagogue of the Chassidim.

[*Photo—American Colony*

England and France, were the cause of a fresh immigration of the sons of Israel into the Holy Land, and accordingly, about the year 1200, we find that some 300 rabbis came from France and England to settle at Jerusalem.

About twenty years later the celebrated Rabbi Nachmanides was successful in making a collection and purchasing from the Moslems the above-mentioned Crusading Church of St. Martin [22], which was a handsome building with columns and a dome. After some repairs it became the Jewish synagogue. In 1493, just after the expulsion of the Jews from Spain, many of the exiles came and settled in Jerusalem. After various trying experiences, those of the Ashkenazim rite were obliged to flee, the Moslems confiscating the synagogue.

It was probably some time after this that the Sephardim who had hitherto worshipped at the Khurveh with the Ashkenazim, and appear somehow always to have managed better than did their brethren from Germany and Eastern Europe to get on with their Mohammedan neighbours, acquired and erected the curious group of synagogues connected with each other and built almost underground. These are still used by them and situated in the elbow of the crooked street leading from Harat al Yahud to Harat al Meidan. The oldest of them is a small dark perfectly subterranean apartment called " the synagogue of Elijah," from the legend that some centuries ago, in the time of persecution, when the handful of Jews who lived in the Holy City were in great fear and danger, and could therefore only meet in secret for the purposes of public devotion, it happened one Sabbath day that the service could not be held because there were only nine Jews present, and a tenth could not be found in order to form a minyan or congregation of

33   C

ten. At this juncture a venerable Jewish stranger, who had never been seen before by any of those assembled, and suddenly disappeared as soon as the service was ended, entered the synagogue and joined the congregation which, as it had now reached the minimum number needed to form a devotional quorum, proceeded with the service. The unknown stranger was the prophet Elijah,

[22] Distant view of Great Synagogues and the minaret or site of St. Martin's. [*Photo by Author*

who is believed to be the guardian saint of Israel, appearing suddenly from time to time to avert danger from the chosen race and to prevent or punish wrong.

The ancient and curious underground synagogue of the Karaites, said to date back to the earliest Moslem occupation, is also worth visiting. It is in the basement of an old house in ruins, situated on the opposite side of the street in which the great synagogue of the Chassidim stands. The Karaite community, which three and a half centuries ago numbered two hundred souls, has since then dwindled down to scarcely twenty, comprising at present only three men. They possess a beautiful manuscript of the Pentateuch illuminated with gilt initial letters and arabesques. The name of the scribe and the date of his work is stated in the following words on the last page :

> "*I, Moses, son of the late Menachem Dalbures, have written this book called ' Maknische,' and delivered the same to the honoured Rabbi Mordecai son of the late Isaac, as a worthy gift, in the month of Siwan, in the year* 6028. *May God grant that he, his children and children's children may meditate thereupon to the end of all generations. Amen. And may there be fulfilled the word that is written, (namely) ' The book of this doctrine shall not depart from thy mouth, thou shalt meditate thereon day and night in order that thou observe to do all that is written therein, for then shalt thou be happy and wise in all thy ways—Be strong ! Amen ! Selah ! '*"

The dwindling numbers and poverty-stricken condition of the Karaites is accounted for by the following strange legend current amongst the other Jews resident in the Holy City.

In the year 1762, the Jews of Jerusalem being very poor, the Turkish Government demanded an exorbitant sum of money from the community. The Chief Rabbi therefore directed that a secret consultatory meeting should be held in the Karaite synagogue which, as we have seen, being subterraneous, was suitable for such a purpose. Whilst descending the stairs leading to it, the Chief Rabbi suddenly felt faint and he stumbled. This led the other Jews present to suspect that evil agencies were at work. They at once began to tear up the stones forming the staircase and discovered copies of the works of Maimonides which the Karaites had buried there in order to prove their contempt, by treading them underfoot. In order to punish them for this act of sacrilege the Chief Rabbi condemned the Karaites to pay the money demanded by the Government, and besides this, he pronounced as a curse upon them the wish that they should never be able to furnish a " Minyan," or the quorum of ten male adults needed to form a congregation for public worship. The curse still rests upon them.

About the year 1836 several families of Karaites came from the Crimea, to the great joy of their co-religionists in Jerusalem, who hoped to be able to hold public congregational worship again. Their joy was, however, turned into terror, for, suddenly attacked by the plague, the male immigrants dropped down dead in the street one after another, before they reached the abode of their brethren, and the survivors died in the house itself soon after ; so that to this day the Karaites are unable to bring " a Minyan " together for worship. (*See Ludwig Aug*

Frankl " Nach Jerusalem." Vol. ii. p. 65). I have verified the existence of this strange tradition amongst the Jews of Jerusalem at the present day.

The Ashkenazim did not return to Jerusalem till 1690, when Rabbi Jehudah Chassid came with a large following of Ashkenazi rabbis and others, and they re-purchased the old synagogue buildings. Thirty years

[23] Der Deutsche Platz.   [*Photo by Author*

later, however, the Ashkenazim were again driven away, and the said buildings once again seized by the Moslems ; nor was it till after the Egyptian occupation of Palestine, in 1831, that the Ashkenazim were allowed to settle again in Jerusalem, and received back the ruined " Khurveh," which was restored and re-opened for

37

public worship after having been closed for 116 years, two months and three weeks. Up to 1870 there was a large tract of waste ground to the south of the Jewish

[24] Zion Gate.　　　*[Photo—American Colony*

quarter, and situated between it and the southern city wall. Of late years, however, a great part of this tract has been built over by German Jews, and it is now known as " der Deutsche Platz " [23]. In order to annoy the Christians the Mohammedans centuries ago opened a tannery close to the Church of the Sepulchre; and in like manner, and to vex the Jews, they placed the shambles at the southern entrance to the Jewish quarter. Both these nuisances still existed when the writer was a child, but were removed after the close of the Crimean war, as a result of pressure brought to bear upon the local authorities by the different Consulates, at the representation of Dr. Macgowan, who, with his assistants, Drs. Sims and Atkinson, were the only European medical men in southern Palestine, and had great influence. The memories, however, of both these nuisances, tannery and shambles, are perpetuated by the name El Dabbaghah, the tannery by which the site of the Knights of St. John's Hospital and churches is known; and that of Harat al Maslah, or Shambles Street, which still clings to the southern part of Harat al Yahud. At the southern end of this street and the Harat Neby Daud, and between them and the Zion Gate [24], there was an open space partly occupied by the leper village. This was removed many years ago. Then for a time the place became the weekly cattle market, but now that market is held in the Birket es Sultan.

CHAPTER V.

THE greater part of the space included within the north-western corner of the city walls, and reaching as far south as the great thoroughfare leading from the Jaffa Gate eastwards toward the Temple area, was sixty years ago unencumbered by buildings, and comprised open enclosures or fields, which in winter and spring were sown with grain and in summer lay bare. It was the prowling ground of dogs that flocked thither to fight over the dead carcases of asses and horses, left there to rot and breed pestilence. So serious did the nuisance become that at last the French Consul, his various colleagues, and the one or two European medical men then in Jerusalem,

[25]   Fragment of Roman tile.
[*Photo by Author*

were obliged to protest to the Governor, who ordered

40

reforms. Since then students of Scripture have often had an opportunity of witnessing the scene described in Jeremiah xxii. 19— "The burial of an ass, drawn and cast forth beyond the gates of Jerusalem."

Buildings have now risen to fill up this void. Just facing the northern wall of the Castle is the Grand New Hotel, the foundations of which were laid in 1885.

The spot is interesting for two reasons. In the first place the hotel stands over an ancient pool, now covered in with a roof so as to furnish a cistern for the building above it. This pool was traditionally known as "Bathsheba's," from the supposition that the wife of Uriah was bathing there when first seen by David. Another and more likely suggestion is that the pool was part of the great trench to the ancient fortifications at this point.

The second reason is the discovery during those excavations of a fragment of what, in our Lord's time, was the second wall enclosing Jerusalem on the north, outside which was the spot where He was crucified. Here also Roman tiles of the tenth legion were found and part of the shaft of a column bearing a votive inscription in honour of the Augustan legate, Marcus Junius Maximus. The monument was erected by the tenth legion, and in particular by Caius Domitius Sergius Julius Honoratus, who was the legate's strator or equerry. We give a view of the fragment of one of these ancient tiles bearing the stamp of the tenth legion. " (Eu) fretensis," photographed to a scale of centimetres (5 *cent.* = 2 inches) [25].

The piece of column with the inscription now forms the

[26] Ancient Roman column and street lamp.
[Photo by Author

pedestal of a street lamp stand [26], and now has been fixed close to the spot where it was originally found. Its discovery here is of peculiar interest, because we are expressly told by Josephus (*Wars vii.* 1, 3) that, when Jerusalem was taken, *A.D.* 70, Titus left the tenth legion as a garrison amongst the ruins, instead of sending them again to their former station in the Euphrates valley. The position of their new camp may be determined from the statements of Josephus, who says that Titus left a

[27] View from site of the Asmonaeans' Palace.

[Photo by Author

part of the west wall standing, that it might serve as a protection to the garrison. He also left the three great towers of Hippicus, Phasael and Mariamne, probably for the use of the garrison, though the Jewish historian suggests that it was with a view of impressing future ages with the strength of the city which he had conquered.

It is just at this point that the recovered inscription comes in to verify the statement of Josephus about the camp of the tenth legion *inside* the city. The place where the broken column was dug up, and where the Grand New Hotel now stands, is just inside the west wall, and on one side close to the Tower of David, which is probably formed by part of the ancient Phasaelus, with which its plan dimensions agree. On the other side it is as near to the great tower south of the Jaffa Gate, and standing, in all probability, on the site of Hippicus.

[28] Church of St. Salvator.
[*Photo by Author*

There is a good view from the roof of one of the buildings on the site of the house of the Asmonæans [27] (*Josephus, Wars, Bk. II. chap.* 16 § 3). We see the Wailing Place; the Mahkameh—on the site of the Sanhedrin Council Chamber; the minaret built over the modern Gate " Bab es Silsileh," which stands on the site of the ancient Temple-gate, "Shallecheth" or "Coponius"; the Dome of the Rock and part of surrounding courts. In the background is the northern summit of Olivet, called "Viri Galilei," from a worthless tradition not traceable further back than Crusading times, that it was here that the angels said to the disciples, gazing heavenwards at the Ascension, "Ye men of

[29] Church of Notre Dame de France.   [*Photo by Author*

Galilee, why stand ye gazing up into heaven." Another tale, equally valueless, is that this spot was "the mountain in Galilee," where the disciples were to meet Christ after His Resurrection. The buildings now crowning the hill belong to the Greek Convent. The spot is, however, interesting for two good reasons. Firstly, that it was here that the tenth Roman legion encamped at the commencement of the siege of

Jerusalem (*A.D.* 70). Roman tiles, bearing the legionary stamp LEG. X FR., and, in some cases also the sketch of a hog or of a galley, sometimes both, have been dug up here. Secondly, that a remarkable catacomb of early Christian times has been discovered here.

To the north of, and behind, the Grand New Hotel are the new substantial buildings of the Greek Hospital,

[30] Latin Patriarchate Church.   *[Photo by Author*

and the Greek College just facing it on the eastern side of the street leading to the Franciscan Casa Nuova, and their lately rebuilt Church and Monastery of St. Salvator [28].

To the Augustincan Assumptionists belong the Church and Hospice of Notre Dame de France [29]. To the west of these are the piles of the Latin Patriarchate Church and clergy-house [30], and the great French boys' school, superintended by the " Christian Brothers."

The re-establishment of the Latin Patriarchate of Jerusalem dates back to the middle of last century. Besides the Latin there is a Greek, an Armenian, and a Syrian Patriarch, and no end of archbishops, bishops, and other ecclesiastical dignitaries—many of them merely titular—of various old historic churches and sects.

Jerusalem may be considered from many points of view. It certainly is, in one aspect, a museum of fossilized forms of religious profession. During the period between the final expulsion of the Crusaders from Jerusalem (*A.D.* 1243) and the re-establishment of the Latin Patriarchate, the interests of the Roman Church in Jerusalem and the East were represented by the Franciscan, Minorite or Cordelier monks, whose brown habit and rope-girdle may be met with everywhere. The founder of this order himself visited the Holy Land and Egypt *A.D.* 1219, and obtained from the Fatimite Sultan permission for the members of the Brotherhood to remain in the Holy Land, for the entertainment of European pilgrims and the care of the so-called holy sites. Since then, according to the Franciscan publication " The Crusader's Almanac for 1906," during the course of centuries more than 4,000 Franciscans have offered up their blood in the service of Christ, and more than 2,000 in the office of ministering to lepers. Though, of course, this statement should be taken " cum grano salis," yet, when one reads old books of Eastern pilgrimage and travel, truth obliges one to confess that this Brotherhood was very useful to travellers in bye-gone centuries, when Eastern travel was dangerous and difficult and there were no hotels whatever. At present, the order has, according to the almanac above-mentioned, convents and " sanctuaries " at Jerusalem, Bethlehem, Ain Karim, Emmaus, Ramleh, Nazareth, and Capernaum ; at Jaffa on the coast, as well as in the Galilean place of the same name ; at Nain, Mt. Tabor, Cana, Sepphoris, and Tiberias. In the service of their " missions " in the East the Franciscans have 218 priests, 44 clerics, and 245 lay-brothers. According to latest statistics 2,141 European and American Roman Catholic pilgrims received hospitality at various Latin Convents in Palestine.

The Franciscan Convent of St. Salvator above mentioned was first occupied by the fraternity during the latter part of the sixteenth century and after their expulsion from the Cœnaculum in 1560. St. Salvator, recently re-built, probably occupies the site of the famous Iberian monastery erected by King Vachtung in the fourth century (*A.D.* 446-499), and afterwards repaired by Justinian. Beside the church and cells for the monks it contains a steam press, an excellent library, and several large workshops. It has boys' and girls' schools and a free dispensary. The latter is well worth a visit because in its cellars there is a fine collection of old majolica medicine pots and jars. It stands to the credit of the Franciscans that the Order not only introduced the first church organ into Palestine in *A.D.* 1616 (" *Infidelibus ad re novitatem mirantibus*" Golnbooricz " *Serie Cronologica* " *p.* 67), but that in their monastery gardens they did much to improve agriculture.

[31] Greek Convent with dome of the Church of the Holy Sepulchre and bell-tower in foreground, behind which are the straggling Greek Convent buildings, with Church of St. Salvator in background.

[*Photo—C. Raad, Jerusalem*]

Somewhat South of the Franciscan establishment, and adjoining it is the great Greek Convent of Constantine [31], where the orthodox Greek Patriarch resides. This monastery is said to have been originally the Palace of the Crusading Kings of Jerusalem. After the year 1118, on the institution of the Order of Knights Templars, the buildings adjoining the Aksa Mosque, which till then had been occupied by royalty, were given up for the use of these military monks. The convent itself is a huge straggling building, extending southwards as far as the crooked street leading eastward from Grand New Hotel; and reaching

49

eastward beyond Christian Street and right up to the Church of the Holy Sepulchre. It contains a magnificent library, including most valuable books and MSS. from the libraries at Mar Saba and the Convent of the Cross, which were incorporated with it about thirty years ago. There are over one hundred ancient Greek MSS. on vellum, a large folio MS. of the whole Bible in excellent preservation, a folio copy of the book of Job, written in large letters, with notes in a smaller hand, and having on almost every page, Twelfth century miniatures of Job and his three friends. It is a great treasure. The convent contains besides several small chapels, a printing press, schools, etc. There are about 200 monks and priests in residence, and many apartments for pilgrims. This is only one of several Greek monasteries in Jerusalem.

In the angle formed by the great street leading eastward from the Jaffa Gate, and that leading northward, as above described, past the Grand New Hotel toward the Casa Nuova, we note a nunnery of the Roman Catholic Sisters of St. Joseph, a Coptic Convent of St. George, a Greek nunnery, and, besides other buildings, the Great Coptic Khan or caravanserai, built during 1838 inside the northern part of the great pool—Birket Hammam al Batrak—" Pool of the Patriarch's Bath." This is called by tradition the Pool of Hezekiah, but was in ancient times the Pool Amygdalon, or the " Almond Pool," if we suppose the name to be Greek. It is, however, not Greek, but Hebrew, or Aramaic, and means, " the Pool

of the Great Tower," that is of the north-east massive
tower of the Citadel, only a few yards distant. Josephus
(*Wars, Bk. v. xi.* 4) tells us that the Pool was situated
close to the spot where the soldiers of the tenth legion
were, during the siege of the city, carrying on military
operations against the second wall.

[32] Pool of Hezekiah. [*Photo—American Colony*]

Some remains of this wall were, as above related,
discovered in 1885, just west of this Pool. The reservoir
is now 240 feet long and 144 feet wide, but it was
ascertained in 1838, when, as already remarked, the
Coptic Khan was built inside its northern end, that it
was originally 57 feet longer than it is at present. As the

Pool was inside the second wall, which ran encircling the North part of Jerusalem as far as the Castle of Antonia, which was situated at the north-west of the Temple-area ; and as our Lord was crucified outside this second wall, it is very difficult to believe that the present Church of the Holy Sepulchre could have been outside this second wall. However, this is a question about which over a score of learned works, many as dry as dust, have been written, and with which I shall not bewilder the reader.

In the illustration of the so-called Pool of Hezekiah, [32], the Coptic Khan is on the left, and, in the background are the domes of the Church of the Resurrection, popularly known as that of the Holy Sepulchre. I will only add that the name " Pool of Hezekiah," is given to this great artificial basin, because it is traditionally identified with the one made by that king, of whom the Bible and Apocrypha relate (2 *Kings xx*. 20 ; 2 *Chronicles xxxii*. 30 ; *Sirach. xlviii*. 17) that he " made a pool, and a conduit, and brought water into the city," and also that he stopped the upper water-course of Gihon, and brought it straight down to the west side of the city of David. Several modern scholars, have, indeed, of late years tried to prove that the pool and conduit were in Siloam, in a quite different part of Jerusalem. On the other hand, others still adhere to the idea that the traditional view is the correct one, and that the aqueduct which, till the last few years fed the pool with water from another outside and west of the city, was the " conduit " referred to in the Scripture passages quoted above.

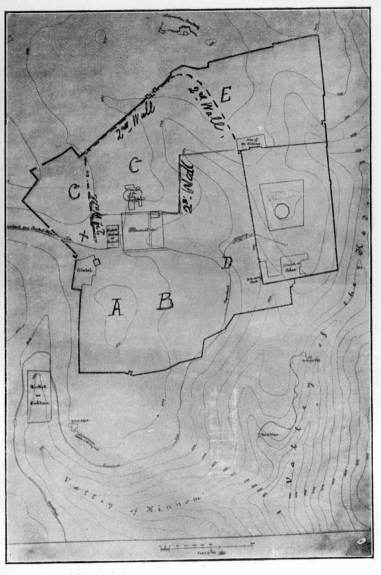

[33] A Plan of Jerusalem.

[*Photo by Author*

53

CHAPTER VI.

HE level of the ground inside the walls of the Holy City varies as greatly as it does outside. The highest point, just inside the north-western angle, where the modern gateway, " Bab es Sultan Abdul Hamid " [34] was opened about the year 1887, is

[34] Bab es Sultan Abdul Hamid Gate.

[*Photo by Author*

2,580 feet above the Mediterranean. The lowest is in the corner east of the Dung Gate and South-east of the city, and this must not be confounded with the south-east corner of the Temple area, for it is quite, as the contour lines on the plan of the city show, two hundred feet lower. From the North-western angle the ground falls steadily Eastward and Southward. At the Jaffa Gate the British Ordnance Survey Bench mark ⏁ cut in 1864 on the city walls

[35] Ordnance Survey bench mark on City Wall. *[Photo by Author*

[36] shows the level to be some 2,528 feet above the sea at that particular spot. Passing South-ward the ground rises twenty feet at Christ Church and in the Armenian quarter. It falls again, as we move east-ward, to 2,450 on the verge of the great cliffs at the Eastern edge of the Jewish quarter, and overhanging the low ground of the Tyropœon valley, at the Jews' Wailing Place, the Mohammedan Mughrabi (*North African*) quarter, and the neighbour-hood of the Dung Gate ("*Bab al Magharibeh*").

Returning to the New Gate, we observe that the large French boys' school in the angle of the city wall, south-west of it, is built on the site of a ruined Crusading fort called " Kala 'at El Jalud," *i.e.,* " Goliath's Castle," sometimes also " Tancred's Tower." Some of the remains of these old middle-age fortifications are shown

[**36**] Model of original rock site of Calvary.

[*Photo—S. A. Hanauer*

to inquisitive visitors or pilgrims. They are preserved in the cellars of the school, and are supposed to be the remains of Herod's great tower of Psephinus. Thanks to the courtesy of Frère Leon, the Principal of this excellent Institution, I am able to furnish a photograph of these remains as they appeared before the French school house was built [**37**], and also other views of the new buildings in this quarter.

56

The contour-line, passing respectively the north-west corner of the city, the Damascus Gate, the Church of the Holy Sepulchre, and Bishop Gobat's school to the south-west of the town, bears the number 2,479, showing that these points are approximately at the same level, and one hundred feet lower than the New Gate. Hezekiah's

[37] Remains of Tancred's Tower, now built over.

[*Photo—B. Leon*

Pool (*Birket Hammam el Batrak*) south-west of the Church of the Sepulchre, occupies the head of a deep and broad depression, or valley basin, which is 800 feet wide at its mouth, and sweeps eastward, ever deepening till it joins another valley coming from the neighbourhood of the Damascus Gate, and usually called " El Wad," or the Tyropœon.

These two united valleys continue Southward and Eastward after having passed beyond the city's southern limit, and at last open into the Kedron, or Valley of Jehoshaphat, at the lower pool of Siloam, a little north of the place where the Wad-el-Rababi, the traditional Valley of Hinnom, comes sweeping from the west and south of the high land on which the town stands. It

[38] Ground model of Church of the Holy Sepulchre.

[*Photo—S. A. Hanauer*

opens into the Kedron at a spot marked on the Ordnance Survey by a bench-mark cut into a rock-scarp, as being 2,035 feet above sea-level, or exactly 555 feet lower than the level at the New Gate.

Another valley, the head of which is indicated by the bend of the contour-line 2,479 between the Mohammedan cemetery to the north of the city (*Gordon's Calvary*) and the North-east angle of the city wall, descends in a South-easterly direction, crossing the Haram, or Temple-area at its North-east corner, about halfway between the St. Stephen's and the Golden Gates, and opening into the Kedron opposite the traditional Gethsemane. This valley, however, is now so filled up with debris that it is only discernible from certain points, such as the high ground on Bezetha, just inside Herod's Gate. In its bed lie the mysterious double Pools of Bethesda, close to the Church of St. Anne, and the huge Birket Israel, now being purposely filled up with rubbish but which, before the re-discovery of the double Pools just mentioned, used to be pointed out as the Pool of Bethesda.

In the preceding remarks I have tried to make it clear that the unequal heights of the ground inside the walls of the Holy City are produced by the presence of three valleys that intersect the mountain-site. First, there is a broad depression running Eastward from Hezekiah's Pool; next, a great ravine running from the Damascus Gate to the South-east corner of the city, just east of the Dung Gate; and in the third place, the valley running from between Gordon's Calvary and the North-east angle of the city through Bethesda and the North-east portion of the Temple-area.

Between this valley and that coming from the Damascus Gate lies a great long hill slope or ridge, the top of which steadily descends towards the South-east. The Ordnance Survey has determined its highest point, just opposite the Mohammedan cemetery, to be 2,524 feet above sea-level.   At the North-west corner of the former

[39] German Church.   [*Photo—American Colony*

Turkish barracks, on the site of the Antonia, it is 2,448.
Inside the North-western angle of the Temple-area it has

fallen to 2,429, to rise again on the summit of Moriah. The levels show this to be connected by a narrow neck or saddle with Bezetha and the ground to rise to 2,440 and then gradually to descend again till, on the verge of the great precipice overhanging the Pool of Siloam, at the southern end of the Ophel spur outside the city, it is 2,129, or almost four hundred feet below its highest point. Between the Damascus Gate valley and that starting from Hezekiah's Pool is the hill called Acra, covered on its higher levels, as we have seen, with large modern buildings. Its highest point within the walls, as already mentioned, is at the north-western angle of the city close to the modern gate of Sultan Abdul Hamid.

The Church of the Holy Sepulchre is situated on its south-eastern slope, but fully one hundred feet lower than the New Gate. Joined to Acra by the neck or saddle on which the Jaffa Gate stands, and to the south of the Pool of Hezekiah valley, is the traditional Zion, occupied, as we have seen, by the Citadel, the mission premises of the London Jews Society, the Armenian convent, and, on its lower and eastern terraces, by the Jewish quarter.

Now the plan of the city [33]—reduced by photography from a large one kindly given me by Dr. Merrill— shows the present city walls. I have marked the course the second wall must have taken if the Church of the Sepulchre really and truly marks the actual spot of Golgotha and our Lord's tomb which were outside the wall. The outer dotted line shows the course of the second wall as described by Josephus, including the site of the Church of the Holy Sepulchre. The minute numbers on the series of contour-lines show the height above the Mediterranean in English feet. The letters refer to the following :—*A.*, Armenian quarter. *B.*, Jewish quarter. *C.C.*, Latin and Greek, etc. *D.*, Moslem (North African). *E.*, general Moslem quarter, on Bezetha. *X.*, Grand New Hotel.

Having thus tried to describe the general line and respective elevations of the different parts of Jerusalem within the walls, we shall now start on our projected visit to the Church of the Holy Sepulchre. My object, as already stated, is not to uphold or promulgate any theory. In a former chapter I alluded to the difficulties of the theory that the Church marks the actual site of the Crucifixion and Resurrection of the Saviour. I now, in justice to those who maintain the contrary, give photographs of two fine models [36 and 38] made from the drawings and notes of the late Dr. Schick. The former shews the nature or appearance of the rock site, as it must have presented in our Lord's time. Namely, 1. Calvary. 2. The Sepulchre. 3. Traditional sepulchre of Joseph of Arimathea and Nicodemus. 4. Quarries. 5. A slight valley. 6. Tomb of Adam. The other is a photograph of a model made from Dr. Schick's drawings, to show the alterations that have taken place, as a result of the cutting away of the rock in order to receive the foundations of present buildings—1. Calvary. 2. The Sepulchre. 3. Tomb of Joseph and Nicodemus. 4. Chapel of St. Helena. 5. Cathedral of the Greeks.

6. Chapel with traditional tomb of Adam. A unique photograph of the Tomb of Joseph of Arimathea appears on page 382.

Whether the reader accepts or doubts the genuineness of the site of the famous Church as being that where, in our Lord's time, Calvary was situated and the garden of Joseph of Arimathea, no one will deny that the place has a marvellous history, reaching back nearly sixteen centuries. Here, between the years *A.D.* 327-336, the Emperor Constantine the Great erected his fine buildings. On the west a great Rotunda, the circular Church of the Anastasis or Resurrection, with what was really believed to be the Holy Sepulchre in its centre. Further east, a large open court with colonnades running along its northern and southern sides. Further east still, a handsome and spacious basilica or cathedral, built on a plan res.mbling that of Roman law courts. The cathedral had a great central nave and side aisles, the roofs of which were supported by columns, and having at the east end three deep apses or semi-circular recesses. At the extreme east of all there was a grand pillared entrance from the street, now called Khan Ez-Zeit, an atrium or great square court, with colonnades running along all its four sides.

The area covered by these structures is stated by Dr. Schick to have extended 500 feet east and west from the Khan Ez-Zeit to Christian Street, and from the present Via Dolorosa north to the street now running along the south side of the Church of the Sepulchre block, or about 200 feet—the area covered being more than 10,000 square yards. A few vestiges of the grand edifices of Constantine may still be seen in the Russian Hospice east of the Church of the Sepulchre, consisting of two of the pedestals of the entrance porch, and a fragment of a massive wall; whilst inside some vaults just North-east of the Hospice, the jambs of the great eastern entrance have been discovered and may be seen. Inside and underneath the buildings on the eastern side of the street there are vestiges of the great colonnaded forum or market which once existed hereabouts.

Other interesting remains on this spot are of later periods—Byzantine and Crusading. The buildings of Constantine having been destroyed by the army of Chosroes II. of Persia in *A.D.* 614, a new set of edifices, on a much smaller scale, was erected between the years 616-626 by the Abbot Modestus, who received pecuniary help from the Christians in Syria and Egypt, and used such of the old materials as were available. As a result, four separate buildings were raised; viz., the Church of the Resurrection, or the Rotunda; the Church of the Cross, situated over the site of the present Chapel of St. Helena; the Church of Calvary, on the present site; and the Church of the Virgin, which probably stood on the spot now occupied by the great bell tower and the south transept. When, in *A.D.* 637 Jerusalem opened its gates to the Khalifeh Omar ibn El Khattab, the Moslem conqueror generously left the Christians in peaceable possession of their churches. Later on, when Haroun Al Raschid, of Arabian Nights' celebrity, came to the throne, among the presents he sent to his equally famous contemporary Charlemagne (*A.D.* 800) were the keys of the Church of the Sepulchre. These monarchs were practically contemporaries of Alfred the Great.

[**40**] Stairs leading from Christian Street to the courtyard of the Church of the Holy Sepulchre.
[*Photo by Author*

Charlemagne took advantage of the favourable political relations between himself and the Oriental ruler, in order to establish a hospice on a site South-east of the Church. A church, that of St. Mary of the Latins, was afterwards erected here, and when, long after the Crusading period, it had gradually fallen into ruin, the site and remains were in 1869 presented to the King of Prussia, and taken possession of by his son, afterwards the Emperor Frederick, whose son, the present ex-Kaiser William, had the church rebuilt on the old lines. It was consecrated on the occasion of his visit to Jerusalem in 1898, and, under the name of the " Erloser Kirche," is the place of worship of the German Protestants.

The churches on the site of the Church of the Sepulchre, having suffered dilapidation from various causes, and on two occasions from fire, were again repaired in the years 830 and 969. Having been quite destroyed in 1010 by the orders of the mad Egyptian Khalif El Hakim, whom the Druses to this day worship as a god, they were rebuilt as separate chapels on the various holy sites. After the Crusaders had obtained possession of the country in 1099, they erected the present building, which includes the shrines which till their coming had been shown under different roofs. It was in this church that several of the Latin Kings were crowned, and here, around the so-called stone of unction, their tombs were preserved, till in 1224, the Kharezmians, a fierce Tartar horde, having overrun Palestine and taken Jerusalem, destroyed the monuments and rifled the graves, in hope of finding treasure.

Though at that time and subsequently, the last occasion being the great fire of 1808, which destroyed the Chapel of the Resurrection and the great dome over the Rotunda, the inner arrangements of the Church of the Sepulchre have experienced various vicissitudes and alterations, yet, on the whole, the outer shell and walls of the building remain practically, except for the wear and tear of eight centuries, much the same as they were when the Crusaders were turned out of Jerusalem in 1187.

CHAPTER VII.

HE present iron dome and galleries over the Rotunda in the Church of the Holy Sepulchre were put up in 1868, the work being done with the consent of the Sultan and at the joint expense of France and Russia, which countries sent architects and workmen.

The only approach to the church is by the great courtyard in front and south of it. The courtyard may be entered either from a door at its south-east corner, or by another at the top of a staircase at its south-west corner. We will visit it from the latter direction, starting from the great open space to the east of the Citadel. At the north-east corner of this space is the head of a long street of stairs leading down eastwards to the Temple-area, 500 yards distant and 106 feet below us. We begin to descend this street, and, having proceeded about 200 feet, turn sharply to the left, following a straight and level street leading northwards. It is now called Christian Street, because, till about twenty years ago, the shops on either side were occupied solely by Christians, no Jew daring to show himself in the vicinity of the Church of the Sepulchre. Now all this is changed, most if not all the shops being occupied by Jews. In Crusading times this was called Patriarch Street, because it led to the residence of the Patriarch, at the corner where it joins the Via Dolorosa, and where the present mosque and minaret El Khankeh are situated.

[41] Christian Street.
[Photo—C. Raad, Jerusalem

Christian Street [41] is very remarkably straight, and for the first half of its course, level, the reason being that in that part it passes along the top of a huge, and very ancient, dam or causeway, which forms the eastern limit of the Pool of Hezekiah. The western side of the dam-top has houses built along it, and that is the reason why this remarkable specimen of ancient engineering, which is about 200 feet long and 50 wide, escapes notice.

We now take the first turning to the right and descend
a winding street of stairs, at the foot of which is the great
court in front of the Church of the Sepulchre.   On the
left hand side, in line with the lowest step of the staircase
[**40**], is the South-east corner of the great Greek
Convent of Constantine, and just here we notice an old
pilaster with a beautiful Twelfth century basket work
capital, and the spring of an arch rising from its abacus.
In line with this pilaster we notice, stretching Eastward,
the broken bases of columns.   These remains are the
only existing vestiges of the beautiful arcade which
stood along the Northern front of the great Hospital of
the Knights of St. John.   There was at the time another

[**42**] Chapel of the Twelve Apostles.

[*Photo by Author*

70

approach to the courtyard from the west, and it is related
that on one occasion, when there was a dispute between
the Latin patriarch and the Hospitalers, who claimed
to be independent of his authority, the militant monks,
knowing that the church dignitary and his clergy were
about to visit the Church of the Sepulchre in solemn
pomp and order of rank, ranged up under this arcade and
received the train with flights of arrows, which, by the
way, we hope were blunt ones. This obliged those in
the procession to run away as fast as they could,
relinquishing every attempt at dignity, into the shelter
of the church, amidst the derisive shouts of laughter

[43] Rival olive tree in Abyssinian Convent.   [*Photo by Author*

raised by the Knights. "As are the times, so are the manners." "Every age," says the corresponding Arabic proverb, "sports with its own generation." In those days the "sports" seem to have been rather rough (*Besant and Palmer, History of Jerusalem, p.* 322).

The courtyard in front of the church, which, during the pilgrim season is thronged by vendors of beads,

[44] Porch of the Chapel with walled-up olive tree.

[*Photo by Author*

crosses, etc., is about 80 feet long and 54 wide. There are vaulted chambers underneath it. It is bounded on its eastern side by the Greek Convent of Abraham, which contains on its upper terrace the small chapel of Abraham, where Anglican clerical visitors are allowed to celebrate Holy Communion by special permission of the Greek Patriarch; the chapel of the Twelve Apostles [42] and the carefully walled-up olive tree [44]. This tree, according to a Greek legend, was the very plant amongst whose branches the ram was found entangled by his horns at the time of the offering of Isaac by Abraham. The Abyssinians, however, protest against this legend as rank heresy, and claim that they possess the veritable olive tree in their own convent [43],

[45] Ruins of Abbey of the Canons of the Sepulchre.

[Photo—Rev. A . E. Mitchell

a cluster of hovels amongst the ruins of the Crusading Abbey of the Canons of the Sepulchre [45], east of the Great Church. In the background of the view are seen part of the Church of the Sepulchre, and some remains of the walled-up cloisters of the Crusading Abbey of the Canons of the Holy Sepulchre. An illustration of the Abyssinian Convent is also given [46].

46] Abyssinian Convent with dome of Chapel of St. Helena in foreground.
[*Photo by Author*]

In the lower storey of the Convent of Abraham, with doors opening into the court, are the Armenian Chapel of St. James, and the Coptic Chapel of the Archangel Michael, whilst in the north-east corner of the court, underneath the Latin Chapel of Mary's Agony, is the Greek Chapel of Mary the Egyptian. Who was she? The Greek priest in charge of the shrine, a little room scarcely twelve feet square, pitying our ignorance, points to a series of coarsely executed pictures illustrating her

74

story. *Picture* 1. Mary, who has been leading a gay life in Egypt, embarks at Alexandria in order to visit the Holy City in pilgrimage. *Picture* 2. An angel meeting her at the gate of Jerusalem forbids the sinful woman to enter. *Picture* 3. Mary, the penitent, retires to the desert to live a life of penance. *Picture* 4. Starving and in rags, she was discovered by a holy hermit, who instructs her in the truths of the Gospel. *Picture* 5. Being convinced of her sincere repentance and piety, the hermit, whose name I forget, gives Mary the Holy Communion. *Picture* 6. Coming one day to visit his convert, the hermit finds that she had died since his last visit. He is just in time to say the funeral service, for a god-fearing lion having dug her grave, is on the point of burying Mary the Egyptian, when

[47] Church of the Holy Sepulchre, with bell tower.
[*Photo—C. Raad, Jerusalem*]

75

the hermit comes up.   The story is characteristic, and typical of many other such, and illustrative of the doctrine held by so many Easterns and others that men can be saved by their own works.   It is remarkable that lions play a part in several of these Oriental saint-stories.   " In paintings St. Jerome is often represented accompanied by the lion whose wounded paw he cured in the deserts of Chalcis, and who in gratitude became the protector and faithful servant of the healer " (*Prothero's Psalms in Human Life, p.* 27).   Mar Saba is allowed by a hospitable lion to share his den, and when the couple find that the quarters

[48] Remarkable carving above entrance to Chapel of Mary
the Egyptian.   [*Photo—A. S. Hanauer*

are not roomy enough for two, the lion generously seeks other lodgings. A lion, as we have seen, buries Mary the Egyptian, and, about three-quarters of a mile West of the Jaffa Gate, the cave is still shewn to which in *A.D.* 614, when the Persians had massacred sixty thousand Christians at Jerusalem, a lion reverently conveyed their bodies for burial. It really seems a pity that such a race of pious animals no longer exists !

Built into the wall, just above the entrance to the Chapel of Mary the Egyptian, is an old carving representing two lions. It is much mutilated. The richly carved cornice above the lions is supposed to be a relic of the time of Constantine, *A.D.* 333. [48].

On the West of the great court are ranged, side by side, the three Greek Chapels of St. James, St. Mary, and the Forty Martyrs. The last-named is in the lower storey of the great bell tower, which, together with the projecting exteriors of the apses of the three chapels, is seen to the left of the illustration of the facade of the Church of the Sepulchre, the latter surmounted by the white-washed dome of the Greek Church of the middle of the world [47]. In the North-east corner of the court, to the right of the blocked-up gateway, is seen the Latin Chapel of Mary's Agony, roofed with a small drum and dome, and with a staircase leading up to its door. The question as to who had the right to sweep that staircase was the cause of a sanguinary encounter between the Latin and Greek monks some years ago.

Stretched in front of the cluster of columns, between
the two great portals of the Church of the Sepulchre, is
a marble slab, bearing the epitaph of Philip D'Aubeny,

[49] Tomb of Sir Philip D'Aubeny.   [*Photo by Author*

and a Norman shield with his armorial bearings [49].   In
1887, by reference to several ancient records, I succeeded
in proving that this is the tombstone of Sir Philip
D'Aubeny, tutor of Henry III. of Winchester, who,
crowned when only a child of eight years of age, was

entrusted to his care during the protectorship of the able Earl of Pembroke. Before the accession of Henry III., however, and during the reign of King John, we find the name of Sir Philip D'Aubeny amongst the barons who signed the Magna Charta. Sir Philip D'Aubeny left England for the holy wars in Palestine in 1222. He resided in the country for fourteen years, dying in 1236. Matthew Paris, the famous historian, describes him as " *miles strenuus, ac morum honestate commendabilis,*" " a valiant soldier of honourable and commendable manners," and refers to his death in the following terms : " *Circa illos dies, nobilis ac Deo devotus, in armis strenuus miles, Philippus de Albineto, postquam militaverat Deo in Terra Sancta, peregrinando pluries, tandem in eadem diem claudens extremum, et finem faciens laudabilem, sanctam meruit in Terra Sancta, quod vivus diu desideraverat, sepulturam,*" which may thus be translated : " About this time " (*A.D.* 1236) " the noble devotee to the service of God, the unflinching warrior, Philip de Albineto, after that he had fought for God in the Holy Land, and oft made pilgrimage there, at last closed his days in the same, and, making a laudable end to his godly life, merited, what living he had long fervently desired, holy burial in the Holy Land."

The identity of the personage buried here has been incontestably proved by the armorial bearings, as well as by historical references, with the family of D'Aubeny, still existing in England, the chief seat of which appears to have been the manor of South Petherton, Somersetshire.

CHAPTER VIII.

THE lintels over the portals to the Church of the Holy Sepulchre are ornamented with choice Twelfth-century carvings, those sculptured over the left-hand entrance gate [50] being scenes from the life of our Saviour, whilst those on the right-hand walled-up gateway [51] are of a mythological character, with a spirited figure of a centaur in the centre. A

[50] Sculpture on portal to Church of the Holy Sepulchre.
[*Photo by Author*

fragment of the scene depicted on the western portal was broken away some centuries ago, but, having been recovered, is now preserved in the Louvre [52] (*Professor Ganneau's " Archaeological Researches "*).

Entering the Church, which is open only at certain hours, we notice, first of all, on our left, the deep-cushioned recess constantly occupied by the Moslem door-keepers. These having official custody of the key, open and close the building at the appointed times, and are said to be willing to open at other hours as well—for backsheesh. The office of door-keeper to the Church of the Holy Sepulchre is hereditary in the very old Moslem family of the Ensaybehs.

In the corner opposite the recess for the door-keeper we notice some quadrant-shaped stairs, which form the lower part of an ascent to the large vaulted chamber called " Calvary." There are other staircases to it from

[51] Sculpture on portal to Church of the Holy Sepulchre.
[*Photo by Author*

other parts of the church as well. Just in front of us, as we step Northwards, lies stretched east and west the traditional Stone of Unction, on which the body of the Saviour is said to have been laid in order to be anointed for burial. At either end are great tripod candlesticks, and suspended over it ornamental lamps. These accessories are the property of the different religious communities, Orthodox-Greek, Armenian, Roman, and others, who possess " rights " in the great church. The stone itself, which is said at one time to have lain further north, is nine feet long, four feet six inches wide, and one foot high [53]. It is of the native red limestone, and has, it is asserted, been placed here only in order to protect the real stone, which lies underneath, from the hands of eager pilgrims. The first

FRAGMENT OF SCULPTURE REPRESENTING CHRIST'S TRIUMPHAL ENTRY INTO JERUSALEM ON PALM SUNDAY.

[52] A fragment of the portal in Paris.
[*Photo by Author*

mention of it is found in the Twelfth - century narrative of Saewulf's pilgrimage. At that time the stone was shewn in the Chapel of the Virgin, which, as above noted, is supposed to have occupied the position now in part occupied by the bell tower. It lies in what is really the south transept of the church, though, because of the filling up of the great arch behind the stone and the separation of this part of the building from the central Greek Cathedral, which is actually the nave of the church, it is difficult to realise this without having a ground plan of the building before one.

On our right hand, as we stand before the stone of unction, we notice a doorway admitting the visitor to a chapel situated underneath the Greek Chapel of the

[53] Stone of Unction.   [*Photo—American Colony*]

Exaltation of the Cross, or " Calvary." Just inside the door-way are two benches, one on either side. That on the left marks the spot where once stood the cenotaph of Duke Godfrey de Bouillon, the first Crusading King of Jerusalem. The tombstone disappeared at the time of the great fire of 1808, though, fortunately, descriptions and sketches of it are extant, from which we learn that it was " a roof-shaped monument of fine porphyry, with vertical gable ends and ornamental edges—supported on four twisted dwarf columns, resting on a plinth of marble. On the sloping surface was the following inscription :—

" *Hic jacet inclytus*
Dux Godefridus de Bulion
Qui totam istam terram
Acquisivit Cultui Christiano :
Cujus Anima regnet cum Christo. Amen."

The epitaph may thus be rendered :—" Here lies the celebrated Duke Godfrey de Bouillon, who won the whole of this country to the Christian religion. May his soul reign with Christ. Amen." It is noticeable that in his epitaph the hero is not styled Rex, a king, but Dux, a duke, because, though elected king, he would not, in his humble piety, accept the royal title, and refused to wear a kingly diadem in the city where his Saviour had worn a crown of thorns. Surrounded as we are on this spot by sites of doubtful genuineness, and by absurd traditions, it does one good to realize that one is standing beside an actually historic site commemorating a man of Godfrey's character.

The tomb of Baldwin, his brother and successor, is marked by the bench on the opposite side of the doorway.

Further on in the chapel we are shewn the tomb of Melchizedec, the place where the skull of Adam was buried, and also the lower part of the rent made in the rock by the earthquake at the time of the Crucifixion of our Lord. The upper portion of what is said to be the

[54] Calvary Chapel.   [*Photo—Anonymous*

same crack is shown in the " Calvary " Chapel [54], overhead, and the tradition is that some of the blood of the Saviour dropped through the fissure on to the head of Adam and raised our first ancestor to life. The idea may be traced back to the days of Origen in the second century. In the south wall of this chapel of Godfrey, Baldwin, Melchizedec, and Adam, is a doorway leading to a chamber used as an office by the Greek ecclesiastical officials. From this room there is access to another, in

which are preserved various antiquities and relics, which
are shewn to visitors who care to look at them.

Leaving this place we pass the Eastern end of the stone
of unction, and a couple of steps round the corner to our
right bring us to the foot of another staircase leading up
to the Calvary Chapel, belonging to the Greeks.   Under
the altar at the eastern end is a round metal-lined hole.

[55] Chapel of the Resurrection showing piers of Rotunda.
[Photo—C. Raad, Jerusalem

in a marble slab, said to be the very hollow in which the
Saviour's cross was fixed.   Just to the right of the altar
is a long slit in the marble, covered with a moveable
metal lid.   This is visible in the photograph, and does
duty for the upper part of the cleft in the rock.   The
altar further to the right is Latin property, and dedicated

to the Virgin Mary; and yet further to right, the southern half of the large chamber, above the chapel of Adam and the Greek Ecclesiastic's office, belongs to the

[56] Nearer View of the Chapel of the Resurrection.
[Photo—C. Raad, Jerusalem

Latins, and is furnished at its east end with their altar. Though it is really only an upper floor room with chambers

[57] Entrance to Chapel of the Angel. *[Photo—C. Raad, Jerusalem*

underneath, it is gravely pointed out to credulous pilgrims as the place where our Lord was nailed to the cross.

Through a barred window, which was formerly a

doorway, we look into the Latin Chapel of Mary's Agony, said to mark the spot where she stood during the Crucifixion. It is remarkable for its painted glass window, and was originally a porch with steps leading up to it, by which the Calvary Chapel chamber could be reached from the outside, without entering the great Church doors.

Descending to the southern transept we once more pass the Stone of Unction, and, proceeding westwards, notice, on our left, a circular slab in the floor covered by a sort of metal cage. It is said to mark the place where the women stood afar off beholding the Crucifixion, and afterwards where the Virgin Mary stood whilst the body of Jesus was laid on the stone of unction to be prepared for burial. Behind this a staircase, with very high and slippery steps, leads up to the Armenian part of the lower gallery, at the back of the eighteen great piers encircling the Rotunda [55].

The entrance porch leading into the front chamber is called the "Chapel of the Angel," [57] because on a pedestal in its centre is shewn a fragment of the very stone which was rolled from the door of the tomb, and on which the angel was seen sitting on the Resurrection morning. Another piece of the same stone is shewn built into an altar in the Armenian chapel of the Palace of Caiaphas outside the Zion Gate.

CHAPTER IX.

TWO oval windows in the north and south walls respectively indicate the places where the Holy Fire first appears on the Greek Easter-Eve [59]. It is well known that the popular notion amongst the lower classes in the Greek Church is that this fire comes direct from Heaven as a result of the prayers of the titular Bishop of Petra, who is the special official to perform the ceremony. More educated and enlightened Greeks believe that it is merely a symbolical ceremony commemorative of the light of hope, joy and life bursting upon the darkened and mourning Church by the good news of our Lord's resurrection from the tomb.

Much has been written on the subject rightly deploring and denouncing the abuses the ceremony has led to, and calling it an imposture. How it first came to be observed seems to be generally unknown. One usually reads in works on Palestine a repetition of the statement in *Robinson's "Biblical Researches," vol. I. page* 393, that the monk Bernhard, who visited Jerusalem *A.D.* 870, is the first traveller to mention the jugglery of the Greek holy fire. May I therefore venture to call attention to what I believe to have been the forgotten origin of a commemorative anniversary service, which has unfortunately led to disgraceful abuses? Descriptions of scenes witnessed in the Church of the Sepulchre on occasions whether remotely or more recently past, are numerous, and I need not dwell on that side of the subject.

[58]   In the courtyard of the Church of the Holy Sepulchre at the time of the "Holy-Fire." [*Photo—C. Raad, Jerusalem*

The Church historian, Eusebius, quoted in *Williams' " Holy City," vol. I., page* 226, relates that during the episcopate of Narcissus (*A.D.* 180-222), one of the most godly of the early Bishops of Aelia Capitolina, several notable miracles were performed in answer to that prelate's prayers. One is specially mentioned :

" It was on the great Vigils of the Feast of Easter, when oil was wanting for the church, and the drawers were greatly perplexed, that he ordered them to draw water out of the nearest well, which, being consecrated by his prayers, and poured into the lamps with sincere faith in the Lord, contrary to all reason and expectation, by a miraculous and Divine power, was changed into the fatness of oil."

Whilst dwelling on this subject I may add that the present crowding and grouping of so many holy sites

[59] Place of the Holy-Fire in the Church of the
Holy Sepulchre, showing oval Holy-Fire windows on side of
Chapel, near centre of photograph.

[*Photo—Sarrafian Bros.*

together, in so incongruous a manner, under one roof, may probably have in a like way not have originated in an intentional purpose to deceive, but have grown out of services held in remote periods at different spots for the instruction of ignorant pilgrims, a very small percentage of whom, it must be remembered, were able to read the Gospels for themselves in the dark Middle

Ages. There may have been special arrangements that the pilgrims should have an opportunity of hearing one part of the Gospel story read in one memorial chapel, whilst at the same time in another a different portion of Scripture was read at another service. As the pilgrims came by thousands then, just as they do now, and as the Church of Christ was not then as divided as it unhappily is in our days, there must have been some arrangement made for different congregations to meet in

[60] Interior of the Tomb Chamber of the Holy Sepulchre. [*Photo—C. Raad, Jerusalem*

differing places of worship. As time went on, the purely commemorative character of the church, chapel or oratory, would gradually be lost sight of, and the memorial church of St. James or St. Peter, for instance, would come to be considered as the very place where the former was beheaded, or the latter wept, when he heard the cock crow after he had denied his Master. A next step would naturally be the exact localization of the details of the story, and the square yard would be identified on to which the martyr's head rolled, or where it was buried, and the pillar would be found and recognized upon which the cock happened to be standing. Thus, round a perfectly innocent and even praiseworthy beginning, misunderstandings, misrepresentations, and finally shameful abuses would gradually grow. I write this as the most likely and most charitable explanation of much in the Church of the Sepulchre and its surroundings, as well as in other parts of Jerusalem, that offends us as being grotesque, absurd, grossly idolatrous, and dishonouring to the name of Christian.

Just behind the pedestal, which is supporting the stone on which the angel sat, is the low entrance, which must perforce be entered in a stooping posture, to the tomb chamber itself [60]. The artificial bench formed of white marble, cracked through the centre and much worn by the lips of pilgrims, has, suspended over it and constantly burning, forty-three handsome lamps, which are fed with olive oil. Of these, thirteen belong to the Greeks, thirteen to the Latins, and the same number to the Armenians, whilst the Copts are only allowed four.

The curiously shaped tent-roofed turret upon the roof of the chambers is hollow in its centre and has windows for ventilation. The room itself is so narrow that only three or four persons can at the same time kneel before the stone bench. The whole of this Sepulchre-chapel, built of native rose-coloured limestone, with marble accessories, in the year 1810, by the architect Comnenos, of Mitylene, whose name is recorded on an inscription just inside the inner doorway, is modern.

Of the original tomb, discovered by the excavators of Constantine the Great—leaving aside the question as to whether that really was the sepulchre in which our Lord lay, or not—it is most unlikely that a vestige exists. The following is, in brief, the utterance of a leading modern Roman Catholic authority on Palestine. " History teaches us that of the ancient rock-cave of which the Holy Scripture tells us, which rock-cave was seriously injured, first by Constantine the Great, out of love to Christ, and then by the Persians *A.D.* 614 out of hatred to Christianity, nothing but the site where it stood remains ; seeing that in *A.D.* 1010 it was destroyed down to the very ground by Hiaroth, governor of Ramleh, and by the orders of the Khalifeh El Hakim." (*Mommert's* " *Golgotha*," *ch. xii., p.* 110).

CHAPTER X.

AVING examined the interior of the Tomb-chapel which stands in the centre of the Rotunda, we will now walk round the little building which is 26 feet long, 18 broad, and pentagonal at its West end. It is built of the native rose-coloured and white crystalline limestone, and ornamented in front with slender spiral marble columns, etc. Clinging to the west end, inside an iron cage, is a small oratory belonging to the Copts, and just opposite this, and between two of the columns of the Rotunda, is a door leading into the dark Syrian chapel, which is simply the rock-hewn western apse of the church. Through a low doorway in the wall of this chapel, the real ownership of which is claimed and sometimes fought over by both Armenians and Syrians, we enter a small chamber, one side of which is formed by the circular outer wall of the Rotunda, and the others by those of an ancient Jewish rock-hewn tomb with " kokim," or oven-shaped recesses to receive the dead. There are two of these loculi in the Southern wall, with a lamp burning before them. These are said by tradition to be the graves of Nicodemus and Joseph of Arimathæa, the last-named of whom is supposed to have made arrangements that when he and his colleague died their bodies were not to be laid in the tomb originally intended for himself, and in which the body of the Saviour was laid until His Resurrection, but in this tomb close by.

On the Western side of the chamber are the blocked-up entrances to other kokim, which, by the removal of the rock partitions between them, have been made into one chamber, which is fitted with a wooden door. It is generally kept locked, but on the occasion of the last visit of the late Sir Charles Wilson to Jerusalem, it was opened for him by the orders of the Greek Patriarch, and I was honoured by receiving an invitation from Sir Charles to accompany him and Mr. Dickson, the late British Consul, and Mr. C. A. Hornstein, when they went to examine it.

In the floor just in front of the entrances to the kokim of Joseph and Nicodemus is a shaft cut in the rock, and at the bottom of this are other kokim. Similar tombs exist in the Coptic Convent just outside the church at its north-eastern end, so there is no doubt that at one time or other the place where the church now stands was really a cemetery.

This fact, however, does not bring us any nearer the solution of the problem as to whether the Sepulchre of our Lord was here, because, in the first place, nobody doubts that, during the time of the kings of Judah, and before the building of the second wall, the place was outside the first wall which was much further south, and ran from the citadel, near the Jaffa Gate, straight to the Temple-area. Secondly, we know

G

[61] Ventilating turret on roof of the Sepulchre Chapel.
[*Photo—A. S. Hanauer*

from several passages in Josephus (*Wars v., chapter ix*
§ 2 ; *chapter xi. 4, etc.*), that during the siege by Titus
there actually was a sepulchral monument, that of the

high priest John, situated somewhere very close to, if not on the actual site of, the present church itself. It adjoined the spot where the Roman fifteenth legion was engaged in constructing banks.

It is therefore quite possible that the mound of earth which in *A.D.* 327 the workmen of Constantine the Great removed, when they discovered what was taken to be the Sepulchre of our Lord, was really part of

[62] Church of St. Helena.   [*Photo—American Colony*

the bank raised by this fifteenth legion. Who can tell? From Josephus ("*Wars*," *book v. ix.* § 2), we learn that the mound or "bank" in question was cast up, "at John's monument," and *after* the taking of the second wall. It, therefore, seems clear that the monument was situated *inside* the second wall. But one cannot now be quite sure.

Returning to the Rotunda we notice, as we now pass to the north of the Tomb-chapel, that between each pair of the great circle of piers, there are chambers, which have been formed at some period after the Crusading time by dividing up the ambulatory that originally ran round this part of the church and between the piers and the outer wall. The series of rooms thus formed is apportioned out amongst the various sects, and used as store-rooms. Above this set of rooms are galleries.

Having noticed this we reach an open space to our left, forming a vestibule to the Franciscan Chapel of the Apparition. In the floor of the vestibule two stones, a little distance from each other, mark the traditional spots where the risen Lord and Mary respectively stood when He appeared to the latter and she took Him to be the gardener. In the Franciscan Chapel the visitor is shewn a piece of a pillar to which our Lord is said to have been tied, and in the vestry, which is on the left-hand side as we leave the chapel, the sword and spurs of Godfrey de Bouillon. People who are made Knights of the Order of the Holy Sepulchre are invested with these and pay high sums for the doubtful honour and privilege. I am told, on good authority, that the price of the lowest grade is £40.

East of the vestibule of the Chapel of the Apparition is the Northern transept of the great church, and here, in the shape of arches supported by masonry, flying buttresses, etc., we note vestiges of structural alterations of different dates. At the Eastern end of the transept is a low white-washed chapel belonging to the Greeks, and called "The prison of Christ." At its entrance one is shewn "the stocks," two round holes in a marble slab.

In prolongation of the Northern transept is the great Eastern ambulatory, very dark and gloomy, containing two apses fitted up as chapels, and named respectively, beginning with the most Northerly, the Greek chapel of Longinus, and the Armenian chapel of the division of the Garments of Christ by lot. Situated between the two last-named is a great, steadily widening staircase, with cross marks and names of pilgrims carved on its side walls, and leading down to the underground Church of St. Helena [62].

It is a very picturesque structure, the Northern and Southern sides being partly rock, cased with masonry. The rough floor is fully 16 feet lower than that of the Rotunda, and the chamber measures, according to a statement which the present writer has not verified, but supposes to be fairly correct, 51 feet by 43. It is divided into a central nave with lateral aisles by four ancient Byzantine columns with dilapidated massive basket capitals patched with plaster. The roofs are groined, and from the central one, above the four capitals, rises a low drum, pierced with four windows, lighting up the chapel, and supporting a semi-spherical dome. The exterior of this drum and dome rises, like a mountain standing in the middle of a plain, from the courtyard of the Abyssinian convent.

The Church of St. Helena is said formerly to have belonged to the Abyssinians, but was seized by the

Armenians at the time that the Abyssinians in Jerusalem died out, during the plague of 1838. It contains two altars, that to the north being dedicated to the penitent

thief, and that next to it to St. Helena. Close to the latter is shown the stone seat which that lady rested on whilst superintending the excavations in search of our Lord's Cross, but unfortunately for the legend, it cannot be historically proved that Helena did institute such a search. The tradition con-

[63] Cave in which, it is said, the Crosses were discovered. [*Photo—C. Raad, Jerusalem*

necting her with the Invention of the Cross and the building by Constantine of the Church of the Sepulchre, did not originate till over half-a-century after her time, and her contemporaries mention none of the circumstances related in the legend.

A rough rock-hewn staircase in the South-east corner of the church leads down into the cavern where the three crosses are said to have been discovered [63]. The exact spot, belonging to the Greeks, is pointed out where they lay. The true one was identified by the circumstance that when laid beside a dying woman it restored her to perfect health, the other two having failed to do her any good. Such tales must be taken with much salt. Of genuine, but melancholy, interest is the altar with a statue in the northern part of the cave. It belongs to the Latins, and commemorates the visit to Jerusalem, in 1855, of the ill-fated Maximilian, then Archduke of Austria, and afterwards Emperor of Mexico, shot at Queretaro in the year 1867 by the victorious insurgents.

Before leaving the Church of St. Helena, we are shewn on the Northern wall, not far from the altar of the Penitent thief, what seems to be a plastered-up window, and we are gravely informed that there was originally an orifice here which reached down into purgatory, so that people could distinctly hear sighs, cries and groans of anguished souls undergoing punishment. As these sounds proved too trying for the nerves of modern sinners, the crack was very wisely closed up. A similar absurd story is related concerning the stone said to mark the middle of the world in the great central nave of the Church of the Sepulchre, set apart as the Greek Cathedral. Remounting the stairs and proceeding Westwards along the ambulatory, we pass on our left another small apsidal chapel belonging to the Greeks and commemorative of the Crowning with Thorns.

The Greek Cathedral [64] lies east of the Rotunda, and opposite the Tomb-chapel, and is best approached from that direction, although there are two doors opening into it from the ambulatory north and south. It is divided from the Northern and Southern transepts of the Church

[64] Greek Cathedral.

[Photo—C. Raad, Jerusalem

of the Sepulchre by stone walls lined with carved gilt and painted wooden wains-coting. On the west it opens from the Rotunda by a great pointed arch. Within is the great central lantern of the church formed by three similar arches, north, south and east, and rising like the western one from four huge masonry piers about 40 feet apart, north and south, and 98 feet east and west. These arches support a drum with a masonry dome, the inside of which was once ornamented with a Twelfth-century fresco painting of the mystic Vine of David.

To the east of the lantern is a great apse, separated from the Catholicon, or body of the church, where the congregation assembles, by a richly gilt screen, the Iconostasis, which is intended, as in all Orthodox Greek churches, to hide the priest consecrating the elements of the Holy Communion from the gaze of the people. No female is allowed to pass behind this screen. Ranged round this apse, are stone benches, raised in steps one above the other, like a Roman theatre in miniature, for the clergy to sit in Ecclesiastical order of precedence on either side of the Patriarchal chair, which is placed in the centre higher than all. From this apse, called the "Hagion," or Sanctuary, there are staircases to the Calvary-chapel and other chambers, built over the great ambulatory, round the church of the centre of the world, which is thus named from a low stone pedestal in the centre of the nave, and said to mark that spot. An old Greek priest once solemnly informed the writer that there is a tradition that before this pedestal was placed there, a hole was there to purgatory, or rather hell, for the Greeks profess not to believe in purgatory.

Along both the Northern and Southern walls of the nave are arranged stalls for clergy, and two episcopal thrones ; that on the north for the Patriarch of Antioch, the southern for his brother of Jerusalem. Between these and the Iconostasis are two ancient stone pulpits, rarely if ever used.

[65] Old drawing of Mount Calvary. [*Photo—W. Franklin*

Another " centre of the world " at Jerusalem is in the Temple-area, and revered by Jews and Moslems, though the former may not visit it. The idea of a centre of the world in the Holy City, though a quaint one, is not actually absurd. It has, as Dr. Schick remarks, " a typical meaning, as Jerusalem is to the Jews, Christians, and Moslems, a Holy City."

I am indebted to Mr. W. Franklin who furnished me with the negative of a reproduction of a picture in an old book (" *Zuallardo's Travels* ") in the library of the Franciscan Convent [65]. The author and artist were here in 1586, and the picture is interesting, not only because it shews the chapels on the traditional Calvary in very much the same condition as they are now, but because in the chapel below, the exact positions respectively of the monuments of the first two Crusading kings, Godfrey and Baldwin, are indicated, and drawings of the same shewn. The following explanation of the letters may be interesting :—

A. The Calvary Chapel (Greek).

B. Chapel where according to tradition our Lord was nailed to the Cross (Latin).

C. Underneath same roof as the Calvary Chapel, and to the right of the altar, " The rent in the rock."

D. Underneath Calvary Chapel, Chapel of Melchizedec and place of Adam's skull.

E. Monument of Godfrey.

F. Do. Baldwin.

G. Stone of Unction.

H. In ambulatory to left of picture is the staircase leading up to Calvary Chapel in 1586.

In a remarkable address, by the Rev. Dr. Munro Gibson, one of the speakers at the Sunday School Convention, delivered in Jerusalem, in 1904, he said :

" *We can all put the centre of the earth where we like now-a-days. The most interesting map I ever saw was a map that made Chicago the centre of the earth. . . . I have at home a classical map of the ancient world. . . . . I measured the length of it and breadth of it, and took the exact centre, and it was right in Jerusalem.*

" *Palestine, though small, was in no corner of the earth. South of it was Egypt ; east, Babylon ; north-east, Assyria ; north, Tyre, Sidon and Syria ; and west, Greece and Rome. If you take Jerusalem as the centre of a radius of twelve degrees of latitude, and describe a circle you will include the capitals of all the countries which figured in the world's history up to the time of Alexander the Great. There is no other capital of which this can be said. . . . The world of course was not nearly so large in ancient times as it is now, but such as it was, the Holy Land was in the centre of it. Think of it and you will see that it would have been impossible to have chosen a better position. This rocky ridge—lifted up above the great river plains around where grew and flourished the empires of antiquity— was a magnificent rostrum from which to reach the nations with the Word of God. Well might the Hebrew prophets lift up their voices to the nations far and near, with a cry like this : ' O earth, earth, earth, hear the word of the Lord.' Or, this : ' Hear, ye people, all of you ; hearken, O earth, and all that therein is.' *"

CHAPTER XI.

LEAVING the great courtyard in front of the Church of the Holy Sepulchre by the small door at its South-eastern corner, we enter a short street leading eastwards. This is generally called "Palmers' Street," from the supposition that it was here that, in the middle ages, pilgrims from Europe, who had fulfilled their vows and were about to return to their native land, purchased the palm branches which they took with them

[66]   Ancient masonry in Russian Hospice.   *[Photo by Author*

in attestation of the journey. As a matter of fact, the old "Palmers' Street" was a few yards further North, though it ran parallel with the modern one. The large vaulted refectory in the lower part of the Convent of Abraham, was originally part of the older street of the palm-sellers.

[67] Ancient ruins in Russian Hospice. [*Photo by Author*

Palmers' Street is called by the natives, " Harat ed Dabbagha," or " Street of the Tannery," from a tannery, the smells and refuse water from which, constituted a nuisance which made it almost impossible to pass that way. This state of things continued till after the close of the Crimean War.

From the earliest times it has been the custom amongst victorious Oriental nations to endeavour to cast ridicule upon the adherents of a rival faith, by giving to their places of public worship names of reproach sounding very similar to their real appellations ; and, whenever they had the power, by installing nuisances either upon or, at any rate, as close as possible to their sites. We find in Scripture a good many allusions illustrative of this mode of action (2 *Kings x.* 27 ; *Daniel iii.* 29), and the way in which proper names are used to play upon, in such passages as *Micah i.* 10-15, where we may read :—

" *In Dust-town (Beth Aphrah) I wallow in the dust. Ye people of Fair-town (Shaphir), in shameful nakedness pass away. The people of Flock-town (Zaanan) have not gone forth like a flock. The calamity of Neighbour-town (Beth-ezel) makes it no neighbour to give you refuge. For the people of Bitter-town (Maroth) have writhed with pain for something good and pleasant. . . . Ye people of Horse-town (Lachish) bind the horse swift for flight to the chariot. . . . Therefore must thou, O Israel, give up possession of Gath's possession (Moreshethgath). The houses of False-town (Achzib) shall be as a false fountain to the kings of Israel. I will yet bring an inheritor who shall lay claim to you, ye people of Heritage-town (Mareshah)."* *

---

* It has been suggested by some commentators that the name " Mount of Corruption " (II. Kings xxiii. 13), in like manner originated in an offensive caricaturing of playing or punning upon the word anointing. Mischah משחה anointing thus becoming " Maschith " משחית corruption.

In like manner, though much more offensively, the Moslems, who for centuries have been the ruling class in Jerusalem, call the Church of El Kiamah or the Resurrection, the Church of El-Kamamah, that is, of the dunghill; and that of St. Martin, or Mar Martin, where

[68] Old Roman gateway in Russian Hospice.

[Photo by Author

the great synagogue of the Perushim now stands, El-Maraghah, which means, " The place where donkeys roll."

The appearance of Palmers' Street has altogether changed for the better since the days when I first knew it in 1856. Not only has the offensive tannery disappeared, but also the great mounds of rubbish and ruin which then towered above the narrow pathway on either side;

and in their stead there are handsome two-storied structures in the ornamental French and Italian style. Some of the most important and interesting bits of ruin

[69] Ancient wall in Russian Hospice.

[Photo by Author

have been carefully preserved inside the new Russian Hospice, at the eastern end of the thoroughfare, and just opposite the German Emperor's Erloser Kirche, a reproduction of, and standing on the site of, the old Crusading Church of St. Mary of the Latins [70], which belonged originally to the famous Order of the Hospitalers of St. John of Jerusalem. Our illustrations shew interesting pieces of ancient masonry as they

[70] Ruins of Church of St. Mary of the Latins.

[*Photo—American Colony*

appeared before the erection of the Russian Hospice [66 and 67]; the ruins of an old Roman gateway [68] which was repaired at an unknown period with materials taken from the ruins of some Byzantine structure, and a remarkable fragment of ancient wall [69] discovered more than half-a-century ago, and around which excavations were made by the late Sir Charles Wilson. He found that it had formed part of the great buildings of the Emperor Constantine, and, as the holes in its face prove, had at one time been covered with marble slabs. The remains of the copper clamps, which held the latter in their places, are still clearly visible inside the holes. Nevertheless, the supporters of the view that the Church of the Holy Sepulchre contains the actual and true site of Calvary maintain that this is a genuine fragment of the second wall of Jerusalem on the north in our Lord's time, outside which He was crucified. The Southern end of this relic may now be seen. Until recently it was covered with heaps of stones, and adjoining masonry of much later dates, most of which are now removed. The above-mentioned Russian Hospice, where this wall and other ancient remains can now be easily examined, is worth a visit.

All along the Southern side of "Palmers' Street" lies the "Muristan," or site of the magnificent buildings once belonging to the Knights of St. John of Jerusalem. The Western part, occupying about two-thirds of the whole, belongs to the Orthodox Greek Church. All traces have been quite removed of the splendid Church of St. Mary the Greater, which stood a few yards to the west of St. Mary of the Latins [70], and was so called in order to distinguish it from the latter, which was a smaller edifice. The apse [71], and also the Saracenic staircase, the latter built after the Crusaders had been driven from the city by Saladin in *A.D.* 1187, had to be removed when the " Erloser Kirche " was built, as above related.

[71] Crusading cloisters, South of Church of St. Mary of the Latins.
                                    [*Photo—American Colony*

A few of the beautiful capitals have been preserved and may, at present, be seen in the entrance hall to the Convent of Abraham, where also are some fragments, including a magnificent group of an archer (Sagittarius) attacked by a wolf, and other stone carvings that formed part of a sculptured "Zodiac," like that over the portal to St. Mary the Less (Erloser Kirche), but on a grander scale. An illustration of one fragment is shown below [72].

Immediately adjoining the Erloser Kirche on the south are still existing ruins of the building supposed to have been occupied by the Sisterhood attached to the Order of St. John. These mediæval and very interesting remains belong to Germany, and stretch Southward as far as David Street, the old vaults bordering which, on the north, are used partly as shops and partly as the vegetable bazaar.

[72] Relic from Church of St. Mary the Greater. [*Photo by Author*

The Greek portion of the "Muristan" is separated from that belonging to the Germans by a new street, cut a few years ago right through the ruins from north to south, and called the "Kaiser Friedrich's Strasse," in memory of the Emperor Frederick of Germany, who, in 1869, when he was Crown Prince of Prussia, visited the Holy

City, and took possession of the ruins which had been presented to his father by Sultan Abdul Aziz. Remains of the old cloisters [71] adjoining the Erloser Kirche are also to be seen, and a handsome mediæval doorway opening into them [73].

[73] Mediaeval doorway in cloisters adjoining the Erloser Kirche.
[*Photo by Author*]

In the South-western part of the " Muristan," in the angle formed by the junction of David Street with Christian Street, is the hospice and church of St. John the Fore-runner [74], the latter being a mediæval struc-ture, restored in 1847. It is very peculiar in shape, consisting of three apses and a corridor running across from north to south, to the west of them. Still more remarkable, however, is the much more ancient crypt or underground church, lying some twenty feet or thereabouts below the level of Christian Street, and just beneath the church we have described. It was apparently a Byzantine building, which suffered alterations at some later period. In shape it resembles the building above it with the three apses and a Western corridor, or narthex, but the existence of large windows and a door, all of them walled up,

74] Entrance to modern Church of St. John the Forerunner.

[*Photo—W. Franklin*

reveals the startling fact that its floor, now so far underground, was, at the time it was built, the ordinary ground level of this part of the City, perhaps fifteen hundred years ago.

As a matter of fact, this subterranean and forgotten Christian place of worship, together with a series of very large cisterns which honeycomb the ground both north and east of St. John the Forerunner, occupy the hollow on the Eastern side of the great dam upon which Christian Street runs Northward. Some authorities believe that this is a vestige of " the Broad Wall " of Nehemiah iii. 8; xii. 38. The underground church and cisterns also furnish a further proof that the present " Muristan " occupies and fills up the head of what was, at one time, a wide valley.

We give illustrations [74 and 75] of the entrance to this Church of St. John, above ground, and also the interior of the western corridor or " narthex " of the underground church. When first discovered, in the year 1847, it was evident from earthenware pipes, visible up till 1904, that in bye-gone centuries this subterranean place of worship had been used as a baptistery receiving its water supply from the Pool of Hezekiah (*Father Burnabe " Meistemann's " Guide, page* 95).

In the spring of 1926, the crypt or underground church having been cleaned out and restored for purposes of worship, by kind permission of His Beatitude the Orthodox Patriarch of Jerusalem, was placed at the disposal of members and friends of the Order of St. John of Jerusalem, for *occasional* services, such as the celebration of St. John the Baptist's Day held annually on June 24th.

On the east the " Muristan " is bounded by the Westernmost of three parallel bazaars or market-streets. These are one of the most picturesque parts of the city,

as far as concerns the variety of costumes one meets with
as one traverses them. Fellahin from different parts
of the country; government officials in red fezzes and
ill-fitting European clothing, and wearing coats somewhat
clerical in shape; townswomen in long white or coloured
sheets, enveloping them from head to foot; Christian
ecclesiastics, wearing long dark robes, and headdresses
of different shapes; Ashkenaz Jews in long kaftans and
black hats; peasant women in dark blue gowns and with
white veils over their heads; Bedu from the Belka
pasture-land east of the Jordan; Greeks from the Archi-
pelago; Persians, wearing long conical and funny brown
sugar-loaf
shaped hats,
with green
turbans wrap-
ped round
their bases;
negroes,
Hindus,
Arabs, gipsies,
Italians,
Frenchmen,
Orientals,
Europeans,
Americans,

[75] Interior of Western aisle of underground Church of St. John the Forerunner.
[*Photo by Author*

and Africans; in short, all sorts and conditions of men
and women, in all sorts and conditions of clothing,
meet and jostle each other as they pass through the
narrow thoroughfare, or try to do so.

CHAPTER XII.

HE bazaars themselves, may perhaps be best described as very long-vaulted corridors or tunnels, built of ancient and very ruinous-looking masonry, with small chambers, by courtesy called shops, on either side [76 and 77].

These shops are deep recesses, not more than twelve feet square at the most, inside. The passage-way along the bazaars is perhaps fifteen feet wide, not more. The only light and air come in from the ends of the tunnel, some hundred yards distant, or from holes in the centre of the vaulted roofs, twenty feet overhead, which also serve as vents for the escape of blue smoke and vapour from numerous cook and blacksmiths' shops located in the above-mentioned recesses.

The Westernmost of the three tunnels is set apart for the use of butchers, blacksmiths and coppersmiths, and makers of the rough camel-leather shoes worn by the peasantry. Here and there, spread upon the floor of the street, just in front of one or the other of these shops, we find a huge raw camel's hide put out to be tanned, and whether we approve of the occupation or not, we have to help, by walking over it, to turn it into leather. It is hardly necessary to say that the atmosphere, in the Western bazaar especially, is most unwholesome.

The middle corridor is called "Suk el Attareen," or "Market of the Apothecaries," because it is occupied chiefly by Eastern druggists, who, seated cross-legged and generally smoking at the doors of their respective places of business, sell spices, nails, sulphur, oriental saddle

[76] Vaulted bazaar

[*Photo—American Colony*

bags and saddlery, rope and string, and many other dissimilar articles which are not easy to get in other parts of the town. The pathway between the two rows of shops in this bazaar is so narrow that it is hardly possible for two persons to walk through it side by side, and the shopkeepers on the opposite side of the street sit scarcely two yards apart, looking into each other's shops and faces.

Now and then you will find an open shop, whose owner is absent. In case his neighbour in the right or left hand shop, or those just opposite, happens not to have the special article you are in search of, but knows that the absentee shopkeeper has it, one or the other will not only offer you a seat, and perhaps a cigarette, or a cup of coffee, in order to induce you to await his return, but will even leave you in sole charge of his own shop, whilst

[77] Part of David Street.
[*Photo—C. Raad, Jerusalem*]

he himself goes to call him, always supposing that he be not very far off. Such is Eastern courtesy.

Here is an open shop without a shopman, but you notice that a piece of twine-netting has been stretched over the wares exposed for sale, or that a chair has been laid on its back upon them. This is a sign that the merchant has been called away on special business, or has gone to the mosque to pray, and has left his property and his business, under the guardianship of his brother trades-men. Woe to the impudent thief who, under such circumstances, would venture to stretch out his hand to abstract the smallest object from this shop!

The third and Easternmost of the three bazaars is about one-half as long as the two others, and is used by silversmiths and oriental drapers. It is worth visiting, because it alone, of all the streets of Jerusalem, has as yet remained unaltered from the condition in which it was sixty, perhaps a hundred, or several hundreds of years ago.

Along the sides of the street, and in front of the shops, are stone benches, about two feet high and a yard wide. The two leaves of the shop-doors are not hinged on to the side-posts, as in ordinary doorways, but, respectively, to the door-sills and the thresholds, and meet in the middle, half way up the door way. When the shop is open, the lower leaf lies flat upon the stone bench, and if covered with a carpet, forms a convenient dais or platform on which the merchant and his customers sit whilst conversing, or else as a counter upon which the shopkeeper lays his wares. The upper door-leaf is lifted up, and kept in position either by an iron bar, which fastens it to the wall behind, or is propped up in such a manner that it hangs stretched either horizontally or else sloping

upwards over the bench below, so as to form a canopy or pent-house. From the lower side of this various goods are hung as advertisements to passers by, on the same principle that European shop-windows are " dressed." Here and there some Koranic text or religious motto, in curiously interlaced ornamental Arabic characters, and placed under glass inside a frame, advertises

[78] A chained prisoner. [*Photo by Author*

the piety of the shop-owner. From the centre of the upper and overhanging door-leaf, there hangs a knotted and often very grimy piece of rope, at which the merchant, who has been sitting cross-legged, clutches, whenever he wants to raise himself to an erect posture.

Up till about the year 1864, all the native shops in Jerusalem were like those in this part of the bazaars, but about that time, as has been elsewhere related, the local authorities had all the " mustabehs," or raised benches running along the streets and on both sides of the latter, removed, and the thoroughfares repaved. About 1885 this pavement was taken away, and the streets paved as they now are, with the middle raised, and the channels for rain-water at the sides. Till the latter date, there had been only one gutter, and that down the middle of the street. We give a view of one bazaar [77] in line with those just described, but further north, which shews, in the immediate foreground, the place where the great street, running southward from the Damascus Gate, is crossed by the " Via Dolorosa," at the point said by a worthless tradition to have been the Seventh Station, or halting place of our Lord during His progress from Pilate's House to Calvary.

I mention the above apparently trivial circumstances because it was at the time that the first alterations were made, by some working parties of chained prisoners [78], that the fine old Roman paving slabs, which might be noted here and there along the line of these three bazaars, disappeared. Fortunately, however, a portion of the same pavement was uncovered some years ago, in the Russian property in Palmers' Street, and has been preserved in its original place and condition in the Hospice.

As we walk through the old bazaars we notice other proofs of their antiquity. Here and there, where the whitewashed plaster has fallen from the walls, we remark old lettering cut deeply into the stones; generally a capital T, or the words " Scta Anna." The former shews that the shops or buildings on which it occurs belonged to the Knights Templars, and the latter marks the property of the Crusaders' Church and nunnery

[79] Medeba mosaic map of Jerusalem showing Street of Columns. [*Photo by Author*

of St. Anne, just inside the St. Stephen's Gate. The crozier marks property that belonged to the Crusading Patriarchate. The shops in the fine new buildings which, during the last twenty years, have been erected by the Greeks, are in like manner marked with ⫟ the sign or monogram for " taphos " the Sepulchre. Thus in modern days we still have survivals of mediæval customs.

The late Dr. Schick and some other competent authorities believe that even in the time of Christ there was a market on the site now occupied by these bazaars. However, here in the East the Crusading period is considered horribly modern, and therefore it is satis-

[80] Remains of traditional Porta Ferrea.   [*Photo by Author*

factory to find in these bazaars other proofs of yet greater
age. Not only have we the mention, by Bernard the
Wise, *A.D.* 867, of the market existing here in his time,
but here and there the shafts of erect columns, still in
sight, peeping through the surrounding masonry, are
relics of the magnificent colonnades erected by Hadrian.
These, as the now famous mosaic map of Medeba attests
[79], ran straight through his Roman town of Aelia
Capitolina, from the Gate of Neapolis, a triumphal arch
on the site of the present Damascus Gate, southward to
the neighbourhood of the modern Zion Gate. A reproduction is now in the library of the College of St. George,
of the city of Jerusalem as it is represented on the Medeba
mosaic, and shews this grand Street of Columns.

CHAPTER XIII.

HE Muristan is bounded on the south by a part of the great street which, starting from the Jaffa Gate, traverses the city, and ends at the western wall of the Temple-area. Amongst the Frank residents in Jerusalem it is generally called " David Street," but amongst the natives its three different parts are known by as many different names, with which, however, we need not burden the reader. The first and westernmost part of it ends, after a descent of twenty-six steps, at the point where " Christian Street " starts on its course northward.

From this point the great street continues to run eastward past the Muristan, and as far as the easternmost of the three bazaars described above. Here the second part of its course ends, and it suddenly turns to the right, that is, to the south for about ten or fifteen yards, when it again turns eastward and continues its course in that direction to its end. Just where the street forms an elbow, before starting on the third portion of its course, is the entrance to the Jewish quarter in this direction.

At the point where the first part of the great street ends at the foot of the first twenty-six steps, and on the side exactly opposite to the entrance to Christian Street, we ascend a very narrow staircase, or short street scarcely seven feet wide on an average. Having got nearly to the

I 2

top, we turn sharply to the left, that is to the East, and having mounted the twenty-third step after leaving the level of Christian Street we follow a short but rather crooked street which runs in a general way parallel to the second part of David Street, though at a considerably higher level.

[81] Saracenic arch on site of Porta Ferrea.
[*Photo by Author*]

The fact is that David Street lies, on the plan, along what, in the days of the kingdom of Judah was the great high road along, but outside, the Northern wall of Jerusalem ; and there is reason to believe that the other rather crooked street, which we are about to traverse, runs along the very top of the said Northern city-wall, part of which still exists, buried under debris.

We pass the Maronite convent on the right. At its north-east corner the street of stairs turns off to the south, leading upwards past the eastern side of the convent,

which was originally the house built for a former British Consul; it then became the first premises of the Kaiserswerther Deaconesses' school and hospital, before the erection of their new buildings outside the city, after which the school was sold to the Maronites. If we follow the staircase it will bring us past the house which was occupied by the early missionary of the London Jews Society, the Rev.

[82] Archway entrance to Syrian Convent.
[*Photo by Author*]

J. Nicolayson, partly built over the desolate Crusading chapel of St. James the son of Alphæus, situated just behind Christ Church, and now a deserted and ruined mosque.

Instead, however, of going along this staircase, we shall follow the old street on the top of the buried city-wall on its Eastward course. Almost immediately after passing the Maronite establishment, we come past the former House of Industry workshops, belonging to the London Jews Society, and the house originally built by Dr. Macgowan, and left by him to the Society. It was afterwards occupied in succession by their Doctors, Chaplin, Wheeler and Masterman. The former carpentry workshops and the house between them and the doctor's house were the first Girls' School premises of the London Jews Society, and stand on the site of the garden belonging to the house left by Dr. Macgowan.

Although the doors to these two houses open directly from the street on its Northern side, yet we cannot help being struck with the circumstance that to reach the former workshops, we have to descend flights of stairs as soon as we have set foot inside the house doorways. The reason for this is that the houses mentioned are built up against the ancient wall, two towers belonging to which were discovered at the time the foundations for the present structures were dug. In the basement of the house next to the old doctor's house there still exists a curious " tower-chamber," described in the Palestine Exploration Fund "Quarterly Statement" for October, 1906, and which, according to monkish tradition, was the prison in which St. Peter was bound (*Acts xii.*). The portion of wall discovered was, including the towers, 390 feet long and 37 high.

A few yards distant, on the opposite side of the street, we notice a displaced capital [80] once belonging to a pilaster of the Corinthian order, and about half a dozen other old stones in a modern wall. These are, according to tradition, the last vestiges of the Porta Ferrea, or "iron gate" (*Acts xii.* 10). Unfortunately for the tradition the said iron gate has been shewn in other parts of the city at various periods. (*Robinson's " Biblical Researches,"* *vol. ii. page* 200 *footnote.*)

Just beyond these vestiges a Saracenic arch is built across the street [81] over the entrance to the doctor's house above mentioned, and at right angles to the latter runs the traditional street along which the Apostle proceeded, past the place where the hospital of the London Jews Society formerly was, to the house of Mary, the mother of John, whose surname was Mark (*Acts xii.* 12). The Jacobite, or Syrian Convent, is asserted by tradition to occupy the site of this house. The building, having been seriously damaged by earthquake some years ago, has lately been rebuilt, but its mediæval doorway, that at which St. Peter knocked, according to tradition, has been preserved [82]. In the church is shewn a picture of the Virgin, said to have been painted by St. Luke, who is alleged to have been, like one or more of our modern missionary bishops, not only a doctor but an artist as well. The font in which tradition says the Virgin was baptized is also shewn here.

The street passing this monastery gate winds away uphill in a general direction to the South-west, till, having passed the ruined chapel of St. Thomas, it enters the

]83] Archway in David Street. [*Photo by Imberger*

street leading from the Jaffa Gate to the great Armenian Convent and Church of St. James.

We continue our walk from the old doctor's house of the London Jews Society eastward, descending until we come upon the Harat el Jawany [83], running at right angles to our course. On market days this particular stretch of thoroughfare is so crowded that it is difficult to get along. The pavement is covered with peasant-women squatting beside baskets of farm produce, fruit, eggs, vegetables, leben, poultry, etc. Vendors of native-made straw mats and baskets range their goods against the wall of the street

[84] Supposed " Gate Gennath."
[*Photo by Author*

quite covering up the ancient arch, which some erroneously suppose to be the remains of the Gate Gennath [84], mentioned by Josephus as the point from which the second wall of Jerusalem on the North started. It was situated near the Herodian tower called Hippicus, and could not have been so far East as this mysterious and walled-up archway is. On either side of the street are the shops of native dyers, and we find a number of Bedawee women haggling with them about the cost of colouring some of their rough homespun.

In order to escape from the throng, we turn aside into what is now a coffee-shop with a thoroughfare leading right through it to the elbow of David Street, above mentioned. It is a curious place. Four roughly constructed arches, rising respectively from as many massive ancient columns, apparently "in situ," with much battered Byzantine capitals, form a kindred structure to the Church of St. Helena. This coffee-shop seems to have been an old cruciform church. Little is known about it, but tradition says that it was really an ancient place of Christian worship, and built on the site of the house which belonged to Zebedee, the father of St. James and St. John. The Franciscans curiously hold that the reason why St. John was known to the high-priest (*St. John xvii.* 16), was the very simple one that the family of Zebedee used to supply the household of the high priest with fish from the lake of Gennesareth; and, as that was at least three days' journey from Jerusalem, the parents of the Apostle, as a matter of course, must have had a dwelling and a place of business in the Holy City, and this was where it stood. In the khan or caravanserai on the eastern side of the above-mentioned elbow are Crusading vaults which formed part of the mediæval Malquisimat or public cooking-place for pilgrims. (*Robinson's Bible Researches, vol. II., page* 560.)

We pass through this puzzling old coffee-house, which is said to have at one time served as a bath-house, and

also as a mosque, and find ourselves at the spot where the
last portion of David Street commences its descent

[85] Portal of Saracenic building on the site of St. Giles' Abbey
[Photo by Author

eastward. The arched and vaulted tunnel-street is dark and gloomy, and the pavement dirty and slippery all the way, even after we have got out again into daylight, and can more clearly see the squalid and tumble-down buildings on either side. About half-way down the street we notice that it is joined by another coming down from the south, that is from our right. It is the " Haret el Meidan," or Theatre Street, along which are the sites respectively of the Asmonean palace and gallery, the German Crusaders' quarters, etc.

Just at this point are some quaint old Saracenic buildings. An archway spans the street, and close by, on the right, is a picturesque Moorish window balcony, and, just by the lamp, is the entrance to the Haret Meidan.

CHAPTER XIV.

O N the opposite side of the street, and just beyond, and partly underneath the archway, is an old and handsome Saracenic building on the site of the Crusading Church and Abbey of St. Giles, mentioned in the "*Citez de Jerusalem*" [85]. Some remains of the Christian building still exist hidden in the basement of the later structure. The entrance to the latter is in the characteristic pendentive Arab style. This ornamental portal is immediately opposite the entrance to the street by which later on, turning sharply to the right, we descend another steep and winding staircase in the Tyropoeon Valley on our way to the Jews' Wailing Place. Before descending we notice the fronts of several ancient oriental houses. It will be noticed that they are constructed of massive stones of different colours, and in some cases have very elaborately carved Arabesque tracery on the outer walls and stalactite-like ornaments over the doors or windows [87]. The portal of the " Medresset et Tunguzieh," or College of the Emir Tunguz, which is situated at the end of David Street, at the eastern extremity of the more northerly of the two great causeways which in the days of our Lord crossed the Tyropoeon, from the Temple-hill to Mount Zion, furnishes a very fine example of pendentive or stalactite ornamentation [88].

This special building, which is now used as the " Mehkemeh," or court where the Cadi sits, occupies the site of the council chamber of the Sanhedrin, which was situated at the Temple gate called " Shallecheth " and also " Coponius." There were indeed other chambers where the great Jewish tribunal sat, within the Temple precincts, but as they seem to have been situated in those parts of the sacred enclosure which Gentiles were not allowed to tread, we may justly suppose that it was in the council chamber that stood where the Mehkemeh now is that St. Paul was brought under the protection of Roman soldiers, and made the memorable defence of which we have an account in Acts xxiii.

Just outside, and close to the portal of the Tunguzieh College, is a very handsome sixteenth century fountain, which, however, seems to have been constructed out of much older material, some of which appears to be mediæval and some more ancient. The architectural rose ornament seen above the Arabic inscription of Solomon the Magnificent (*A.D.* 1520-60), probably at one time adorned some Crusading church, whilst the highly decorated trough was in all probability at one time a sarcophagus in some rock-hewn sepulchre of the Herodian period. There are several such fountains in Jerusalem, both inside and outside the Temple precincts, and though in general form they are similar, yet this one is by far the handsomest. The water which supplies these fountains comes all the way from Solomon's Pools, through a four-inch iron pipe which was laid a few years ago. Before that time the water came through an aqueduct, which was very frequently out of repair, but which delivered the water through two branches, one supplying the northern part of the Haram and the other the southern, as the present pipe still does.

[86] Saracenic building.   *[Photo by Imberger*

A few yards to the east of this fountain is a curious and domed little structure, through which one could get to the

[87] Arabesques on Saracenic building.   [*Photo by Author*

aqueduct whenever it needed repairs. When standing in the open space in front of the fountain we happen to be just above the famous " Wilson's Arch," as the first vaulted link in the great northernmost of the two cause-ways, which in our Lord's time joined the Temple-hill to Zion, is named. The whole of this causeway still exists entire, but is so hidden by houses built upon it and also against its sides, that it is difficult to realize its existence.

To the West of Wilson's Arch, the causeway is con-structed of a series of remarkable vaults built alongside others, and in some cases over some at a lower level. They end in a noteworthy vaulted passage which was intended to facilitate the bringing of troops into the Temple enclosure from the great citadel near the Jaffa Gate. This passage is fully described in the publications of the Palestine Exploration Fund. There are, in fact, two ancient twin viaducts running side by side, the combined widths of which exceed that of Wilson's Arch, of which they form the continuation, by 18 inches.

The Southern of these twin viaducts is broken in its continuity to the west by a large rectangular vaulted chamber of ancient construction, with a column or pedestal sticking up from the centre. I mention this curious chamber which General Sir Charles Warren calls the " Masonic Hall," from some circumstances connected with its discovery. Dr. Russell Forbes, in his work " *The Holy City Jerusalem*," *page* 33, tries to identify this undoubtedly exceedingly remarkable apartment, with that in which—according to the account by

Philostorgius (vii. 14) of the discovery of the Tomb of David, etc., during the reign of the Emperor Julian— there was found also at the same time, and lying upon a pedestal wrapped in a cloth, a manuscript of the Gospel of St. John.

It is not my object to enter into any controversy, but as I have been more than once questioned by tourists about the matter, I take this opportunity to point out that Sir Charles Warren, on whose staff I acted as interpreter, when the chamber was discovered, did not find an ancient sepulchre situated underneath the "Masonic Hall," full details concerning which are given in the Palestine Exploration Fund " *Recovery of Jerusalem*," *pages* 87-89. The present entrance to the Temple-area, standing at the Eastern end of the causeway, occupies the site of an old Temple gate.

We now retrace our steps in order to reach again the entrance to the street of stairs already mentioned, as leading down from the southern side of David Street into the Tyropoeon and the different interesting spots there situated.

CHAPTER XV.

ETRACING our steps as far as the portal of the Saracenic building, on the site of the Crusading Church of St. Giles, we turn to the left, and descend by a crooked and slippery street of stairs into the low-lying quarter of the town occupying the Tyropoeon Valley south of David Street, and west of the Temple-area. This quarter of the city is popularly known as " Harat el Magharibeh, or street of the Western Arabs," because it is inhabited by Moslems whose fathers, if not they themselves, originally immigrated into the country from North Africa. They may easily be distinguished from others by the white burnoose, or hooded surplice-like cloak which they wear over their other garments. They are mostly tall, well-formed men, with spare wiry frames, and keen fierce-looking features. Many of them are the descendants of the refugees who came over from Algiers about the middle of last century, when the brave and chivalrous 'Abd el Kader with many of his gallant followers went into exile.

The houses in this depression are all low, one-storied and poorly-built. The streets by which we reach the open space in front of the Jews' Wailing Place are very narrow and filthy. Crowds of Jewish and other beggars squat on the sides of the thoroughfare, and though many of them are blind and crippled, yet I cannot recommend the visitor to give any alms here, because that would be the signal for the whole swarm of beggars to beset and pester the good-natured philanthropist to such an extent that he will repent his ever having evinced a desire to be kind.

The Wailing Place has been so often described by others that it seems almost a waste of time to say much about it. In the lower part of the sixty feet high wall are several courses of great stones of the Herodian period in a fine state of preservation, and above them are several courses of large stones of later Roman work, with yet others of more recent date, higher up. Between these stones we notice growing at different heights, bushes of the caper-plant (*Capparis Spinosa*) which some people, on apparently insufficient grounds, have identified as " the hyssop which springeth out of the wall." As this is not the place to discuss this subject, I would refer such of my readers as may be interested in it, to Dr. Post's masterly article in Hastings' " *Dictionary of the Bible*," The total length of the Wailing Place is roughly speaking fifty feet, measuring from the Southern wall of the Mehkemeh, or Tribunal-hall of the Cadi. The magnificent drafted Greek masonry of which the lower courses of the wall, as now visible, are formed, are attributed by universal consent amongst those who are authorities on such subjects, to Herod the Great. The courses are about four feet high.

In the same wall, about thirty feet from the present southern end of the Wailing Place, and two hundred and seventy feet from the South-western angle of the Temple enclosure, there was visible until the year 1880, and inside one of the low houses, the enormous lintel of one of the four gates by which the Temple used to be approached from the west. The lintel itself was apparently first prominently brought into notice about the middle of last century, by Dr. Barclay, of the United States, in his " *City of the Great King*," and was thoroughly examined by Sir Charles Warren, whose account in the "*Recovery of Jerusalem*," *pp*. 110-117, I am using as reference. It is about 24 feet 8 inches long, and excavations revealed the fact that the gate itself, which still exists, buried in debris, is about 28 feet 9 inches high, measuring from the bottom of the lintel to the top of the sill or threshold.

During the excavations at this place, and at the time when I was an interpreter on the staff of Sir Charles Warren, the " Sanctuary " wall was bared to a depth of 78 feet 6 inches from the bottom of the lintel above mentioned, to the rock. It was then discovered that the massive drafted masonry, of which only a few courses are now seen at the Wailing Place, reach right down to the rock. There are twenty-six courses in all, twenty-two below the lintel, two on a level with the lintel, and two above it. These two latter courses do not now exist immediately above the lintel, but can be seen a little further to the north at the Wailing Place. Above these again, are four courses of squared stones, without drafts, except in a portion of the fourth and lower courses at the farther end, near the Hall of Justice, where drafts are to be seen.

The great stones at the Wailing Place are very much
worn and damaged. In the crevices between them we

[88] Portal of Medresset at Tunguzieh. [*Photo by Imberger*

notice a number of iron nails, which have been left there by Jews who, from superstitious motives, wished to leave as mementoes of their visit, a nail in God's " holy place " (*Ezra ix.* 8). Some of these nails are shewn in the illustration in the horizontal line just above the lowest course, and under the stone in front of which the first figure to the right is standing [89]. Our illustration looks Northward toward the Mehkemeh. The little door in the background, in front of which a crowd of Jews is seen, gives admission to a garden enclosure, where the continuation of the great wall is visible. This garden for some years past, has been opened by its owners, for a compensation, of course, to such Israelites as cannot find standing room in the other open space, and are able and willing to pay for the use of a quiet corner.

The great lintel is no longer visible, as, in order to discourage the visits of travellers, it has, for many years past, been purposely covered over with plaster. It has, however, been identified inside the Temple-area, with the upper part of a magnificent portal, the upper portion of which consists of a single stone above " 20 feet long," still visible in the subterranean Mosque of El Borak, which is at present closed against Christian visitors, but has been, in former years, several times examined by the Palestine Exploration officers, and was rightly believed by Ali Bey, who discovered it in 1807, to have been one of the gates of the Temple. (" *Travels* " *vol. ii. p.* 226, *compared with the plan and explanation prefixed to vol. i.,* *as referred to in Williams'* " *Holy City* " *ii.* 39.)

A great cistern, immediately east of this ancient gateway,

and in continuation of the same, has been recognized by competent authorities as the ancient gate-passage belonging to this approach to the Sanctuary. The excavations above referred to, also showed "that the road to this gate

[89] The Jews' Wailing Place.   [Photo—American Colony

from the Tyropoeon Valley may have been by means of a causeway, raised 46 feet above the rock. Whether it was solid or supported on arches is not apparent."

On all days of the week, Jews may be found at their devotions on this sacred spot. It is, however, on

Friday afternoons and the eves of fast or feast days, that they assemble here in great numbers. Here, bowed in the dust they may at least weep undisturbed over the fallen glory of their race ; and bedew with their tears the soil which so many thousands of their forefathers once moistened with their blood. It is often said that this custom is a mere hypocritical formality ; but this is a harsh judgment. Although with many it may have become part of a trade to pray at this place for people in other parts of the world who send money to be prayed for, yet doubtless, in the case specially of newcomers or visitors to the Holy Land, the grief of the mourners is the result of genuine and heartfelt emotion.

The custom is of ancient origin. After the futile insurrection under Bar Cochab had been suppressed in a deluge of blood, *A.D.* 135, the Jews were excluded from the city ; and it was not till the fourth century that they were permitted to look upon Jerusalem from the neighbouring hills (*Robinson's " Biblical Researches," i.* 23). St. Jerome, commenting on Zephaniah i. 15, relates that in his day (*A.D.* 410) they were obliged to purchase from the Roman soldiers the privilege of visiting the city once a year, on the anniversary of the destruction of the Temple (the 9th of Ab), in order to wail over its ruins ; and Benjamin of Tudela, who came to Jerusalem in the Twelfth century, mentions the custom.

CHAPTER XVI.

IN reference to the photographs of the Bab es Silsileh reproduced, the following description of this gateway may be of interest.

It is called Bab es Silsileh [**90** to **92**], or " Gate of the Chain," from the tradition that a " Melik en Namsa," or " King of the Austrians," was put to death here many centuries ago, by being hanged with a chain which was long preserved in memory of the event, but which has now disappeared.

However, leaving this worthless fable out of account, this Saracenic gateway, erected in the early part of the Thirteenth century, and adorned with marble capitals and fragments from Christian Churches, is noteworthy for several reasons. I have already remarked that it is believed with great likelihood, that the site occupied the position where, at the Eastern end of the great causeway terminating in Wilson's Arch, the ancient Temple Gateway " Shallecheth," or " Coponius," once stood. Besides this, it perpetuates what was a special feature of all the Temple gates, the double gateway. There were four such gates in the Western wall of the great enclosure, but though their exact positions are known, their remains are at present inaccessible to Christians ; and so, before describing Robinson's Arch in the ancient " Millo," or " filled up," or " Causeway " quarter of the city—both renderings are equally correct and appropriate—it is interesting to note that in our Lord's time, and before that, it was always customary to use special respect and ceremonial observance in approaching the Sanctuary. Thus one never, even though residing in a higher quarter of the city than was the Temple-hill, spoke of "going down" but of "going up" to the Sanctuary.

[90] Bab es Sılsileh from inside Temple-area. *[Photo by Author*

This usage may be traced back to the time of Israel's sojourn in the wilderness, when, though the camp formed a great square with three tribes pitching their tents on each of the four sides having the Tabernacle in the centre of a great empty space in the middle, and not, in a physical sense higher in level to the other tents, the dignity associated with the place as the abode of

Deity caused the approach of His worshippers thereto to be thought of as an " ascent." Thus we read in Numbers xvi. 12, that when Moses " sent to call Dathan

[91] Inside the Bab es Silsileh gateway. [*Photo by Author*

and Abiram " they said " We will not come up." This idea of the superiority in dignity of the Sanctuary should be borne in mind, as it supplies a key to several Scripture passages which would otherwise be, as indeed they have been, misunderstood. Further, it was a rule that " No one was to come to the Temple except for strictly religious purposes, neither to make the Temple mount a place of thoroughfare, nor to use it to shorten the road.

[92] Another view of the Bab es Silsileh gateway.

[*Photo by Author*

Ordinarily the worshippers were to enter by the right and to withdraw by the left, avoiding both the direction and the gate by which they had come." Therefore, there would have often been two different streams of people, each going in the opposite direction from the other through the right and left hand portals. " But mourners, and those under ecclesiastical discipline, were to do the reverse, so as to meet the stream of approaching worshippers, who might address to them either words of sympathy (' He who dwelleth in this house grant thee comfort '), or else of admonition (' He who dwelleth in this house put it into thy mind to give heed to those who would restore thee again ') " (*Edersheim, " The Temple,"* *chap. iii.*). In fact, the directions given by our Lord to His disciples when He sent them forth without money in their purses, without scrip, staves, etc. (*St. Matthew x. 9-10; St. Mark vi.* 8; *St. Luke ix.* 3) were, as is shewn clearly in *Lightfoot's " Temple Services," chap. x.,* identical with rules to be observed by worshippers approaching the Sanctuary, and the lesson which would suggest itself to the disciples would naturally be that their missionary journey was to be carried out in the same spirit in which their prayers in the House of God ought to be.

Before leaving this gateway, we notice the ancient paving-stones of the Roman period, seen just across the thresholds of the portals, and inside the Temple enclosure. There are about twenty, very much worn and exactly like similar paving-stones of the same period found in other parts of the city. Here they are specially interesting for two reasons, namely, first, our Lord's feet may have trod on this very pavement, and, secondly, their being inside supplies a valuable indication as to the level of the outer Temple-court at this point.

Leaving the Wailing Place, and passing through other narrow lanes, we reach an open space planted in part with cactus or prickly pear (*Opuntia vulgaris*), and partly used as gardens for the cultivation of gourds and cauliflowers. This spot, in New Testament times, was occupied by the Xystus, the southern of the two bridges leading across the Tyropoeon from the Temple hill to the traditional Zion ; and the hippodrome of Herod.

[93] Robinson's Arch restored. [*Photo—American Colony*]

The remains of the first and last named of these structures are invisible, being probably hidden under the immense accumulation of rubbish which now fills up the valley.

Of the bridge a remarkable relic survives in the so-called " Robinson's Arch " [93 and 96], which is quite one of the most interesting remains of antiquity still extant, and for the discovery and identification of which we are indebted to the author of that standard work on Palestine, the " Biblical Researches " ; who, in 1838, noticed in the western wall of the Temple-area, and at a distance of 39 feet from the south-west angle, three courses of huge stones projecting from the wall and forming the segment and spring of an arch, the span of which when entire

[94] View looking North up the Tyropoeon.　[*Photo by Author*

was, as shewn by the excavations of Sir Charles Warren, " a trifle over 41 feet 6 inches."

The distance from the wall across the valley to the precipitous side of Zion where the Palace of the Asmoneans once stood, on the Eastern verge of the present Jewish quarter, was 350 feet, which was the approximate length of the ancient bridge.

The last illustration [94] is a close view looking

Northward up the Tyropœon valley at the present day from the same point of view as that of the restored viaduct, and shewing, in the background, the modern buildings masking the northern and still extant causeway ending in Wilson's Arch. The next picture is a view of

[95] Buildings on the site of the Asmonean Palace as seen from roof of Mehkemeh.

[Photo by Author

the modern buildings on the site of the Asmonean Palace [95] as seen from the roof of the Mehkemeh and illustrating the circumstances recorded by Josephus in *Antiq. Bk. xx.* 9-11 and *Wars Bk. ii.* 15/1 and 16/8, etc.

All authorities are pretty well agreed that the portion of the Western wall of the Temple-area from Wilson's Arch to the South-west angle, and the Southern from the South-west angle to the double gate, is of the Herodian period. The spring of Robinson's Arch, however, belongs possibly to an older structure.

Already twenty years before Herod was made King we find the bridge definitely mentioned by Josephus (*Wars, i.* 7, 2).

[96] Remains of Robinson's Arch to-day.

[*Photo—American Colony*

During the siege by Pompey the adherents of Aristobulus are represented as retreating from Zion into the Temple, and breaking down the bridge behind them. The same historian also tells us that the house of the Asmonean family was situated above the Xystus, opposite the Temple, and where a bridge connected the Temple with the Xystus (*Josephus, Wars, ii.* 16). The said bridge was, later on, rebuilt by Herod, for in another passage of the same History we are told of Titus standing on the Western side of the outer court of the Temple, there being a gate in that quarter beyond the Xystus, and a bridge which connected the upper town with the Temple (*Josephus, Wars, vi.* 6, 2).

It seems certain, therefore, that we have here the remains of the structure so often and so clearly described by the historian. The excavations of Sir Charles Warren consisted of a series of shafts and mining galleries, sunk in a line across the valley from west to east in order to determine, in the first place, the line of the original rock or valley-bed, and next, in order if possible, to discover remains of the bridge. The enterprise was successful. Not only the remains of a colonnade which probably had formed part of the Xystus, but also the pier of the great arch, and of another further west, were found. Stretching from the base of the great pier to the sanctuary wall is a pavement, falling slightly to the east, and on this were found the fallen arch-stones and debris of Robinson's Arch. Twenty-three feet below the pavement there was found rock, and following it up to east, two fallen voussoirs, or arch-stones, of a yet older bridge than

Robinson's Arch, jammed in over a great rock-cut canal running from north to south, 12 feet deep, and 4 feet wide which had probably been in use before the sanctuary wall at this point had been built. The bottom of this canal is 74 feet below the spring of Robinson's Arch and 107 feet below the level of the old roadway. (*Recovery of Jerusalem, pp.* 94-111). The width of the viaduct was 50 feet.

CHAPTER XVII.

I N the same way that a geologist is able, by the study of the section of a quarry, to draw inferences as to the history of the earth's crust, so in like manner it is possible from a study of the different kinds of masonry lying over or beside each other in different parts of the walls of the city, or of the Temple-area, to tell the dates of various parts of those structures and obtain other valuable results. Here, for instance, at Robinson's Arch, and the South-western angle of the Temple enclosure, we have several sorts of masonry contiguous to each other [97]. In the lower left-hand corner of our illustration and behind the leafless branches of a tree, are the upper stones of Robinson's Arch-spring, twenty-five feet long, of Herodian times, and possibly earlier. Next above it, on the right, is early Arab masonry, over which come the bossed stones of the Templars' buildings, whilst to the left again, and over the great Arch-spring, we have the small and insignificant stones of the early part of last century. Round the corner, at the South-western angle, the masonry is different from any of these, and consists of massive cubical stones, measuring about three or four feet in length and breadth, built to a considerable height, each course receding backward an inch or so, in pyramid fashion, and dating apparently to late Roman or Byzantine times. They reach from the South-western angle as far as the heap of ruins, just South of the Mosque el Aksa, seen to the right, and all along and above them stretch the Templars' buildings referred to above, and having a row of large windows [99].

The depth of rubbish in this part of the city is very great; underneath the third window, counting to the

[97] Masonry of various periods.   [Photo by Author

right from the South-western angle it has been found to be ninety feet. Below the present surface the great Herodian stones stretch in complete courses from the South-western angle eastward as far as the Double Gate, underneath the Aksa; and northward as far as Wilson's Arch. As they quite differ from the more ancient masonry which is found to the east of the Double Gate, and as far as the South-eastern angle of the Haram enclosure, and also from that to the north of Wilson's Arch, it is clear that they are of later date. The excavations and investigations have proved that, although the portion indicated, from Wilson's Arch, southward to the corner, and thence to the Double Gate, is Herodian, and was built across the Tyropœon at this point, yet that

[98] A view of Millo   [*Photo by Author*

during the period between the death of Solomon, B.C. 976, and up to the commencement of the Herodian restoration, B.C. 17, it was not included within the Temple precincts. The presence of the two great viaducts, and the enormous amount of debris found there, could not be more suitably described than by the name " Millo," which has been rendered into English by the " filling up," or the "causeway," which at the present day extends southward as far as the Southern city wall East of the Dung Gate, and eastward from the foot of Zion to the city wall, bounding the open space called Hakurat el Khatuniyeh on the East, and also beyond that wall eastward. The three illustrations [98–100] placed side by side furnish a panorama including the whole of

[99] South wall of Temple enclosure.　　　[*Photo by Author*

this part of the city, and embracing on the left, the part stretching from the minaret over Bab es Silsileh as far as Robinson's Arch; and to the right the remainder from the latter point to the South-eastern corner of the " Hakurat." The first picture is looking towards the Dome of the Rock, the second towards the Mosque el Aksa and Olivet, and the third is taken from the same point as the two former and looking over the Southern city-wall, with its crenellations on top and narrow walks along its inside, and over the roof of the Dung Gate towards Siloam and the Mount of Corruption, with a Benedictine monastery on its summit.

These illustrations not only give a view of the present south wall of the city and of Millo, but also show its relation to the Mosque el Aksa and the southern wall of

[100] Another view of Millo.   *[Photo by Author*

the Temple enclosure outside the city.   The huge stones in the lower courses of the south " Millo " wall are old material re-used—one of them, which is only half-dressed, and has a boss bulging from it, is called " Hajar el Hublah," or " stone of the pregnant one " [102].   A similar legend is also told concerning the famous great stone in the quarry at Baalbek, that during Forty years after Solomon's death, the Jan, unaware of his decease, were toiling upon the construction of his stupendous buildings, and a female Jin was at work on this stone when news came of the death of the King, and so she left off work and her task remained unfinished. Another legend is that the stone here shewn was placed in position by the Virgin some time before she gave birth to our Saviour. In the outer angle formed by the

[101] View from the brow of Zion.   [*Photo by Author*

eastern wall of the Hakurat el Khatuniyeh, the excavations carried on by Dr. Bliss in 1897 revealed the existence of very ancient rock-cut dwellings (*Palestine Exploration Fund " Quarterly Statement," 1897, page* 267). These have been covered up again, but similar ones have been found on the eastern slope of Zion, within the space once included in the City of David, and may have been used by the ancient Jebusites. The next view is taken just outside the Dung Gate, by which we now leave the city for a while, looking downward toward Siloam. The grove of olive trees in the dark foreground is on the ridge of Ophel, and marks the place where, according to

[102] "Hajar el Hablah" in South wall. *[Photo by Author*

a learned but strange theory, upheld by many modern scholars, Zion, the City of David, once stood. Let me state their arguments briefly but fairly, as well as the objections to the same.

    1. Zion was an important fortress, and therefore must have been close to the Gihon spring, the only perennial fountain in the neighbourhood. A fortress must have a good water supply.

    2. Most authorities are agreed in identifying the present " Virgin's Fount," at the eastern foot of Ophel, with Gihon, and the famous subterranean

tunnel from the " Virgin's Fount " to the Pool of
Siloam with " the conduit " made by Hezekiah when
he " stopped the upper spring of the waters (*Revised
Version*) and brought them straight down on the
west side of the City of David " (2 *Chronicles xxxii.*
30). As Gihon or the Virgin's Fount is East of
Ophel, and the Pool of Siloam on the South-west of
the ridge, it follows conclusively that " the City of
David " must have been situated on Ophel.

3. Whenever we read of the Kings of Judah
going to the Temple they are always spoken of as
"going up" to the sanctuary. Thus Solomon
" brought up " the ark. As Ophel was the only
hill-top lower than Moriah, it follows that the city
of David must have been on Ophel.

Against these arguments, which at first sight seem very
plausible and even strong, there are the following
objections :—

a. Zion was *not* near the water. It had no
fountain to supply it. The name itself denotes its
being " *waterless* " and is derived from a root which
in Hebrew as well as in the cognate languages Syriac
and Arabic ציה *and* צוה (*in the Hebrew and
English Lexicon of the Old Testament based on
Gesenius, translated by the late Professor Edward
Robinson, and edited in 1906 by Professors S. R
Driver, D.D., Francis Brown, D.D., and Charles A.
Briggs, D.D.*), means " be parched," " dryness,
drought, parched ground, etc." Like several other
strongholds in Palestine, the castles at Banias,

Kula'at e Eshkif, Rabbath Ammon, &c., the citadel
was on a high hill somewhat distant from a spring.
It depended for its principal water-supply on the
ancient rock-hewn cisterns with which the site of
the traditional Zion is honeycombed. A few years
ago such an ancient cistern of Jebusite form was
quite unexpectedly discovered at the Boys' School
of the London Jews Society, close to Christ Church.
It had been hidden for centuries under a depth of
forty feet of debris. It seems absurd to argue that
a place the name of which means " the waterless,"
should be close to a fountain.

b. As regards the argument founded on
2 *Chronicles xxxii.* 30, there is no doubt whatever
that the passage is vague and ambiguous, and that
the words, which in both the Authorised and
Revised Versions are rendered " the west side of the
City of David," may, as is pointed out in the article
on " *Jerusalem*," in Hastings' " *Dictionary of the
Bible*," be equally well translated, " straight down
westwards to the City of David," and this would
strengthen instead of weakening the claims of the
South-western hill or the traditional Zion. It is
clear therefore, that no conclusive argument can be
built on this passage.

c. That the post-Davidic Kings should be said
" to go up " whenever they went to the Temple is
natural, because, as is generally allowed, the palace
built by Solomon was south of the sanctuary, and

lower than it, in the space between the Double Gate and the South-eastern angle of the present Haram enclosure, somewhere near to the site of the celebrated vaults called " Solomon's Stables." But when Solomon " brought up the ark of the covenant of the Lord out of the city of David, which is Zion " to the Temple which actually stood on lower ground, we must remember what has already been said in our remarks on Bab es Silsileh, about the use of the expression " going up " as a term of dignity for the approach to the House of God.

Thus all the chief arguments in favour of the Ophel site for Zion are answered and others may be adduced in favour of the traditional one. This subject is referred to again in another chapter.

CHAPTER XVIII.

FROM the Dung Gate a road leads southward down the western side of the Tyropœon Valley [103], outside the city walls, to the Pool of Siloam. The top of the minaret close to the pool, is in full view from the point where the above-mentioned road is crossed by another coming down along the City wall from the Zion Gate, situated one hundred and forty feet above us, and fifteen hundred distant to the west.

[103] View from the modern Dung Gate. *[Photo by Author*

Beyond the minaret, we notice the large enclosure at the mouth of the Tyropœon, marking the lower pool of Siloam, commonly called "Birket el Hamra" [104]. The

[104]   Pool of Siloam.   [Photo by Author

wall of the city in the time of the Jewish kings ran along the top of the massive buttressed dam, closing the valley mouth on the eastern side of this pool. The mulberry-tree—as tradition pretends, growing on the spot where Isaiah met his death, by being sawn asunder by command of Manasseh—stands on a stone platform at the South-eastern angle of the pool. The Mount of Corruption, with the houses of the Yemenite settlement at Siloam clinging to its steep sides; and beyond, the Kedron valley winding away amongst the hills to the South-east toward the ancient desert monasteries of St. Theodosius (Deir Ed Doseh) and Mar Saba, close in the landscape.

We turn to the left and follow the road leading eastward for about five hundred feet along the City wall, which here forms the southern rampart of the Millo quarter. This wall now turns Northward, for two hundred feet to the spot where, some thirty years ago, might have been noticed traces of a walled-up gateway of Crusading times, called, from its being first observed by a traveller of that name, " Richardson's Gate." When this part of the wall was rebuilt, all exterior traces of this gateway disappeared, but the great passage-way, with lofty groined roof, still exists inside the town underneath the old ruins, already mentioned as having been part of the Templars' buildings south of the Aksa, and at the North-eastern corner of the present Hakurat el Khatuniyeh. A few steps further east, we round two more corners and reach the spot where the city walls abut on to the southern wall of the Temple enclosure, running up against the ancient gate-post between the closed portals of the western Huldah or double gateway. Only part of the eastern part of the gate is visible from without, as a great heap of débris is

piled against it in the corner. Just above the lintel—
under which is another archway with carvings, supposed
to be of the time of Julian the Apostate, *A.D.* 363—we
notice a stone with some letters on it. They stand on
their heads and
belong to the
well-known
inscription
which is con-
jectured to have
formed part of
the pedestal of
the statue of
Hadrian, that
was seen both
by the Bor-
deaux pilgrim
(*A.D.* 333) and
St. Jerome
(*A.D.* 410),
standing close
to another of
Jupiter of the

[105]   Head of statue of Hadrian.
[*Photo by Author*]

Capitol, and on the site of the Holy of Holies—
(Hieronymus " Comment. ad Isaiæ "), " Hadriani statua
et Jovis idolum collocatum est." The inscription reads—

TITO AEL
HADRIANO
ANTONINO.
AVG PIO.
PP. PONTIF AUGVR
D.D.

178

" *To Titus Aelius Hadrianus, Antoninus Augustus Pius, Father of the Fatherland, Pontiff, Augur, decreed by the Senate.*" A magnificent marble head which belonged to a life-size statue, supposed to be the very image of Hadrian in question, was discovered in 1873, and came into the possession of a deceased acquaintance, a Russian ecclesiastic sometime resident at Jerusalem. It is now supposed to be at St. Petersburg, but in view of more recent events it may possibly be irretrievably lost [105].

Leaving this fascinating spot we proceed Eastward for about two hundred feet and reach the Eastern Huldah Gate, also walled up. Stretching between it and the Double Gate, we notice the famous string course of massive stones, each six feet high, double that of the other ancient stones. It extends, with interruptions, beyond the Eastern Huldah to the end of the South wall of the Temple enclosure, and it has been discovered that the architects who laid it must have been men of great technical skill. When the Temple wall along this side was free from the débris which have since accumulated against it, this gigantic course passed from end to end for six hundred feet, touching, near its centre, the crest of the hill which sloped downward, eastward and westward. Had the great course been laid perfectly level, it would, by an optical illusion, due to its contiguity to the curve of the hill, have appeared bent downward at either end. In order to obviate this, the ancient master builders actually laid the course with a slight curve sufficient to correct the error.

The huge corner-stone at the end of this course, seen

at the South-eastern angle of the Haram area [106], used in mediæval times to be pointed out as that referred

The
cor
stor

[106]   Ancient masonry at South-eastern angle of Temple.

[*Photo—Anonymous*

to in *Psalm cxviii*. 22, and alluded to by our Lord in *St. Matthew xxi*. 42, as " the stone which the builders rejected." It was also pointed out as such to the Jewish writer, Dr. Frankel, in 1856 (" *Nach Jerusalem*," *vol. ii. page* 158). It is clearly seen in the third course above the head of the standing figure. The great stones in this picture tower above the ground to the height of

[107] Triple, or Eastern "Huldah" gate. *[Photo by Author*

seventy-five feet, their limit upward being marked by the projection seen near the upper right hand corner. The Eastern Huldah Gate was originally a double gate like the Western, but was altered in the late Roman period and turned into a triple gateway [107], with three parallel passages leading toward the upper levels. Yet further East we reach " the Single Gate," a Crusading one [108], which, when open, gave access to the remark-able subterranean vaults, popularly called " Solomon's Stables," which exist at this point just inside the angle formed by the Southern and Eastern walls of the Temple-area. These were substructions intended to support the great platform at this point, and were called " Solomon's Stables " [110], because the Templars used to keep their animals here. As we wander through the forest of square columns, we notice that many of them are perforated at the corners, in order to receive " tether ropes." Here and there are remains of mangers. It is not unlikely that the royal stables during the period of the Jewish monarchy may have been hereabouts, though at a lower level. During his excavations, Sir Charles Warren discovered, about twenty feet below the sill of the Single Gate a passage running at a lower level, between the piers which support the vaults above. It is built of magnificently dressed stones, and was traced Northward for sixty feet. We may, therefore, conclude that there must be other vaults and chambers at this spot, but at a considerably lower level. Possibly the original stables of Solomon still exist deep below those of the Crusaders. The " Horse Gate " of ancient Jewish Jerusalem was, as is generally believed, somewhere hereabouts (*II. Kings xi.* 16).

CHAPTER XIX.

IN one corner of the present substructions may still be seen remains of the original underground Herodian vaults, whilst in the South-eastern angle there exist the lower courses of a great tower which stood at this spot, and the top of which is identified with " the pinnacle of the Temple " on which our Lord was placed by the Tempter (*St. Matthew iv.* 5), and also, and by a very ancient tradition, with the tower from which St. James the Less was cast by his persecutors. Not

[108]   Single gate near South-eastern angle of City walls.

[*Photo by Author*

being killed by the fall, a fuller, who was amongst them, struck him on the head with his club and thus put an end to his sufferings. In this illustration the

remarkable corner-stone referred to is at the end of the fifth course above the dry-stone wall seen in the lower left-hand corner of the picture [106]. Sir Charles Warren estimates its weight as over one hundred tons. (*Recovery of Jerusalem,* page 121). It is a remarkable fact, that scarcely one hundred yards from this spot, and two hundred feet south of the Triple Gate, a cave furnished with fuller's vats was discovered during Sir C. Warren's excavations. As we wander about amongst the many dim, mysterious and deserted aisles grouped side by side inside the South-eastern angle, we notice

[109] Remains of Herodian vault in Solomon's Stables.

[*Photo—C. Raad, Jerusalem*

184

that materials from other buildings have been freely used for repairs. In one place is a stone richly carved with the classic egg and dart pattern ; in another, the huge lintel of an ancient gateway set on end, and furnished with sockets for bolts, serves to form part of a restored pier; whilst in an obscure corner is a Herodian fragment elaborately ornamented with vine leaves, grapes, and trellis work, like that on the ceiling of the vestibule of the Double Gate, and evidently a relic of the Temple of the time of our Lord. It is well known that underground passages and great cisterns exist in different parts of this old world " souterrain," but we must not weary the reader by trying to describe them.

Passing the Single Gate, we come to the South-eastern corner of the Temple enclosure, about one hundred feet distant. The depth of débris at this point, however, has

[110] Solomon's Stables.   [*Photo—C. Raad, Jerusalem*

been ascertained to be fully eighty feet, and the grand old masonry reaches all the way down, founded on the rock. There still exists therefore at this place a portion, one hundred and fifty feet high, of the ancient structure. The foundation stone is let into the rock. It was on the stones of the lower courses that in 1868 were found old Phœnician mason-marks, some cut into the stone and others painted on it, the discovery of which roused such great interest at the time. Starting from this south-eastern angle and running southward was discovered the great Wall of Ophel, fortified with towers and erected by the ancient kings of Judah. Somewhere here was probably the " Horse Gate " of ancient Jerusalem. This Wall of Ophel was found by General Sir Charles Warren, in 1868. Some years later, about 1880, another portion further South, was uncovered by Professor Guthe, and it is shown on the plan in *Benzinger's* "*Hebraische Archaeologie,*" Bd. I. Tubingen, 1907. Verlag von J. C. B. Mohr (Paul Liebeck).

In 1925 Professor Macalister and the Rev. Garrow Duncan again uncovered and described this portion of wall very thoroughly. The British Antiquities Department have arranged for it to remain exposed as " a national monument."

Now comes a view of the Eastern side of the ancient wall, as one looks Northward on turning the South-eastern angle. In the distance, on the sky line, is seen the projecting column upon which, according to popular Moslem eschatology, Mohammed will sit on the Day of Judgment [111]. For the grotesque details connected with this belief see " *Tales told in Palestine* " (*Jennings & Graham, New York*). As a

[111] Wall of Temple enclosure, looking towards Mohammed's judgment seat. [*Photo by Author*

matter of historical fact I may, however, mention that some three or four hundred years ago, when Jerusalem was taken by a Mahdi, who had arisen amongst the Bedouin

187

east of the Jordan, the leader of the Arabs took his seat
upon this column, and intended to rehearse for the
edification of his followers what would happen at the Day
of Judgment, when he became giddy, as well he might,
and falling headlong, perished on the spot. The tradition
that the division of the wicked from the good at the Day
of Judgment will take place here and on Olivet, goes back

[112] Wall with ends of column and Moslem tombs.
[*Photo by Author*

to the early days of Islam, and is attributed to Safiyah
bint Hai, known as " The Mother of the Faithful," who
visited Jerusalem with the army of Omar, and died about
A.D. 670 (*Besant & Palmer's " History of Jerusalem,"
pp.* 479-80). " Mohammed's Seat " is not the only
column built into the eastern wall of the Temple enclosure. In the time of our Lord, open colonnades ran

along the sides on the edge of the outer court, and as we walk along, we notice many of them of porphyry and other beautifully coloured stones, built in with their ends protruding, and in one place a whole row of them above a group of sepulchral monuments marking the graves of rich Moslem towns-people [112]. The characteristic mark of such tombs is a cenotaph with two short upright

[113] Century plant on a Moslem tomb.

[*Photo by Author*

columns fixed at either end, and little stone-basins of water for the use of passing birds, and also of the departed. I have as yet not been able to get any satisfactory explanation of the symbolical significance of the two upright columns. The graves of the poor fellahin of Siloam are marked by a simple circle of stones, on which in many cases grows a century-plant [113] or giant aloe (*Agave Americana*). The use of this plant is decidedly symbolical. In sound, its name, " sebr " is exactly similar to that of the Arabic word for " patience." It is therefore the dumb expression of the patient and hopeless resignation of the humble Moslem to the inexorable fate decreed by Allah. Moslems believe in the Resurrection, but I have not found that the tardy blooming of this remarkable plant several decades after it has been planted, is in any way connected with thoughts suggestive of a hope after death, such as those to which a Christian mind is awakened by the sight of Olivet in full view, a thousand feet distant, across the Kedron and beyond Gethsemane.

Looking eastwards across the valley we notice thousands of white tombstones marking the graves of Jews, and also three very ancient monuments called respectively "the monument of Zechariah," and by Jews of "Jeremiah," "the cave of St. James," and "Absalom's Pillar." In another chapter we shall give a more detailed account of these.

We are now approaching the Golden Gate. This is so well known that I need not say much about it. It is a late Byzantine structure, on the site of a more ancient gateway, possibly that called " Miphkad " (*Nehemiah iii.* 31). Just before reaching this spot we notice a little closed Crusading postern in the wall [115]. A cross painted in the centre of a circle of rays

[114] Interior of the Golden Gate. [*Photo—American Colony*

191

on the face of the mediæval lintel has survived the weather of Eight centuries, and all efforts of the Moslem to deface it. It is just distinguishable in the photograph. A closed-up entrance between this Crusading postern and the South-eastern angle of the Temple-area leads one to conclude that there may be other unknown vaults besides " Solomon's Stables " there.

[115] Crusading postern in the City wall. [*Photo by Author*

It is generally acknowledged by competent authorities that the space just inside, and along the southern wall from the Double Gate to the South-eastern angle, was at first occupied by the palatial structures of the successor of David, and the kings following him, the South wall west of the Double Gate being Herodian. In New Testament times, the substructions now called " Solomon's Stables," [*page* 182], which bear evident traces of renovation, alteration and repair at subsequent periods, supported the great platform, on which from East to West for a length of nine hundred and twenty-two feet, extended the great Royal Cloister of Herod, with its three aisles, the middle one broader and loftier, cathedral-like, their roofs upborne by four rows of great columns, one hundred and sixty-two in number (*Josephus'* " *Anti-quities,*" *Bk. xv. chap. xi. 5*).

CHAPTER XX.

T HE Golden Gate [**114, 117** and **118**] is a late Roman or Byzantine structure, concerning the exact date of which there is still a great deal of uncertainty, for whilst some authorities are inclined to attribute it to the age of Hadrian (*Robinson's " Biblical Researches," i. p.* 296), others think it a work of Constantine, who, however, does not seem to have built within

[116] Ancient fountain at Jerusalem.   [*Photo—Anonymous*

194

the Temple-area, in which, as late as the time of St. Jerome, who died *A.D.* 410, there were still standing the equestrian statue of Hadrian and an image of Jupiter (*see footnote*). Others, again, attribute the Golden Gateway to the time of Justinian (*Professor Hayter Lewis, in his " Holy Places of Jerusalem"*), possibly overlooking the fact that the Persians and Jews who took and sacked Jerusalem in *A.D.* 614 are not likely to have spared a building like this. Whatever the exact date may be, however, it cannot be later than the Moslem occupation, *A.D.* 637, and therefore we may suppose that it was rebuilt by orders of Heraclius. He entered Jerusalem in triumph by this gateway eight years previously, in 629, when he visited the city bearing upon his shoulders the so-called " wood of the true Cross " which he had recovered from the Persians.

This supposition receives colour from a curious mediæval tradition current in 1102, and preserved by Saewulf. " By this gate the emperor Heraclius entered Jerusalem when he returned victorious from Persia, with the cross of our Lord ; but the stones first fell down and closed up the passage, so that the gate became one mass, until humbling himself at the admonition of an angel, he descended from his horse, and so the

---

Hieronymus Comment, in Esaim ii. 8, " Ubi quondam erat templum et religio Dei, ibi Hadriani statua et Jovis idolum collocatum est." Also Comment in Matthew xxi. 15, " de Hadriani equestri statuâ, quæ in ipso Sancto Sanctorum loco usque in presentem diem stetit."

" Where formerly was the temple and religion of God, there the statue of Hadrian and the idol of Jupiter is placed." " Of Hadrian's equestrian statue, which to the present day stands on the very site of the Holy of Holies."

entrance was opened unto him." (*Bohn's* " *Early Travels in Palestine*," *p. 40. and see footnote A.*)

Now as the buildings of Justinian were erected about *A.D.* 527, and the pilgrim Antoninus of Placentia, who came to Jerusalem about forty years later, found " what was once the beautiful Gate," in ruins with the " threshold and posts still standing" (*see footnote B*) it is difficult to believe the present structure to have been built by Justinian. On the other hand, the great monoliths inside the gateway, forming respectively the northernmost and southernmost jambs, are of great antiquity, and probably " the posts " noticed by Antoninus. They appear to have belonged originally to an ancient Jewish Temple Gate at this point, which is about one thousand and twenty feet north of the South-east angle and, as

---

A. This visit of Heraclius brought about a dreadful massacre of the Jews. They had helped the Persians to sack the Holy City and destroy the Christian churches, but when Heraclius " came to Tiberias the Jews who dwelt . . . in that country, came out to meet him, bearing presents, wishing him good luck and begging him to grant them security, which he promised, and set his seal to a written covenant with them . . . The monks and people at Jerusalem told him how the Jews had sided with the Persians." . . . and said " Do us a favour and put away all the Jews." . . . Heraclius answered, " How can I suffer them to be slain when I have already granted them security and have sealed a written covenant with them to that end ? . . . Unless I uphold this covenant I shall be thought by all men to be a liar, a cheat, and a man unworthy to be trusted, besides the great sin and wickedness whereof I should be guilty before our Lord Christ." . . . They answered, " The Lord Christ knoweth that their slaughter will be to thee for a remission of sins, and for an atonement for thy offences . . . and we will take this sin from thee upon ourselves, and will atone for it for thee, begging our Lord Jesus Christ not to lay it to your charge. Moreover, in the week wherein eggs and cheese are eaten— that is, the week before the great fast—we proclaim a complete fast, . . . with abstinence from eggs and cheese as long as the Christian religion shall endure . . . abstaining from all flesh and fat . . . that it may be an atonement for that which you have granted to us." So Heraclius consented to them in this matter, and slew countless numbers of the Jews. (Eutychii Annales, Pilg. Text Soc. version, pp. 47-49). The above is an historical association too often forgotten.

B. " Portam civitatis (quæ cohæret portæ speciosæ, quæ fuit Templi, cujus liminaræ et tribulatio stant) ingressi sumus in sanctam civitatem." Antonius Martyr—Ugolini Thesaurus, tome vii. p. mccxiii.—*Palestine Pilgrim Text Society's translation of Antonius Martyr, p. 15.*

seems likely, marks the North-west angle of the Temple Area in pre-Christian times. Here probably stood the gate "Miphkad" (*Nehemiah iii.* 31). The name "Golden Gate" is the result of two mistakes, viz. :— first, the supposition that this richly decorated Byzantine portal must have been the "Beautiful Gate" mentioned in *Acts iii.* 2 *and* 10. Secondly, the change of the Greek

[117]   Golden Gate from the East.   [*Photo by Author*

word "Horaia," meaning "beautiful," into the Latin "Aurea," meaning "golden."

In Crusading times, as we learn from the "*La Citez de Jerusalem,*" this gate was opened only on two occasions every year, namely on Palm Sunday, and on the feast of the Holy Cross in September, in commemoration of the visit of Heraclius. On both these occasions religious processions passed into the city this way. The gate of Jehoshaphat, now called St. Stephen's, served as an Eastern outlet from the city at other times.

We noticed in the last chapter the little postern a short distance south of the Golden Gate. There was also another little postern, a good deal further South. It has

[118] Golden Gate from the West.   [*Photo—Raad, Jerusalem*

been examined by the officials of the Palestine Exploration Fund and is described in the " Quarterly Statement " for 1882, p. 169, but is now difficult to identify, as a great quantity of rubbish was thrown against it after that date, so that now scarcely anything but the lintel is visible.

With regard to the familiar " dragoman-tale " that the Mohammedans keep the Golden Gate walled up, because they fear, if left open, the Christians will take the city, I would remark that it does not seem to be of earlier date than the Fifteenth century. Inside the gate chamber [114], on the South wall, between the two pilasters, and at the height of about three feet from the ground, I recently discovered traces of ancient square Hebrew lettering, which seem to have hitherto escaped observation.

CHAPTER XXI.

LEAVING the walled-up " Golden Gateway," we proceed Northward. The road still passes through the great Moslem cemetery, which stretches along the whole eastern side of the city as far as its north-eastern angle. The only break is where the road to Gethsemane and Olivet leaves the St. Stephen's Gate. On Thursdays especially the burial-ground is much

[119] Herodian tower, with large stones.   *[Photo by Author*

frequented by the Mohammedan women, who come to visit their dead, and for this reason. By a flight of imagination which is truly Oriental, these women believe that their revered dead are able to hear all that is said to them and accordingly continue to take an interest in domestic matters. And so the women sit down by the side of the grave and tell the dead all that has happened in their families since the last visit. I have often had opportunities of overhearing some sorrowing peasant mother or sister telling the deceased " how the brother or cousin has been taken as a conscript; and the tax-gatherer has seized more than his due; or the black ox has died of the cattle-plague." Moslem towns-women are frequently accompanied by some blind sheikh whom they pay for reciting passages from the Koran for the edification of the souls of the departed, and also for their own comfort. They also generally bring with them bunches of flowers, which they leave on the graves or tombstones. This custom originated, as I have been informed by a very learned Moslem, in the following manner : A certain Moslem of wicked life having died could not find rest in his tomb, but, as was evident to passers-by, from the groans that proceeded from the grave, was undergoing great torments. Being at a loss what to do for the departed soul, his relatives asked the advice of the Prophet, and his counsel was that Scripture should be read by the graveside, and flowers laid on the tomb.

One day, as I was passing through this cemetery, a veiled Moslem woman, carrying a baby, stopped me and asked me to lay my hand upon her little one and say " a prayer of blessing " over it. I could not refuse and she went away quite happy.

Unless told so, nobody proceeding along the Eastern city wall from the Golden Gate toward the gate of St. Stephen, would dream that he was crossing a deep but now filled-up valley; yet such is undoubtedly the case, for the excavations carried on here in 1867-1869 by Sir Charles Warren, have proved that whilst there are from thirty to forty feet of débris just outside the Golden

[120] Open space inside the Eastern wall.
[*Photo by Author*

Gate, there are one hundred and twenty-five feet of débris at a point two hundred and sixty feet further north. From this point the rock rises, till, at the Southern end of the great tower at the North-eastern corner of the Temple Area, the depth of rubbish is one hundred and ten feet, and at St. Stephen's Gate there are twenty feet of débris between the present surface and the rock. Our illustration of the great Herodian Tower at the North-eastern corner of the Temple Area [119], clearly shews the immense stones, one of which is twenty-one feet long. These stones are still visible above

[121] St. Stephen's Gate. *[Photo—American Colony*

ground up to a height of about thirty feet, to which we must, with our mind's eye, add the one hundred and ten feet now covered up at this point, or the one hundred and twenty-five feet to the now effaced valley-bed above referred to.

Instead of continuing our walk further Northwards through the Moslem cemetery and along the great rock-trench dug by Saladin first Northwards as far as the North-east corner of the city to the Burj Luglug or Stork's Tower, and then Westwards, we now re-enter the town through the well-known St. Stephen's Gate [121], called by the Jews "the Lion Gate," because of rude sculptures that adorn it. For the legends connected with this gate I must refer the reader to "*Tales told in*

[122] Church of St. Anne and Seminary.   [*Photo by the White Fathers*

Palestine," *p.* 19, or to "*Folk-Lore of the Holy Land*," *p.* 94, *et seq.*

Right before us, leading Westward, is the great street ending in the Via Dolorosa, whilst on the left is an open space between the City wall and the huge pool called "Birket Israil," which is now being rapidly filled up with rubbish. This, in our Lord's time, formed one of the strongest defences of the Temple precincts on the north, and till about forty years ago, when the now famous twin-pool, close to St. Anne's Church, was rediscovered, it used to be shewn to tourists as the " Pool of Bethesda." Our illustration [120] shows the open space just referred to, with the highest visible courses of Herodian work at the North-eastern angle, and on the right, " Bab el Asbat," a name given to the approach to the Temple-area at this point.

We continue our walk Westward and almost immediately notice on our right the entrance to the grounds of the recently restored Crusading Abbey Church of St. Anne [122] occupying the site, according to a tradition dating, from the Fourth century, of the dwelling of the parents of the Virgin Mary. Foolish as the legend seems, it has, as we shall see later on, a very interesting origin. There is here a valuable Biblical museum containing, according to the claims of the White Fathers who collected its contents, specimens of every object mentioned in Scripture. Amongst other things they show a large stone weight of one Talent [125].

CHAPTER XXII.

THE legend about the Church of St. Anne can be traced back to the Fourth century. It originated in the same way as the name "Golden Gate," which was given to the structure so-called, in the misunderstanding of an older title in a different language. Such mistakes are very common, and fruitful sources

[123] Stone weight in Museum of the White Fathers.

of mediæval traditions and legends. We shall meet with
yet another such instance when we come to the traditional
" House of Veronica," in the Via Dolorosa. In order to

[124] Northern subterranean twin-pool.

Photo—American Colony

explain that of St. Anne's Church we must turn to the narrative (*St. John v.* 1-18), telling of the healing of the impotent man, at the pool called in Hebrew " Bethesda " (*Bethsaida, or Bethzatha*), " having five porches and close to the sheep gate or market." This sheep gate was north of the Temple ; and besides the great pool " Birket Israil," noticed in the last chapter, there existed, in the Fourth century, a very remarkable twin-pool [124], that is, two pools lying side by side and surrounded by cloisters or colonnades on the four sides, whilst a fifth, making five porches, came between the two pools, and staircases led down to the water. This pool is in the same valley which, as has been previously shewn, rises east of the hillock of the Grotto of Jeremiah, and opens into the valley of Jehoshaphat at a point between the North-east corner of the Temple-area and the Golden Gateway. Peter of Sebaste (*A.D.* 381) mentions a church in the same place. Other writers of mediæval times speak of the twin-pools as the Piscina Interior. As time passed on, the fourth century church was probably destroyed by the Persians (*A.D.* 614), and, as the heaps of débris around had encroached upon, and partly filled up the rock-cut pools, it became necessary in the Crusading period to shorten the latter and roof them over. In order, however, to preserve the memorial of the five porches, a church, of " St. Maria in Probatica " [125 and 126], was erected over one of the reduced pools, and the crypt of this church was divided into five transverse sections, to represent the porches. This church was in its turn destroyed, and its very existence, as well as that of the

[125]   Exterior of crypt of Church of St. Maria in Probatica.

[*Photo by the White Fathers*

twin-pools, forgotten, till they were re-discovered during excavations conducted by the French at the time that the

[126] Interior of old crypt of Church of St. Maria.
[Photo by the White Fathers

adjacent church of St. Anne [127 and 128], which had been given to the Emperor Napoleon III. after the Crimean War, was being restored. According to Hunter's "*History of the War in Syria*," the church had been offered to England after the bombardment of Acre, in 1840, but refused.

"The Sanctuary of the House of St. Anne," says Professor Clermont Canneau, in his "Archæological Researches," *vol. i. p.* 119, "built upon the actual site of Bethesda, has for its origin a play upon the words 'Bethesda' and 'Beth Hanna,' both of which mean 'House of Grace.' The legend guarantees the exactitude of the Gospel tradition and fixes its exact locality. We have a decisive material proof of this in the marble foot, discovered at St. Anne's itself, and bearing..... an 'ex voto' in Greek, of 'Pompeia Lucilia, in gratitude for her cure at the Sheep Pool.'"

[127] Church of St. Anne.
[Photo by the White Fathers

On the other hand several scholars, following the suggestions of Dr. Robinson ("*Biblical Researches*," *vol. i.* 342), are inclined to identify the Pool of Bethesda with the Virgin's Fount or the ancient Gihon spring, in the Kedron and close to Siloam, the reason being that they think that the intermittent flow of the latter, due probably to the action of a natural syphon may have been the troubling of the water alluded to by St. John. No such phenomenon has as yet been noticed in the waters of the re-discovered twin-pools.

The interior of the Eastern of these pools, both of which are now underground, is seen in illustration [124]. It will be noticed that the three rectangular masonry piers on the right stand on the fragments of more ancient and massive circular columns. The wall on the left-hand side is rock, that on the right, as well as that in the background, masonry.

Another illustration is a fine view taken in the ruined crypt of the church of St. Maria in Probatica [125], and looking Westward. The door-way seen in the background, gives access to the Western of the twin-pools, and the railing on the left, between two of the transverse arches which divides up the crypt into five parts, as above stated, is to keep visitors from approaching, and damaging by their touch, the remains of an interesting Twelfth century fresco-painting on plaster, representing the angel troubling the water.

Yet another view, taken from the same spot, looks in the contrary direction. It shews a person descending the staircase leading down into the pool and above, in the back-ground, the remains of the semi-circular apse of St. Maria in Probatica [126].

The next illustration is the exterior of the extremely interesting and typical Crusading church of St. Anne [127], which is situated nearly thirty yards South-east of the pools and ruins above mentioned. Just over the doorway in the arched portal, and behind the coat of arms, there still exists the Arabic inscription recording the fact that Saladin turned this church into a Moslem college or Medresseh, after he had wrested Jerusalem from the Christians in 1187. He was a wise and sagacious, as well as a brave monarch, and having other foes of Islam besides, and more dangerous than the Christians, to contend with, namely, the various heretical and sectarian parties, such as the Ismaeliyeh, the Nuseiriyeh, the Druzes, and the adherents of the " Sheikh el Jebel " or Old Man of the Mountain, with the latter's blindly and fanatically devoted " fedawis " or assassins (*Besant and Palmer's " History of Jerusalem," pp*. 359-363), he and other rulers of El Islamiyeh who succeeded him, strove to counteract their dangerous and murderous doctrines by educating the Moslem youth in the real teachings of the Koran. For this purpose there were founded at Cairo, and in other cities, including Jerusalem, great Saracenic Colleges, such as we have already had occasion to refer to in this book.

The fine interior of the Church of St. Anne [128], looking Eastward toward the altar, consists, like several other Palestinian churches of this period, of a nave and parallel aisles. The church of St. Anne has several curious features. For example, by a visitor, standing at the Western end of the axial line of the nave, it is seen to be un-symmetrical. The left hand aisle, for instance, is not exactly like the right hand one, and the small window over the Eastern apse seems to be too much on one side. As I have been told by a learned Roman Catholic priest, these seeming irregularities are

[128] Interior of Church of St. Anne.   [*Photo by the White Fathers*

characteristic not only of this, but also of other churches of the same age, especially in the South of France.

The mediæval architects, most of them "religious," *i.e.*, monks, tried to give " sermons in stones," and to impress upon worshippers, amongst other doctrines, not only that the church was the " navis," or ship in which the believer passed safely over the waves of this troublesome world into the land of eternal rest; but that it was also the " Corpus Christi," or spiritual body of Christ, the temple in the walls of which true Christians were the living stones. In order to express this idea, churches were often built, like the Church of St. Anne, lop-sided, so as to remind one of the body of Christ hanging on the Cross, with His head inclined to one side.

In the southern, or right-hand aisle, is a broad flight of steps leading down to chambers, or crypts, said to have been the apartments in which the parents of the Virgin dwelt, and where she was born. We need not either visit or describe them, for many of the Romanists themselves doubt the genuineness of these churches, and a fierce paper-war has been waged by the Franciscans against the " White Fathers," who own the Church of St. Anne. They have, as it would appear, materially enlarged the chambers, besides adding new ones " for the edification of the faithful," *i.e.*, of the credulous.

Before leaving the precincts of the church and the modern seminary adjoining it, a few further remarks on the history of the place may not be deemed superfluous. From Moslem writers, such as Abul-Feda, we learn that before the Crusaders took Jerusalem it had already become a Moslem " dar el 'ilm," or house of learning, but that " when the Franks took Jerusalem, it was once again turned into a church." A Benedictine Sisterhood was then installed in the adjoining convent, and St. Anne's Abbey rose to great importance in the days of Baldwin I., who compelled his wife Arda, an Armenian princess, to take the veil there.

Not long afterward, the convent of St. Anne had the honour of receiving a princess of the blood-royal, Ivette, the daughter of Baldwin II., who afterwards became abbess of the convent of St. Lazarus at Bethany, the modern El Azariyeh, a wretched little Moslem village, built amongst the ruins, and with the materials of the said convent. When the Crusaders were turned out of Jerusalem, Saladin, as we have noticed in the preceding chapter, again turned the church into a Mohammedan school.

During the Great War the Church and premises were seized by the Turks and restored to Moslem use. With the liberation of Palestine by Lord Allenby, the White Fathers came in to their own again, and they re-opened their institutions for the training of Roman Catholic missionary-priests and teachers for work in Africa. Their Order was founded by the late Cardinal Lavigerie, often called by Roman Catholics, " The Apostle of Africa."

CHAPTER XXIII.

LEAVING the Church of St. Anne, we continue our walk along the street leading Westward. After passing an archway thrown across the street, and generally sheltering a group of coffee-drinkers and smokers from sun or rain, we cross a street leading to Bab Hytta, one of the Northern entrances to the Temple Area. From Bab Hytta we get a glimpse of the Dome of the Rock [129]. We do not turn aside to gaze at it, but still proceed Westward. The Saracenic buildings bordering the street on our left are of later date than the Crusading era, for we notice, built into the lower courses here and there, many stones with the peculiar and characteristic Crusading diagonal dressing and " masons' marks."

" Masons' marks," of which there is an endless variety, are found on Twelfth and Thirteenth Century buildings not only in Palestine, but also, it is said, on many churches and other edifices, of the same period in different parts of Europe, including Great Britain and Ireland. The first writer to notice the existence of such interesting marks on buildings at Jerusalem was the Franciscan Morone da Maleo, in 1669. Of late years they have attracted a great deal of notice and study from Antiquarians. It is supposed that they are the " hall-marks " of various guilds of masons and stone-cutters who travelled

from country to country in order to put up important
buildings, in the same way in which, when Christ Church,

[129]   Dome of the Rock from Bab Hytta.
[*Photo by Author*

Jerusalem, had to be built nearly Sixty years ago by the
London Jews Society, there being then no competent

workmen on the spot, the Society had to bring stone-
cutters from Malta. Thus history repeats itself.

Immediately in front of us, another heavy arch bestrides

[130]   Tower of Antonia.   [*Photo—C. Raad, Jerusalem*

the street, throwing a very deep shadow ; and just before
we reach it, we notice a remarkable ruined minaret

or mosque-tower on the right-hand side. This is often pointed out to tourists as the " Tower of Antonia " [130]. As a matter of fact, it is very likely that the seven courses of massive masonry forming its lower portion, really are a relic of that famous fortress, part of the site of which, before the War, was occupied by the Turkish barracks at the North-west corner of the Temple-area. Just in the corner, a walled-up ancient door-way, flanked by greatly-mutilated limestone colonnettes, used in the early part of last century to be pointed out as the entrance to the former " House of Ahasuerus, the Wandering Jew," The oldest traditions of this mythical and allegorical personage are found in the writings of Roger of Wendover, a monk of St Albans (*died* 1237), and of Matthew Paris (*died* 1259). (*An article on* " *The Wandering Jew*," *pp. 1,568-9, Webster's Great Dictionary*). A few minutes after passing this arch and minaret we have on our left the said barracks, the court-yard of which, once the site of the chapel of the Crowning with Thorns, now long since destroyed, may be considered as the starting-point of the Via Dolorosa. On our right, the recently restored Franciscan chapel and convent of the Flagellation of Christ, is worth visiting, because here there has been laid bare during recent years a considerable portion of massive Roman pavement like that which we have already noticed in other parts of the city. The stones are grooved in order to prevent horses slipping. This pavement, which some suppose to be remains of Gabbatha (*St. John xix.* 13), is formed of great slabs of limestone from three to four feet square and almost a foot thick. It extends Southward for some distance, a continuation of it having been discovered under the adjacent nunnery of the Ecce Homo, and also beyond that under the Greek convent erected in 1906 in connexion with the newly-invented " Prison and Stocks of Christ," of which an account and illustration appeared in the " Jewish Missionary Intelligence " (*August,* 1906, *page* 125).

[131]   Remains of Ecce Homo arch.

[*Photo—C. Raad, Jerusalem*

The central arch of the Roman gateway, called the " Ecce Homo " [131], from the tradition that it was here that Pilate placed the Saviour in view of the clamouring multitude, saying, " Behold, the man ! " has been found by competent investigation to be of later date, having probably been a triumphal gateway built in honour of Hadrian in the Second century. The small Southern side portal no longer exists, its place being taken by the khan or hospice, for Moslem pilgrims from Hindustan and Central Asia. The corresponding Northern one is still preserved, and forms a very picturesque and interesting " reredos " or background to the altar in the nunnery chapel [133].

In the time of Christ, there was here a remarkable double or twin-pool, which still exists underground, and

[132]   Reconstruction of the Ecce Homo Arch.

[Photo—American Colony

part of which is shewn in the picture of the reconstructed arch [132].   It is inacessible now, but could still be visited some twenty years ago through an entrance in the cellars of the nunnery.   A glimpse of the Northern pool can at present only be obtained from a window in the subterranean corridor or gallery running underneath the great pavement in the above-mentioned convent of the Flagellation. It still contains a great deal of water, which

[133] Altar in Chapel of Ecce Homo.

has percolated through the surrounding soil and been drained from the rocky declivity of the Bezetha hill to the north of it. That it once received another supply is

proved by the existence of a mysterious rock-hewn
aqueduct, which runs into it, and has been traced right
through the City as far as the rock-cut foundations of the
present City wall just East of the Damascus Gate, but
no further. The next illustration [134] shews the
entrance to the so-called Solomon's Quarries on the left.
The white stones for the clock tower, which several

[134] City wall near Solomon's Quarries

[*Photo by Author*

years before the Great War was built over the Jaffa
Gate tower, were taken from here. This clock tower,
now removed, was furnished with a timepiece which
struck Oriental time, but had four dials, two of which
marked European, and two the Eastern hours of the
day. As this description may not be intelligible to the
general reader, it may not be out of place to remark

that in the East, before the Great War, the same mode of reckoning the hours of day and night as was used in New Testament times was in vogue. This was amongst the natives generally, and for Moslem religious purposes more especially. The hours were reckoned from Sunset, twelve for the night and twelve for the day, Sunset at all seasons of the year being at the Twelfth hour. It follows therefore, that, except at the equinoxes, when day and night are of equal length, 6 o'clock by day or night might fall at any time between 11 o'clock and 1 o'clock a.m. or p.m.

[135] The Via Dolorosa.
[Photo—C. Raad, Jerusalem

Sixty years ago few people, except Europeans, had watches or clocks, and the hour of the day or night was guessed at by looking at the sun, one's own shadow, or the stars. It was not until the yeat 1846 that ordinary clocks were imported into Palestine by the late Dr. Schick.

Now, of course, watches are common, and there are several public clocks. Besides these there was another ancient and interesting way by which the lapse of time was noted in the Holy City. In some old Roman households it used to be marked, as we are informed by Sir W. Ramsay, by the sound of a trumpet.

"The use of the trumpeter after the Roman fashion to proclaim the lapse of time," says he, "is said to have been kept up until recently in the old imperial city of Goslar, where, in accordance with the more minute accuracy of modern thought and custom, he sounded every quarter of an hour." ("*Letters to the Seven Churches*," *page* 9).

This custom, as it is interesting to note, survived at Jerusalem till the recent British occupation of the Holy City on December 9th, 1917, up to which time the blast of a Turkish bugler stationed on the roof of the barracks on the site of the Antonia was every quarter of an hour answered by another bugler on the ramparts of the citadel close to the Jaffa Gate.

Three points deserve our notice before we leave the Ecce Homo chapel. The first is, that the Northern wall is artificially scarped rock, forming, in ancient times part of the counter scarp of the great rock-hewn trench which separated the Antonia from Bezetha to the North of it. This scarp is continued Westward as far as the great Austrian hospice, and in part is honeycombed with artificially hewn chambers in three tiers one above the other, some of which are accessible in the Greek convent above-mentioned, and situated between the Ecce Homo and the hospice. The second point is that during the excavations at the Ecce Homo and the Chapel of the Flagellation, several curious stone stands or pedestals

[136] House of Veronica.   *[Photo—American Colony*

were found. One of these stands in the porch of the Ecce Homo Chapel, and one is shewn standing under the

cloister on the left of the picture of the restored arch
[132]. These pedestals are supposed to have served as
stands for street orators, and also to have been specimens
of the kind of stones called " Eben ha Toim " in the
Talmud, and on which articles that had been lost in the
streets were publicly displayed in order that they might
be claimed by their rightful owners. The third point,
a very interesting one in connexion with Jewish mission
work, is suggested by the Latin inscriptions seen in
the illustration of the altar in the Ecce Homo chapel [133],
" Blessed is He that cometh in the name of the Lord !
Hosannah ! " and " Father, forgive them, for they know
not what they do."

The Ecce Homo nunnery is one of the principal
institutions in connexion with the Roman Catholic
mission for the conversion of the Jews, and was founded
by the late Father Marie Alphonse Ratisbonne, himself
by birth a Jew, but converted in 1842 to the Roman faith
by a vision in which the Virgin Mary herself appeared
to him whilst on a visit to the church of St. Andrea delle
Fratte at Rome. (*Granville Popular Library Series—
London : Burns & Oates Limited*).

The " Sisters of Zion " resident at the Ecce Homo
have schools for day-scholars and boarders, which are
attended not only by daughters of Jews but also of
Moslems, Greeks and others, who desire for their girls
a better education than they could get elsewhere.
Many of the nuns who teach in these schools are ladies
of rank, several being connected with European royalties.
They have a sister-institution at Ain Karim. There is

also, in connexion with the same mission, a large Boys' school outside the walls of Jerusalem.

Leaving the Ecce Homo we proceed on our way along the Via Dolorosa [135] in which Ecclesiastical tradition, not earlier, however, than the Fourteenth Century—the first allusion to it being in the work of Marinus Sanutus—brought together the scenes of all the historical or legendary events connected with the Crucifixion.

We ascend by the Via Dolorosa to the Northern end of Christian Street, noticing as we do so the traditional " House of Veronica " [136], the only one of the various " Stations of the Cross " deserving a passing notice. It is a modern building erected over a basement of the Crusading period. The legend is that St. Veronica, a pious woman, whose name, whilst still a Jewess, was Berenice, met our Lord as He passed her house when going to His death ; and, moved with pity, handed Him a napkin with which to wipe His face when covered with blood and sweat. When He handed back the napkin, it was found that the stains had produced a " true portrait," " Vera icon " of His face. The true facts are that, as already noticed in previous chapters, in the case of the traditions connected with the " Golden Gate," and St. Anne's, we have here also an instance of a linguistic misunderstanding. Mr. Benjamin Scott writes, that " St. Veronica's name and existence are derived from the words ' Vera icon ' (a true likeness) formerly inscribed under pictures which purported to be representations of Christ. These certified copies came in time to be called ' Veronicæ,' and were known by that name to Christian writers. It was not until the Fourteenth Century that Rome constructed out of legends, based upon the ignorant use of the word ' Veronicæ,' the saintship and history of St. Veronica and established her worship." (" *Contrasts and Teachings of the Catacombs*," *page* 153).

The last thing we notice in this chapter is the remarkable building connected with a mosque and minaret at the corner where the Via Dolorosa strikes the northern end of Christian Street.

This building, now called El Khankeh, was the palace of the Latin Patriarch during the Crusading period, and when Jerusalem was taken by the Moslems in 1187, of Saladin himself. The walled-up Gothic portal close by and in Christian Street, was used by the canons of the Holy Sepulchre, and is connected with a still existing gallery adjoining that church. Within recent years changes have taken place in Christian Street, many of the old buildings having been destroyed and new ones erected in their place.

CHAPTER XXIV.

DIRECTLY after passing the Crusading Patriarch's entrance to the Church of the Holy Sepulchre, mentioned in the last chapter, and now walled up, we proceed along the Northern portion of Christian Street. It is in part arched over, forming a bazaar in which, besides the groceries, wax candles, beads, pictures, and other articles displayed for the use of pilgrims, there may be noticed, on the left-hand side, the entrance to a little, dark, but white-washed chamber, with a prayer-niche or Mihrab in its Southern wall, and sometimes a bit of ragged and dirty matting spread in front of the latter, shewing that it is a Moslem place of prayer.

This small, and generally, but seldom used little mosque, which now-a-days is often utilized as a lumber-room for storing away empty packing-cases belonging to the shopkeepers close by, is said to have been built by Omar. It was once famous, as is testified by various Moslem writers, for its connexion with a legend reminding one of the story of the brazen serpent ; it may possibly contain a reminiscence of it, and perhaps also of the cities of refuge. I shall quote it as given in the pages of Mejr ed-din (*A.D.* 1495, *vol. I. pages* 112, 113, *Cairo edition*).

" El Hafiz ben Asakir said, ' I have read in an ancient book that in Beit el Makdas were great and deadly serpents, but that Allah privileged his worshippers by granting them a Mesjid (place of worship, *i.e.*, mosque) on the road which was taken by Omar bin el Khattab, with whom Allah was pleased, from a church there which is known as the dunghill, and there are two great stone pipes upon the heads (capitals) on which are the images of serpents ; and it is said that they are a charm against them, for if a serpent stings a man in Beit el Makdas, it does him no harm, but if he goes out of Beit el Makdas, even though it be only for the distance of one span, he will die instantly. The remedy against this is that he remain in Beit el Makdas for Three hundred and sixty days, for if he goes out before that time, even though only one day be lacking for the completion of the term, he will perish. This is also mentioned by El Herowee in his book of ' *Places to be visited,*' *etc.*"

Though I have often visited this little mosque I have never seen any trace of these wonderful hollow talismanic pillars or pipes, the use of which is so vaguely mentioned, but I suspect that the legend may have risen from the existence, in a vault a little distance further north, but on the same side of the street, of two old columns with Corinthian capitals—old materials which have been re-used in mediæval times as ornamental sides to a doorway. The location of this mosque of the serpent's talisman is minutely and accurately described by the Arab historian as, " in Christian Street and close to the Church of the Sepulchre on the west."

Arriving at the Southern end of the vaulted portion of the street, we now turn sharply to the left, and, having descended some broad steps, we again turn to the left, noticing, however, on our right, the recently built and very ornamental entrance to another mosque with a Turkish inscription over the doorway. It is the mosque erected or restored about 1858 by orders of the then reigning Sultan Abdul Mejid, on the site wrongly said by the Moslem tradition to be that where Omar prayed, on the staircase leading to the Church of the Sepulchre, when the City was first surrendered to the Moslems in *A.D.* 637. The tradition is wrong,

[137]　Ancient Arabic inscription.
[Photo by Author

because at that time the entrance to the Church of the Sepulchre was from the East, close to where the Khan-ez-Zeit market now is, and, as a matter of fact, just here there was found, about 1895, the ancient Arabic inscription belonging to the mosque commemorating Omar's act of worship [137].

Within recent years, there has been discovered, only a few feet distant from the spot where this inscription was found, the remains of the great Eastern gateway belonging to the famous buildings of Constantine on the supposed site of the Holy Sepulchre.

The following is a translation of the inscription : *" In the name of God, the Merciful, the Compassionate. The command has gone forth from the exalted Majesty that this mesjid (mosque) is to be well guarded and kept in good*

[138] Excavations of St. Maria Latina.
[*From illustration by Dr. Merrill—Photo by Author*

repair, and that no one protected by us (that is, either Christians or Jews) shall be allowed to enter under the pretext that he wishes to swear a legal oath there, or with any other object. Let great care be taken that this order be not contravened, and that the regulations laid down in this matter be obeyed. May this be the will of Allah."

See also Palestine Exploration Fund " Quarterly Statement"
April, 1898.

However, the mosque restored by Abdul Mejid, and its

[139]   Entrance to Cotton Merchants' Bazaar.
[Photo by Author

minaret to the South of the present Church of the
Sepulchre, and forming a pair with that towering above

the Khankeh, is now generally known as " El Omariveh," or place of Omar. There is another mosque of Omar— not the Dome of the Rock, which is often erroneously called by that name—in the Temple-area, which we are now on our way to visit.

This minaret referred to was built A.H. 870=*A.D.* 1465-6. The other, close to the Khankeh, was erected A.H. 820=*A.D.* 1417-18. Christians were greatly annoyed because it overtopped the Church of the Sepulchre, and they offered a great sum of money to the builder, Sheikh Barhan ed din bin Ghanem, to induce him to abandon his design. He, however, refused, and then, as Moslems say, Mohammed appeared in a dream to a man whom he directed to salute Ibn Ghanem in his name, and assure him of his intercession at the Day of Judgment, as a reward for his having built this minaret above the heads of the infidels.

Descending the broad staircase which leads down into the great court-yard, outside the Church of the Sepulchre, we pass through it into the street running along the North of the Muristan.

On our left is the great convent and hospice of Abraham, which we have already visited, the basement of which is built over a huge cistern, one Hundred feet long, fifty broad, and as many deep. Two rows, containing each eight great columns, support the vaulted roof. When empty, and lit up with magnesium light, as I saw it when cleaned out after its discovery, it looks like a great deserted cathedral, dis- mantled and stripped of all accessories. At the time it was found there was great jubilation amongst those who upheld the claims of the traditional Holy Sepulchre, and pointed to it as a fragment of the trench which ran along the second wall of Jerusalem in the time of Christ. Since then, however, another discovery, namely that the Muristan and the German church, consecrated by the Emperor William during his visit to Jerusalem, are built over a broad and very deep, though now filled-up valley, the " Maktash " of *Zephaniah i.* 11 ; and that the great cistern is not altogether rock-cut, but built in the accumulated débris, has disproved the theory. It is of Byzantine origin, and now generally attributed to Constantine. It is accessible to visitors who are willing to pay a baksheesh to the porter at Abraham's convent, and is really worth a visit.

When we passed this way before, I did not mention the fact of the discovery at a considerable depth from the surface, of a great and very ancient wall running east and west deep below the site of the German church. I now furnish an illustration of the same taken from Dr. Merrill's work on " Ancient Jerusalem," page 297 [139]. In the background of the picture are seen the line of shops forming the basement of the convent of Abraham above-mentioned. This wall was found during the digging operations in order to lay the foundations of the German church on the site of the mediæval St. Maria Latina.

Up to the year 1918, European visitors desirous of seeing the Temple-area had to be accompanied by a Consular cawass, who in his turn called on his way with the party at the Serai, or Government house. This house, until about the year 1880, was still located close to the military barracks, on the site of the Antonia, but was afterwards installed in the back-rooms and courts of a very interesting Saracenic building situated on the eastern slope of the Acra hill, and sometimes spoken of as Helena's hospital.

Some authorities have gone so far as to suggest that this is the splendid hospital erected by the orders of Gregory the Great of Rome (*A.D.* 590-604) for the reception of pilgrims. The architecture of the great edifice, however, is in the best Saracenic style, and we are expressly told by Mejr ed-din that it was erected by a very wealthy and charitable lady named " Sitt Tonshok." Her tomb is shewn on the opposite side of the street to the richly decorated northern facade of the imposing palace the date of which is A.H. 794, *i.e.*, *A.D.* 1391-2. The building is now used as an Orphanage for Moslems. The street here is unfortunately so very narrow that it has not been possible to bring the camera to bear on this noteworthy specimen of Eastern builders' craft.

In an old ruined building adjoining is a Mohammedan public kitchen, established, it is said, by another ancient Moslem lady, named Roxelana, the favourite Sultana of Suleiman II., for the daily relief of the poor. The " sportula " is still doled out every day, and the enormous cauldrons in which the food is prepared rival the capacious porridge-pot of Guy of Warwick. This charity, which is superintended by the government, is maintained by the revenues of various houses in the city, and the village of Beit Jala, near Bethlehem, is also its property. This

[140] Saracenic fountain, with staircase on site of the "Holy of Holies" in background.
[*Photo by Author*

kitchen, and the handsome structure close by, are known as Et Tekiyeh, *i.e.*, the hospice or hospital.

From this place, a short though winding street brings

us to the Western entrance of the old Cotton Bazaar [139]. It is a very remarkable structure about Three hundred feet long and Fifty or Sixty broad. Its outer shell is formed of large bevelled stones apparently belonging to some important building of the Græco - Roman period. The interior consists of a great tunnel-like passage with shops, and adjoining chambers built in Saracenic style. An Arabic inscription, flanked by goblets which seem to have been the armorial bearings of the same Emir Tunguz, who constructed the Mekhkemeh

[141] The now deserted Cotton Bazaar, showing on right, door to Turkish bath.
[Photo—Z. Kotter

building, shews that he had a hand in the construction of one of the two Turkish baths occupying some of the chambers in its southern side. One of these baths is noteworthy, because connected with a very deep draw-well at the bottom of which, 86 feet below its mouth, is the entrance to a remarkable rocky chamber and passage 128 feet long, supposed to belong to the Roman period.

At the end of this is a small spring of brackish water, from which the bath is supplied, but which sometimes fails in years of excessive drought. In the outer-room of the bath is an ornamental fountain, to form which an elaborately carved circular marble basin, evidently once a baptismal font, has been utilised.

Before the overland caravan-trade from India by way of Bussorah, Baghdad, and Mosul declined, as a result of the discovery of the sea-route round the Cape of Good Hope in *A.D.* 1497-8, the muslins, calicoes of Mosul and Calcutta, and the silks of the further east, used to be displayed here by Oriental traffickers. When, early in 1897, the approaching visit of the Ex-Emperor William of Germany was announced to the Municipality of Jerusalem, that body of sages, after due deliberation, decided that the Imperial eyes must on no account be offended by the sight of so much dirt, and therefore, as they found that it would be cheaper to hide than to remove it, they had wooden doors put to the shops in order to conceal their contents. From that time, however, several of the doors have broken down and the shame behind is only too apparent.

Since the British occupation some of the old shops and chambers at the entrance to this bazaar have been utilized for weaving, etc., but otherwise, though the great tunnel-like place has been cleaned and white-washed, yet, except as an approach to the Temple-area the bazaar of the cotton merchants is deserted, and the rows of shops on either side of the great passage-way are filled to their ceilings with the accumulated rubbish of centuries [141].

By steps leading up to the doorway at the further end, we enter the sunlit Temple-precincts or Haram Area, with its Saracenic domes, fountains and tree-shaded mastabehs or platforms for prayer [140]. See! that imposing staircase right in front of us, with trees shading its feet, a Saracenic colonnade at its top, and the great Dome of the Rock in the background, occupies the actual site of the Holy of Holies in the Jewish temple.

CHAPTER XXV.

THE Bab el Kattanin [142], by which we emerge from the gloom of the deserted Cotton Bazaar, occupies, together with the Bab el Mathara, a few steps to the South of it, a central position amongst the Eight gates on the Western side of the present Temple-area or Haram enclosure. I need not trouble the reader with the names of the other gates on this side, or of the three along the northern. On the Eastern and Southern sides there are none open at present, and we noticed them walled up when we passed along the outside of the city and the Haram. The Bab el Kattanin is a very fair specimen of a Saracenic gateway, with the characteristic pendentives or stalactite ornaments and parti-coloured stone-work. It is not certain by whom it was built, but Arab authors record its having been repaired A.H. 737=*A.D.* 1336-7, by Sultan Melik en Nasr Mohammed Kelaun. Because of its ornate character it was at one time supposed—like the Golden Gate at another—to have been the "Beautiful Gate" of *Acts* iii. 2.

To the right and left, that is Northward and Southward, there stretch, over the space occupied in Herod's Temple by the double aisles of his Western cloisters, a series of heavy Saracenic arcades or single

[142] Bab el Kattanin. [*Photo by Imberger*]

cloisters resting on massive piers, the spaces between
which have in several places been walled up in order to

244

[143] Porch of Medresset el Ashrafiyeh. [*Photo by Imberger*

form chambers. Just South of Bab el Mathara the continuity of these arches is interrupted by the projection

245

into the area, of the Saracenic College, " Medresset el Ashrafiyeh," its date being A.H. 888=*A.D.* 1483. It was in course of erection when Felix Fabri visited Jerusalem [143].

South of it, and next in order, comes the Bab es Silsileh, described and illustrated in former chapters, and from that point the Saracenic cloisters again continue southward as far as the Bab el Magharibeh, between the Jews' Wailing Place and Robinson's Arch. From the walled-up cloisters, just before we reach the Bab el Magharibeh, a winding staircase leads down into a remarkable subterranean chamber with a massive vault of the Herodian period forming its roof. The ancient floor is hidden by many feet of débris, for this is an ancient gate-passage leading inward from one of the old Jewish temple gateways of our Lord's time. In fact, the huge lintel is still visible just above ground in a recess on the west ; it is the other side of the lintel which we previously mentioned as existing south of the Wailing Place, and known as " Barclay's Gate." Few Europeans of the present generation have ever visited this under-ground chamber, which is called by Moslems the Mosque of El Borak, because here one is shewn the iron ring to which Gabriel is said to have secured that marvellous human-headed and winged creature when Mohammed made his fabulous night-journey from Mecca to Jerusalem. It is true that Four hundred years ago, as Arab writers attest, the place where the celestial beast Borak was tied up was shewn further North, at Bab en Nazir, but what does tradition care for the records of historians? Is it not enough that the place was in the Haram, and has not a Moslem artist left an old picture of the event? And is not the " Kubbet el Miraj " on the

[144] Dome of Mohammed's Ascension.

[Photo by Miss Blyth

Mosque platform, the place whence Mohammed ascended to Heaven? Christian antiquaries indeed assert that the latter, which was repaired by the Emir Isfehsalam Uzz-ed-din, son of Amru Othman, Governor of Jerusalem in A.H. 596=*A.D.* 1199-1200, was in times previous the Baptistery of the Christian Church which occupied the site of the Dome of the Rock during the Crusading period [144].

[145]   Model of Herod's Temple, by Mr. J. M. Tenz.   *[Photo by Author*

The present Western cloisters form the basement of a line of Saracenic buildings, former schools, the endowments of which have long since lapsed; the houses themselves being used as dwellings for people now connected with the Haram [146]. In Herod's Temple there were no such buildings forming a second story to the cloisters. Instead of the pointed arches springing from heavy quadrangular piers we must imagine long double aisles with a flat cedar roof, resting on slender marble Corinthian columns about Thirty-seven feet high, and running all round the Temple enclosure, the outer row of columns resting on the City wall as is shewn in an illustration of a model by Mr. J. M. Tenz [145], and in which we have the Southern and Western sides portrayed.

[146]   Saracenic arches in Haram enclosure.

[Photo by Miss Blyth

Bearing in mind that there were no buildings above the cloisters, we can now recall vividly one of the terrible scenes that took place along this part of the Temple Area in *A.D.* 70. It was on July 27th; the Romans had, three weeks previously, obtained possession of the Antonia, occupying the top of the great artificially isolated rock on which the former Turkish barracks and minaret stand, dominating the Temple Area at its North-west corner. The cloisters connecting the fortress with the Temple had been purposely set on fire by the Jews, in order to prevent the enemy using them to reach the Sanctuary courts. Part of the Northern cloisters had also been burnt down by Roman fire. The troops of Titus now attacked the Northern end of the Western cloisters at a spot close to the site of the present Bab en Nazir and fierce fighting ensued ; when, suddenly, as if panic-stricken, the defenders clambered down off the cedar roof. In the ardour of the fight a large number of their assailants, applying ladders, climbed to the deserted coign of vantage and then prepared to descend into the courts of the Temple. Suddenly flames, issuing from below, burst out all around them. Too late came the discovery that they had been led into becoming the rash victims of a stratagem of war. The space inside the cloisters had, unknown to them, been some time previously, and in pursuance of a deliberate plan, filled with combustibles now on fire. This was the secret of the well-feigned panic of the defenders. One man excepted, the Romans on the roof all perished by fire or sword. Was not suicide considered by the Romans the approved way for desperate men to end their lives ? The one who escaped from the frightful situation was Artorius. His ruse is thus described :—

" When he had with a loud voice called to him Lucius, one of his fellow-soldiers that lay with him in the same tent, he said to him, ' I do leave thee heir of all I have, if thou wilt come and receive me.' Upon this he came running to receive him readily ; Artorius then threw himself down upon him"—Lucius stood about forty feet below—" whilst he that received him was dashed so violently against the pavement by the other's weight, that he died immediately." It was but one small incident in a terrible tragedy, but we can realize the scene vividly as we stand looking at these Arab cloisters. The fire then destroyed Herod's Temple as far as John's tower, which stood probably close to the present Bab es Silsileh. The leap of Artorius took place somewhere close to the present Bab en Nazir.

The Temple in the time of our Lord had four gates on the west. The exact position of these is well ascertained. The remains of three at least still exist, though they are not all accessible at present. Beginning from the South we have first of all the approach over Robinson's Arch, then the remains of Barclay's Gate, and then the gate which once occupied the site of the Bab es Silsileh, built over Wilson's Arch. Last and northernmost of all, though like Barclay's Gate at a level considerably lower than the floor of the Temple Area, is a great gate-passage, now inaccessible because it has been blocked up at either end and turned into a huge cistern which has been found to reach right through the Western wall of the Temple-area. The position of this is indicated on next page by that of the picturesque Saracenic sebil, or drinking fountain of Kayet Bey [147], erected *A.D.* 1445, by the same Egyptian ruler whose mosque at Cairo (*built about A.D.* 1475) is generally acknowledged to be one of the finest remaining specimens of the Saracenic architecture

[147] Drinking fountain of Kayet Bey.

[*Photo—American Colony*

of the Fifteenth century. The dome of the sebil is
artistically ornamented with arabesques in relief as seen

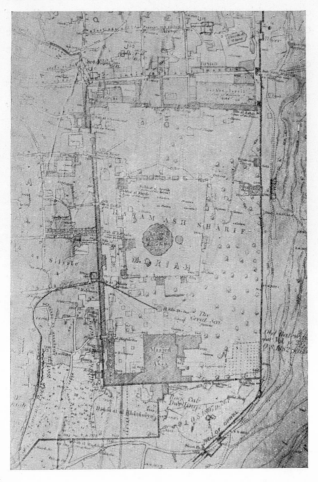

[148] Plan of the Haram Area.   *[Photo by Author*

in the illustration. This precise knowledge of the exact position of the gates of the " Outer Temple " is of course of the greatest help in determining the approximate situation of other buildings that once existed inside the enclosure, but of which no trace remains nowadays.

The plan of the Haram Area and its surroundings [148], is copied from the Palestine Exploration map, and may be consulted for the various sites.

CHAPTER XXVI.

UR present knowledge of the exact positions
in which the Gates of the ancient Temple
stood—and where some and the remains
of others still exist in the great "peribolos,"
or enclosure wall of the Haram Area—a
mighty and ancient monument of which,
strange to say, Josephus has no mention—makes
it a comparatively easy task to locate, and with the
help of the two descriptions of the Sanctuary given in
the pages of the Jewish historian (*Josephus* "*Antiquities,*"
xv. 11 ; and "*Wars*" v. 5) as well as the detailed account
furnished by the Mishnic treatise, "*Middoth,*" to re-
construct the Temple as restored by Herod on the lines
of that built by Nehemiah, who erected his on the same
foundations which had supported Solomon's. The
result of study and exploration, therefore, enables us to
point out on the plan of the "Haram esh Sharif" the
approximate positions of the different parts of the famous
edifice.

Until about the year 1880, although all authorities were
unanimously agreed that the Jewish Temple stood somewhere within the great enclosure, yet there was a
considerable difference of opinion as to the exact site it
occupied. Some placed it in the South-eastern corner,
whilst some believed that the Holy of Holies stood on
the remarkable perforated Rock from which the " Kubbet

es Sakkhrah " or " Dome of the Rock " takes its name—
though Europeans often misname it " the Mosque of
Omar." And there were not a few who believed the said
Rock to have been the foundation of the great Altar of
Burnt Offering, and these recognized that the curious
bore through the rock into the cave underneath was
connected with the cesspool which is known to have
existed under the Altar. This served as the entrance to

[149] Model of Herod's Temple.   [*Photo by Author*

the canal through which the blood of the victims, mixed
with the water that had been used for ablutions, passed
out into the Kedron. ("*Middoth," with the commentary
of R. Bartenora, P.E.F. " Quarterly Statement," for
April,* 1887, *page* 118, *and* 2 *footnote* 15).

At the present day this is the prevalent view, and one
great argument in its favour is, that if in attempted

256

reconstructions the Holy of Holies be placed on the Rock it is found that there is too much space to the West and too little to the East for the buildings, whereas if the Altar be placed on the Rock over the cave, the different parts of the Temple fit into position and to the natural lie of the ground. This proof has become actual demon-

[150] Haram Area, looking North-East.   [*Photo by Author*

stration in the celebrated models made by the late Dr. Schick and Mr. J. M. Tenz and other students of this interesting subject. Our illustration gives a view of the Eastern and Northern sides of the Temple [149].

Bearing these facts in mind we will now proceed on

our visit to the different parts of the Haram, and the kind reader will not be incredulous when we state that such a Herodian building stood here or such another, there.

We show first a view of the Area from the minaret at its South-west corner and looking North-east [150]. At the left hand side we have, in the background, the barracks and minaret on the site of Antonia, on the right-hand the slopes of Mount Scopus, and in the middle the beautiful Dome of the Rock, in the centre of the great platform which coincides in position, and approximately in dimensions, with that on which stood the group of buildings technically known as " the Inner Temple," and comprising the Holy House, with special edifices North and South, and the Women's Court to the East of it. On the left we look along the West side of the Area Northward.

The next illustration [151] is a general view from a point exactly opposite to the preceding, and looking South-east. Taken from an elevated point at the North-western corner, it shews the Western half of the Northern side of the platform, with an arcade at the extreme left and another at the top of the great staircase at the North-western corner of the platform. These stairs to the platform, of which there are three on the Western side, two on its Northern, one on the Eastern, and two on its Southern side, were built or restored by various Saracenic Emirs and Sultans. Each has an arcade at its top, constructed of old materials. These arcades [152] are popularly known as " El Mawazin " or " the Balances," because of the belief that from them will be suspended the scales in which will be weighed the souls of those who, at the Day of Judgment, have safely crossed the terrible bridge " Es Sirat " which, constructed of one single horse-hair, will stretch across the Kedron from the top of the minaret on Olivet to the projecting column known as " Mohammed's Judgment Seat." " Then," to use the very language of a Moslem muleteer with

[151]   Haram Area, looking South-East.

[*Photo—O. Raad, Jerusalem*

whom I travelled now many years ago, " every believer will have a palace given to him for his very own, containing every sort of delight, and if he desire to converse with any of his former relatives on earth, the palace will, of its own accord, move till it approach that of the person its owner wishes to interview.   The believers will speak to each other from the windows of their respective mansions, after which each palace will, of its own accord, return to its appointed station."

To return to the staircase in the illustration [151], the tiny dome, supported on slender marble columns on the corner of the wall above the foot of the staircase, is called the " Kubbet El Khudr," or dome of Elijah—St. George—Phinehas, the son of Eleazar the high-priest, who is looked upon as an ancient saint that, having discovered and drunk of the fountain of eternal youth, never dies, but appears from time to time as a sort of personification of retributive providence, in order to right and protect the helpless and wronged, and to punish evil-doers. The row of small domed buildings along the Northern side of the platform are used for lodgings, for Mosque-servants, &c. Just behind one of them is seen the small cupola of the " Kubbet El Arwah," or Dome of the Spirits, where, according to popular belief, the ghosts of departed Moslem saints assemble for worship at night time. This building is interesting because its floor is formed of the polished rock. We have over Forty observations for rock levels within the Temple Area, and these prove that to the North of the Dome of the Rock there was a naturally fairly levelled rock floor, which would be admirably suited for an oriental threshing floor such as was that of Ornan or Araunah (2 *Samuel* xxiv. 18-25; 1 *Chronicles xxi.* 18-28). Besides this, the locality just above the North-western staircase, the " Kubbet El Khudr," and the " Kubbet El Arwah," is interesting because hereabouts, in the time of Herod's temple, was situated the Beth " Moked," or " House of the Hearth," so-called because of the fires which were kept burning in order to enable the bare-footed priests to warm themselves. We must imagine a great vaulted apartment, on either side of which, and projecting from the wall, was a double row of stone benches, forming

[152] Arcades or Balances at North-West corner as they appeared in the year 1914.

NOTE.

The ornaments above the columns were painted on plaster, which has now been removed.

[*Photo by Miss Blyth*

steps one above the other, and serving as bedsteads on which the elders of the house of the fathers slept on pillows or mattresses—whilst all night long the priests kept their guard of honour.

Four small rooms opened into this central guardroom. In the South-western room were kept the lambs selected for the morning sacrifice ; the South-eastern was used for making the shew-bread ; the North-eastern was an office called " the Chamber of Seals." Here sat the overseer whose duty it was to receive the money from those who

[153]   Arcade and marble Pulpit, on site of Water Gate.
[*Photo—American Colony*

needed fine flour for the meat offering and wine for the drink offering, and who received, in exchange for their cash, a seal or voucher, which they had to present to the person who supplied these things. In this office or " Chamber of Seals " were also preserved the stones of the altar that had been desecrated by Antiochus Epiphanes, who sacrificed a sow upon it (2 *Maccabees* x. 3).

The fourth or North-western chamber communicated with the subterranean sacerdotal bath-room, and this again with an underground passage by which priests who had incurred ceremonial defilement could, after bathing, leave the Temple precincts unseen.

One of the curious things discovered hereabouts, during the examination of the huge rock-cut cisterns with which this part of the great platform is honey-combed, is, that one of these cisterns, situated under the spot where part of the Beth Moked stood, shews by its remarkable shape that it probably was part of this very same bath. A little distance East of it is another, that in its present condition, is a portion of an ancient tunnel which probably was the very same underground passage by which the defiled priests reached the gate called " Tadi," or obscurity. This cistern is one hundred and thirty feet long, Twenty-four feet wide, and Eighteen feet deep. It runs Northward, pointing underground in the direction of the present Northern gate of the Haram Area. This gate, by a curious coincidence—perhaps the survival of some tradition about the gate Tadi—is known as " Bab el 'Atm," or Gate of Darkness.

In the background, in the centre of illustration [151], we have the Dome of the Rock viewed from the North, and shewing its Northern entrance called " the Gate of Paradise," because, during the middle ages, there was a garden belonging to the Convent of the Canons of the Temple north of the great platform. East of the Dome of the Rock, i.e., left of the photograph, is the much smaller " Kubbut es Silsileh," occupying approximately the position of the Gate of Nicanor, East of the Altar, and between the Court of the Women and that of Israel. West of the Sakkhrah, and behind the low square-domed building close to the North-west " Balances," we see the cupola of Mohammed's Ascent. Beyond this is the Arcade at the top of the staircase, of which an illustration has already been shown [140] as occupying on the plan the site of the Holy of Holies. In the background of illustration [151] between a cypress tree, close to the West of the Dome of the Rock and the South-eastern minaret, we see the buildings of the Aksa. The larger minaret on the right marks the position of Bab es Silsileh, etc.

Before closing this description it may be well to remark that extending Eastward from the Beth Moked, on a site in line with the Kubbet el Arwah and the arcade West of it, and reaching to the Western limits of the Women's Court, we picture, in our mind's eye, a series of other structures which stood here in the time of our Lord. These were the Corban Gate by which the victims for sacrifice were brought into the Temple, the Gate Nitsots, with adjacent magazines for salt, which had to be offered with every offering (*compare Leviticus ii.* 13 ; *Numbers xviii.* 19 ; *St. Mark ix.* 50 ; *Colossians iv.* 6) ; the room where the insides of the sacrifices were washed ; and the House named Parbah, with a special bath-room, used by the High-priest on the Day of Atonement. Over the Gate Nitsots was a verandah or balcony where young priests kept watch, a guard of Levites being stationed below. Inside the row of chambers, and looking Southward, ran a line of single cloisters. (*Josephus* " *Wars*," *v.* 2.)

A similar row of buildings, but used for different purposes, occupied the Southern side of the platform. These were the chambers for wood selected and assorted for the Altar, the House called " Abtines " where in a special apartment the High Priest used to be secluded for a week previous to the Great Annual Day of Atonement, in order to be safe from ceremonial defilement, and also prepare by study, meditation and prayer for the solemn

[154]   Dome of the Rock from South-East.
[*Photo by Author*

and special ritual of the Great Fast Day.   Besides these there was the draw-well room ; and, more especially, the great Liscath ha Gazith, of which more hereafter. Between these chambers came the Southern gates of the Inner Temple, named respectively—" Of Flames,"

" Of First-lings," and the " Water Gate." The position of the last coincided practically with that of the arcade and marble pulpit erected by the Cadi Barhan ed Din in the Sixteenth century, with old materials taken from Christian churches [153]. Amongst other carvings and ornaments in marble there are the remains of a mermaid, purposely mutilated by iconoclastic Moslems.

We also give a view of the Dome of the Rock from the South-east, showing in the foreground the arcade or " balances " next in order [154]. In the interval between the two arcades probably stood the Liscath ha Gazith, or Great Hall of Paved Stones, where the sessions of the great Sanhedrin sat, and where St. Peter and St. John (*Acts iv.* 1-21 ; *v.* 21-41), like St. Stephen some time later (*Acts vi.* 12 ; *vii.* 57), made their defence before the high tribunal.

This great hall stretched East and West. A line on the marble pavement showed the limit, North of which was a part of the Court of the Priests, within which no lay Israelites except Kings of the house of David might sit. South of the line, and at the Western end of the great apartment, were the seats for the judges.

The Eastern part of the chamber was in daily use, for here, in the early morning, the priests assembled, in order that their special shares in the ministerial work for the day might be apportioned by lot, " which assigned to each his function. Four times it was resorted to : twice before, and twice after the Temple gates were opened." (*Edersheim, " Life of Jesus," page* 134.) Clothed in white the priests trooped in and stood in a row, with hands uplifted and fingers extended, awaiting the announcement of the number of the lot by the superintending officer, touching at random the head of some individual priest, in order to indicate that there the counting of fingers was to begin. (*Lightfoot's Horae Hebraicae* "*Prospect of the Temple*," &c.) The lot for the designation of those who were to trim the Golden Candlestick and prepare the Golden Altar of Incense took place at the second time of assembling, when it was scarcely daybreak.

As we look at the view shown in this illustration, we cannot help thinking, not only of the two apostles and the first Christian martyr, but also of Zechariah, the father of St. John the Baptist and his wonderful vision.

CHAPTER XXVII.

IMILAR causes produce similar results all the world over. Hence it not infrequently happens, in Palestine and the East at any rate, that history repeats itself though under modified conditions. Having in a former chapter cursorily surveyed the great platform in the Temple-area, we now proceed to visit the remarkable and beautiful building occupying nearly its centre. We are reminded that it was Abd el Malik ibn Merwan, the ninth Caliph or successor of Mohammed, and the fifth of the Dynasty of Omawiyeh, who in *A.D.* 684 gave orders for the erection of the building. Whether he was conscious of the fact or not, he was really following a policy similar to that of Jeroboam the son of Nebat, who, sixteen hundred years previously, had set up a new sanctuary to prevent Israelites from making pilgrimage to Jerusalem. Yet so it was, though now with Jerusalem as the attraction, for the building was designed in order to discourage Moslems from visiting Mecca.

The reason of the decision of Abd el Malik was that for some eight years the Moslem world had been distracted by factions and petty quarrels, and the people of Mecca and Medina rising in rebellion against the authority of the lawful Khalifeh, had proclaimed Abdallah ibn Zobeir their spiritual and temporal head ; and despite the efforts of Yezid and Mo'awiyah to suppress the insurrection, the rival commander of the faithful had succeeded in making his authority acknowledged not only at Mecca but throughout Arabia, Egypt and the other African provinces. Trembling for his own rule, and in order to divert Moslem pilgrims from visiting Mecca and becoming tainted by the religious and political influence of Ibn Zobeir, Abd el Malik conceived the plan of diverting their minds and inducing them to make the pilgrimage to Jerusalem instead.

The task was not a difficult one. El Kuds is frequently mentioned in the Koran, and closely connected with Scriptural events which Mohammed had taught as part and parcel of his own creed. Lastly, his night-journey, to which reference has been made in former chapters, from Mecca to the Holy Rock at Jerusalem, and thence through the seven heavens—these were all points which appealed directly to the mind of Islamiyeh. Added to these was the charm of novelty sanctioned by antiquity, so that we need not be surprised that the appeal of Abd el Malik to his subjects was enthusiastically responded to, or that letters of approval and congratulation should have been addressed to him from all quarters.

Having assembled a number of skilled artizans and set apart for the work a sum of money equal to the whole revenue of Egypt for seven years, the work was successfully completed in the year 72 A.H. = *A.D.* 691. This is attested by a magnificent and still extant Cufic inscription inside the Dome of the Rock and running all round the outer colonnade within the walls. The name of the original founder has indeed been erased, and that

of Abdullah el Mamun, son of Harûn Er Rashid fraudu-
lently substituted, but the forger has over-reached
himself as those of his kind are wont to do, in having
omitted to erase the date when he removed the name of

[155]   Haram Area.   Arcade at top of stairs occupying site
of Holy of Holies.   [*Photo—American Colony*

NOTE.—*The ornamental work at the top of the columns
was only painted plaster and has now been removed.*

" Abd el Malik," and the writing still remains as
evidence of the munificence of the latter. I need not
trouble my readers with the wording. They will find

it given at length in *Besant and Palmer's "History of Jerusalem," Bentley and Sons,* 1888, *pp.* 94-96.

The best position for seeing it is inside the Western doorway with the afternoon sun shining in over the Arcade at the top of the broad staircase, occupying the

[156] Mosaic work and clerestory windows in the Dome of the Rock. [*Photo—American Colony*

site on the plan of the Holy of Holies [155]. The sunshine falling obliquely on to the floor of the Sakkhrah is reflected upward and illuminates, without directly striking the narrow band of ancient Cufic lettering in mosaic just above the arching of the colonnade inside the building.

The history of the edifice subsequent to its restoration by El Mamun is briefly as follows :—The cupola having been destroyed by an earthquake was rebuilt in *A.D.* 1022 by Ali Daher al 'Izaz, the son of the mad Khalifeh El Hakim bi amr Illah, who is worshipped by the Druzes as an incarnation of the Deity. When the Crusaders took Jerusalem they changed the building into a church, called it the " Templum Domini " and established, in close

[157] Dome of the Rock and Dome of the Chain

[*Photo— American Colony*

proximity, a body of Canons Regular with a mitred Abbot at their head. The rock in the centre was hewn in order to receive a marble casing on which was erected a high altar. The chippings are said to have been sold by the Christians for their weight in gold to the relic worshipping people of Sicily and Constantinople (*Besant and Palmer, p.* 434). The Crusaders' platform, altar and crosses were demolished when Saladin retook the Holy City in *A.D.* 1187, and the rock was thoroughly cleaned and washed with rose-water and other perfumes, but no amount of cleaning could obliterate the marks of the Frank picks and chisels. They are only too plainly visible, but serve a purpose, some being very conveniently supposed to be foot-prints and finger-marks of the Angel Gabriel. Saladin not only purified the rock, but in *A.D.* 1194 he had the whole building restored. This is testified by a still existing inscription in gold letters and divided into a series of panels, running round the lower inside part of the Dome and just above the clerestory windows [156]. Below these are seen some of the mosaics and mosaic windows in the drum, the former Ninth, the latter Sixteenth century work. After Saladin's time the Sakkhrah was restored by Mohammed Ibn Kelaun in *A.D.* 1327, by Suleiman the Magnificent in the Sixteenth century, and by the late Abd el Hamid, ruler of Turkey and his immediate predecessors in our own days.

The building is an octagon [157], the angles of which would, if placed in a circle 180 feet in diameter, touch its circumference. Rising from the centre of this octagonal roof surrounded by a low parapet or wall, and borne up on a cylindrical drum, is a great dome or cupola not quite symmetrical in dimensions, but for that very reason all the more striking. It is Seventy-eight feet in diameter, and its summit is One hundred and eight feet in height from the pavement outside the edifice. On the very top is a large crescent, the symbol of Islam, supported by a pillar consisting of three globes placed one above the other. It stands Twelve feet high. At its base the dome is slightly narrower than it is higher up, and is covered with strips of lead.

Taken as a whole the Eight-sided structure forming its pedestal, may seem at first sight to be too low to harmonize with the dimensions of the dome, but the impression soon

[158]   South door of the Dome of the Rock.
[Photo—American Colony

wears off, especially when one beholds it from a distance towering above and elevated by the great platform which itself is, on an average, about Twelve feet higher than the surrounding and fairly level court.

At the four cardinal points are doors, overshadowed by porticos supported by columns that formerly belonged to more ancient buildings. In front of the Southern door-way [158] is a masonry pedestal said to have been the stand of a sun-dial. Somewhere, a few yards to the left of this upright structure of masonry, probably stood the great laver or molten sea in the Jewish Temple. Underneath, and at the back of the portico, are some of the curiously joined and veined marble slabs which case the whole lower part of the great octagon to the height of Eighteen feet. To the right, between the first and second pair of columns, and inside a black border, are two smaller slabs, which having been sliced from the same block, show the same veining. These have been fixed up edge to edge in such a way that a figure is formed somewhat resembling the picture of two birds perched on opposite sides of a vase. According to the current legend, resembling the story told by Mr. Rudyard Kipling about "the Butterfly that stamped," these birds were turned into stone by King Solomon "as a warning to men not to boast, and to women not to encourage them." ("*Tales told in Palestine,*" page 81 ; or "*Folklore of the Holy Land,*" page 48.)

It is supposed by some that at one time an outer corridor or portico, of which those still extant are vestiges, ran round the entire building, but this is unproven. The upper part of the wall above the marble-casing, some of which is ancient material and carved with wreaths, is pierced by a row of pointed windows and faced with earthenware. Before the Sixteenth century, as is evident from the representation of the structure given on Breydenbach's map and picture of the Haram Area [159] the windows were double and the balustrade round the eight-sided roof was ornamented with little arches supported by small columns. These still exist, and may sometimes be seen when the old glazed tiles which cover them fall off, or are otherwise removed.

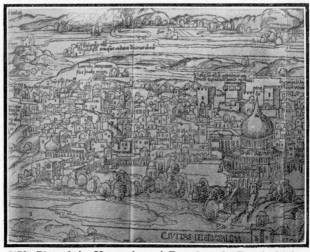

[159] Plan of the Haram Area, A.D. 1483-4, by Breydenbach.

[*Photo by Author*

The first and oldest set of tiles was placed here by *Suleiman the Magnificent* (*A.D.* 1520-60). They have been restored several times since those early days. Some of the older ones had inscriptions shewing that they were made at Damascus, where, however, this branch of industry has long ceased to be carried on. Traces of the ancient furnaces were recently discovered outside the East Gate of that city.

Since the British occupation of Jerusalem, a glazed-tile factory has been started there.

Our illustrations [160] show in a general manner the forms and details of the exterior ornamentation, but being

[160] Tiled ornamentation of exterior of Dome of the Rock.

[Photo— American Colony

monochrome they cannot in the slightest degree reproduce the remarkably beautiful blending of colour in the intricate enamelled arabesques, amongst which wind in interlaced Arabic ornamental lettering, long passages from the Koran, inscribed in white on an azure-blue ground, producing a marvellously beautiful effect.

We make our way to the Eastern side of the structure, where [157] there is what seems, except that its sides are open all round, a miniature copy of the larger building. Here we must stop whilst our feet, shoes and all, are encased in large slippers, or else bags made of rough sacking, before we are allowed to enter the dome of the Rock. This smaller building constructed like its greater companion, mainly of older materials, is the celebrated Kubbet es Silsileh, or Dome of the Chain, because of the belief that in the time of King Solomon a miraculous chain was suspended between heaven and earth over this particular spot. It was possessed of such remarkable virtue that whenever two litigants were unable to decide their dispute they had but to come together to this place and try each to lay hold of the chain " which would advance to meet the grasp of him who was in the right, and would elude all efforts of the other to catch it." One day two men appealed to the ordeal, one accused the other of having appropriated some money which he had confided to his keeping, and, swearing that he had not received it back, laid hold of the chain. The sly debtor, who had cunningly hidden the money in the interior of a hollow staff which he had in his hand, handed the said staff to the claimant, whilst swearing that he had restored the money to its owner and he also was enabled to grasp the chain. From that moment the chain disappeared, feeling no doubt that it had no chance of maintaining its reputation for legal sagacity in a " holy city " where such tricks were played.

The place, however, long retained some of its judicial functions, and according to Moslem writers perjury is an exceedingly dangerous weapon in the vicinity of the Dome of the Rock. It is said that the Khalifeh Omar Abd el Aziz ordered the stewards of his predecessor Suleiman to give an account of their stewardship upon oath in front of the Sakkhrah. Only one of them refused to swear, and paid a thousand dinars rather than do so.

CAPITAL OF WHITE MARBLE, IN ONE OF THE MINARETS OF THE HARAM ESH SHERIF, AT JERUSALEM.

[161] Crusading capital from the Dome of the Chain.   [*Photo by Author*

The result was that twelve months later he was the only survivor of the number.

Leaving these fables aside the Kubbet es Silsileh is, for many reasons, an exceedingly interesting little structure. Its plan is one of two concentric figures with respectively six and eleven columns at their angles. The hexagon enclosed in a polygon allows the seventeen handsome pillars to be all seen at one time from whichever side you look at them. It is said that Abd el Malik himself designed this little dome, and that he " personally gave the architect instructions as to its minutest details. When finished, he was so pleased with the general effect that he ordered the Kubbet es Sakkhrah itself to be built on the same model." (*Besant and Palmer, page* 87.)

During the Crusading period the Dome of the Chain was fitted up as the Chapel of the Presentation of our Lord in the Temple. After the Franks were driven out in 1187 the place was restored to its original condition and the mediaeval capitals, which the Christians had added, were used by the Moslems for other buildings. Some of them, see illustration [161], taken from Prof. Clermont Ganneau's " Archaeological Researches," have been built into the minaret at the North-west angle of the Haram Area. The date of this minaret is A.H. 697= *A.D.* 1297-8. The idea, however, that the Kubbet es Silsileh stands on the spot of the Presentation is not by any means an absurd one. As a matter of fact the great gate between the Court of the Women and that of the Israelites in all probability stood within a few feet of the spot, supposing that the great rock inside the Kubbet es Sakkhrah was the foundation of the Altar of Burnt-Offerings.

CHAPTER XXVIII.

I N the preceding chapter we remarked that during the Crusading period the Kubbet es Silsileh was known as " The Chapel of the presentation of Christ in the Temple." According to another tradition preserved in the Norman Chronicle, written about *A.D.* 1187, there was also here " a chapel of my lord St. James the Less, the Apostle," because of the supposition that he met with his martyrdom on this spot, being thrown by the Jews from the battlements of the Temple. The writer of the Chronicle confounds James the brother of our Lord, surnamed " the just," with James the son of Alphaeus, who was surnamed " the Less." When speaking of the remains of the tower at the South-east corner of the Haram Area we noticed the older and original tradition concerning the death of St. James the Just. It is given by Eusebius (*H.E. II.* 23), who quotes from Hegesippus (*about A.D.* 160), and an account of it will be found in Hastings' " Dictionary of the Bible," *vol. ii., page* 542, to which I must refer the reader. Another mediaeval tradition was that Kubbet es Silsileh was the place where our Lord saved the woman taken in adultery from her accusers. (*St. John viii.*)

We now enter the grander Dome of the Rock by its Eastern portal, through a mean and rudely white-washed passage, noticing the Corinthian capitals peeping, as if in

protest against their concealment, through the stucco.
Three paces land us within the magnificent edifice, and
our first impression is one of amazement at its contrast

[162] Interior of Dome of the Rock, commonly called
the Mosque of Omar.

[*Photo—C. Raad, Jerusalem*

with the wretched entrance-hall; and also at the mysterious, unearthly effect produced all of a sudden, after
leaving the dazzling sunlight outside, by the play of
subdued light and shadow in the immense building, which
seems, at first glance, to be a forest of magnificently
coloured columns of parti-coloured marbles, breccia,
verde-antique, porphyry and granite, with beautifully-
gilded capitals [162].

The eight walls of the octagonal structure enclose a
space occupied by three concentric enclosures. The
outermost, bordered by the exterior wall of the building
on one side, is separated from the next inner enclosure by
eight piers corresponding to, and about sixteen or
seventeen feet distant from, the outer wall. The many
coloured mosaic windows differ from the stained glass
ones seen mounted in lead in European churches, in
that they are " true mosaics," or tiny fragments of glass
of different colours, each bit being placed in a separate
plaster frame, the sloping or bevelled edge of which
reflects the same colour as the glass it encloses. These
fragments of glass are most artistically arranged, and their
colours, harmonious though differing, are toned down by
a perforated screen of tile-work, which covers the outer
side of the windows, and whilst protecting them from
weather, allows just sufficient light to illuminate and show
up the glass and to pass through into the edifice.

Between every pair of the eight piers above-
mentioned are two columns with gilded capitals. At
first sight all seems beautiful and harmonious, but by
the time our eyes have become accustomed to the

curious alternations of light and shadow, our perceptions have also grown more critical, and we notice that a great quantity of old material has been freely used in the building. The columns are of unequal length, some of them, which had seemed to be costly marbles, being merely fragments of shafts pieced together and covered with cunningly painted stucco, their bases being of unequal height, as are also the marble-faced blocks surmounting the capitals and supporting the richly carved and gilded architrave which, in its turn, bears up a set of semi-circular arches, Three between each pier, richly adorned with handsome mosaics.

Of the general beauty of the whole, photographs can only give faint ideas. The eight great piers are faced with slabs of veined marble, ingeniously placed edge to edge so as to form various patterns like those of olive-wood work. A large number of chandeliers and lamps of various shapes, for burning the sacred olive-oil, are suspended from iron bars between the piers or at the end of chains pendant from the ceilings. These, in the outer and second enclosure, are of wood covered with stucco and richly ornamented with painted and gilt arabesques and geometrical designs.

The second enclosure is bounded on the outside by the eight piers and intervening sixteen columns just described, and its inner limit is a circle composed of four very massive pillars, with three great columns between every couple of piers [163]. Four of these huge columns are monoliths of rose-coloured native limestone, which probably came from the well-known quarries West of the city and near the Convent of the Cross, and are remarkable for at least two reasons. In the first place they belong to a much more ancient building which stood on this spot, and of which they are relics. This was proved in the year 1870 in a strange way. The Kubbet es Sakkhrah was undergoing repairs, in the course of which it became necessary to remove part of the flooring, and then it was found that the Attic pedestals on which these columns now seem to stand, are mere shams, the true and more ancient ones being still in position at a lower level than that of the present flooring.

This discovery of course opened the question as to what building the Four monoliths originally belonged to. Were they parts of a circular colonnade surrounding statues of Jupiter Capitolinus, and of Hadrian in the Temple built by the latter? or are they of later date? and did they, as some suppose, belong to the Church of St. Sophia, or the Divine Wisdom, which is mentioned by the anonymous author of the "Jerusalem Breviary," and in the tract of the pilgrim-writer Theodosius, both of whom are supposed to have written about *A.D.* 530, that is, during the age of Justinian?

This question is difficult to decide, especially as a recent Franciscan writer has tried to make out, that these two pilgrims visited Jerusalem some time before the accession of Justinian. (" *Le Pretiore de Pilate* " *par Pére Barnabé, page* 147.) In any case, however, we have in the second place, in these great monoliths, specimens illustrating the description given by Procopius the biographer and panegyrist of Justinian, of the buildings erected by that Emperor at Jerusalem, a place so distant from the sea that it was " difficult for the contrivers of the Temple to introduce columns from elsewhere. But, as the Emperor was distressed at the difficulty of the task, God showed a kind of stone in the nearest mountains well adapted for the purpose, whether it existed previously or was now created. In either case," says Procopius, quaintly, " there is credibility in the account to those who refer the cause to God. For though we, measuring everything by human power, believe many things have been excluded as impossible ; yet nothing could be either difficult or impossible to the God of all. Hence, then, extraordinary columns of great size, and resembling in their colour the brightness of flame, support the Temple on all sides."

Though indeed this passage refers more especially to the columns in the Church of St. Mary, the site of which is occupied by the present Mosque El Aksa, yet the description exactly suits the great monoliths in the Kubbet es Sakkhrah.

From the capitals of these columns, and also from the four great piers, spring semi-circular arches supporting the drum which is divided into two stories, upper and lower, by a thick cornice. Of these stories the lower corresponds to the roofing of the lower sides of the building, and the upper is pierced with windows, most of which are fitted with glass mosaics. The whole surface of the interior of the drum is covered with Byzantine mosaics of different dates, between the Seventh and the Fifteenth centuries, and comprises various graceful designs intermingled with Koranic texts in letters of gold. Above the clerestory rises the great dome, seventy-five feet in diameter, and at its centre, measured from inside the building, ninety-six feet above the floor. It is double and constructed of wooden laths nailed to rafters and girders, and the inner dome is lined inside with richly painted and gilded plaster, whilst the outer one is covered outside with sheets of lead.

Four entrances—North, South, East and West—give access from the second enclosure to the great central one. The doors are in a beautifully gilt screen of hammered iron-work, the handicraft of the Crusaders, and the gift probably of some Bourbon monarch as yet unidentified. This grille, with its finials of the lilies of St. Joseph runs between the columns and pillars supporting the dome, and is fixed on a marble bench, so that the visitor has to be careful when crossing the latter, because it is rather higher inside than it is outside. However, this bench and the pedestals of the columns afford good standing points whence to overlook the most interesting object, namely, the sacred and mysterious Rock or Sakkhrah, which has bestowed its name on the whole building that encloses it as in a triply-lined casket. This rock, which is now believed by most authorities to have been the foundation of the great Altar of Burnt-Offerings in the Jewish Temple, is surrounded by a high wooden balustrade or screen, which makes it difficult to overlook it conveniently [163].

According to Jewish traditions adopted by the Moslems, this marks the exact centre of the world, and the spot whence the Almighty took the dust out of which He formed Adam. More interesting is it that the South-eastern corner of the rock, abutting on a great pier, is

[163] Rock under Dome.   [*Photo—C. Raad, Jerusalem*

quite unapproachable. It was just over this corner that, according to the Talmud, the boundary-line between the territories of Benjamin and Judah passed, so that " the

South-eastern corner alone " was " in the portion of Judah." (*Tractate " Middoth," with Rabbi Bartenora's Commentary—see Palestine Exploration Fund " Quarterly Statement,"* 1887, *pages* 117, 118). And as Jacob blessed Benjamin saying, " Benjamin shall ravin as a wolf : in the morning he shall devour the prey " (*Genesis xlix.* 27), which is interpreted " in his possession the Sanctuary shall be built " (*Targum of Onkelos*), that which sanctifies the blood must be in no other than the portion of Benjamin. On this account they did not make a foundation to the altar at the South-eastern corner, because it was not in the portion of the " Raviner." As mentioned in most Guide Books, many other traditional associations and legends cluster around this rock.

At the South-western corner, enclosed in a shrine, is a slight depression now said to be the foot-print of Mohammed, even as in the Twelfth century, it was said to be that of our Lord. Above it, and in the same domed shrine, is a gilt urn, enclosing, it is said, " two hairs of Mohammed's beard." Besides this the banner of " the Prophet " wrapped round his lance, and the banner of Omar, are also shewn. A couple of yards distant, and built against the great piers at this corner, is a sort of triangular ledge, supported on curious little marble colonnettes, with shafts like plaited work, and mediaeval capitals once adorned with carved heads of cherubs, whose faces have been mutilated by iconoclastic Moslems. Colonnettes exactly similar, are said to exist in buildings in Italy, but the guardians of the Haram gravely tell us that these are the handiwork of Solomon, who knew the are of kneading and moulding stone, in the same way that a pastry-cook kneads dough and forms it into different shapes. There are similar colonnettes in the cave below.

In the year 1861, when I paid my first visit to the Dome of the Rock, there was fixed on this ledge or stand " the Shield of Hamza," which has now disappeared, as mentioned in Chapter II. (*page* 18). Close to this " Shield " were some fragments of arch-stones carved with the ornament technically known as a " Chevron." These, too, have now vanished, but were then shewn as bits of the saddle-trappings of El Borak.

Sir Charles Warren records that the " entrance to the cave," underneath the rock " is by a flight of steps on the South-east, passing under a doorway with a pointed arch, which looks like an addition of the Crusaders; the chamber is not large, with an average height of six feet; its sides are so covered with plaster and whitewash, that it is impossible to see any chisel-marks, but the surface appears to be rough and irregular."

Moslems believe that when Mohammed ascended from the Sakkhrah to Heaven on El Barak, the Rock wished to follow, but was held down by the Angel Gabriel, whose finger prints are seen above. Ever since then the Rock has been suspended in the air, thus forming the cave, the hollow-sounding wall of which was placed there because pilgrims who passed under the rock feared lest it should fall and crush them.

An ancient Arab author relates very naively that " when I first visited the Sakkhrah, I durst not enter the cave, because of its darkness, and of sins which I had committed, but afterwards, when I beheld greater oppressors and sinners than I knew myself to be, going in and coming out safely, I, after watching for some time, gathered courage and also entered and beheld the marvels."

The said marvels now shewn, are the praying-places of Abraham, Elkhudr, David, Solomon and Mohammed. In the rock above the latter, is a large hollow or dent. Concerning this it is related that Mohammed's prayer was so eloquent that the rock approached and listened spell-bound. However, the prayer ended so abruptly, that, on rising from his knees, the prophet struck his head against the rock, and caused the before-mentioned dent.

We need not waste the time or patience of the reader by relating other legends equally childish, as for instance, about the tongue, still shewn, with which the rock sang the praises of Allah, or the column shaft, by which it is kept in position, so that it cannot be blown away by the wind.

CHAPTER XXIX.

BESIDES the spots connected with absurd traditions three things claim our attention as of great and genuine interest. These are the hole through the rock, the cave itself, and the so-called " Bir el Arwah," or " Well of the Spirits," the opening into which is covered with a marble slab.

This hole has in all probability been formed by enlarging into one, the two " narrow nostril-like " orifices through which, as the Talmud tells us, " the blood poured upon the western and southern foundations " of the altar, might run down (*Middoth, chapter iii. 5. Palestine Exploration Fund* " *Quarterly Statement,*" 1887, *page* 118). As Bartenora explains, the blood then " became mixed together in the canal for water which was in the court, and thence passed out into the valley of Kedron, where the gardeners purchased it for fertilizing purposes from the treasurers of the Temple. Long after the destruction of Jerusalem by Titus, the Bordeaux pilgrim, *A.D.* 333, speaks of this opening, and tells us that at that time, the Jews came once a year to anoint " the pierced rock, ' *lapis pertusus,*' when they gave themselves up to their lamentations."

This identification, first proposed by Williams in his " *Holy City,*" is now generally accepted, as is also the belief that the cave answers " to the hollow or pit which

was under the altar " and from time to time had to be
flushed out and cleansed. In this case the hollow sound
produced when one stamps upon the slab closing the Bir
el Arwah, would lead one to believe that the cavity
underneath the floor of the cave must be the sewer
through which the water and blood were drained from
the sanctuary.

164]   Southern Staircase and Basin el Kas. [*Photo—Anonymous*

We must not, however, forget that the great underground passage in connexion with the bath-rooms of the
priests in Beth-Moked, by which those who had con-
tracted ceremonial defilement could leave the Temple
precincts unseen, through the gate Tadi, is supposed by

Sir Charles Warren to pass right under the cave, and that its presence may account for the hollow sound. This, however, is a question which, though very interesting, is not likely to be solved for a long time to come, as even "baksheesh," all powerful in other cases, has utterly failed

[165]   Open-air Pulpit near Dome of the Rock.

[Photo—Anonymous

to obtain permission for explorers to lift the slab, and discover what is underneath, or whether, as some people think, both the above theories are wrong, and that beneath the floor there are secret chambers containing

the long-lost Ark of the Covenant and other treasures of
the Jewish Temple referred to in *Chapter xxxviii.*
That the holy vessels are still concealed somewhere about
the sanctuary precincts is the universal belief amongst
the Orthodox Jews in Jerusalem ; and for that reason no
strict Israelite will venture to set foot within the enclosure,

[166]   Sebil Kaiet Bai from Temple platform.

[*Photo—Anonymous*

for fear lest he tread upon the spot where the Temple furniture is buried, and, as a punishment, die during the year. To this day, the older sheikhs of the Haram relate how, in the year 1860, one of the Rothschilds, on visiting Jerusalem, had himself carried in a chair through the Temple-area rather than venture to set his foot on its holy ground.

We now leave the Dome of the Rock. As we emerge from the cave we notice a long platform upborne by little marble columns where an ancient copy of the Koran, said, wrongly of course, to have belonged to the Khalif Omar, is preserved. Inside the great South door on the right and left, are railed off spaces where learned Moslems may be seen seated cross-legged on the rich carpets presented to the Haram by the late Sultan Abd el Hamid, and engaged in studying their sacred books. A few steps land us outside the building, and again passing the open-air marble pulpit [165] and through the four-fold arcade close by, and on the approximate site of the Water Gate of the " inner temple," we descend Southward by a broad flight of twenty steps, each nine inches, or half a cubit of eighteen inches high, the exact height of the steps in the ancient Temple, as I have ascertained by personal measurement. At its foot, to the right and left, are " mastabehs," or prayer platforms, overshadowed by stately cypresses and olive trees, whilst right in front of us is a great circular basin called " El Kas," [164] about three feet deep, with steps leading down into it. In its very middle is another round basin formed by a circular wall of marble slabs. In the centre again of this, and resting on a pedestal, is a semi-spherical font-like stone vessel, from which, through eight perforations in its rim, gushes water that has come through the iron pipes, recently laid, from the famous " Sealed Fountain" close to Solomon's Pools, South-west of Bethlehem.

A little further to the east are groups of men filling skins and jars from the cisterns with which this part of the Temple Area is honey-combed. These cisterns are of

[**167**] Porch of Mosque el Aksa, with El Kas in foreground.
[*Photo by Miss Blyth*

very great size and of remarkable form. One just under the South-east corner of the great platform, from which we have just descended, is cut deeply into the rock and looks on the plan like an anchor with one of its arms broken off. Another close by and called " the Great Sea," will contain, as was ascertained by Sir Charles Wilson, during the years 1864 and 1865, two million gallons of water, whilst the total number of gallons which could at that time be stored in the different reservoirs inside the Area probably exceeded, as he estimated, ten millions. (" *Recovery of Jerusalem*," *page* 17).

During the time since the investigations of Sir C. Wilson, the storage-room has greatly increased, many new cisterns

[168]   Galleries to Western Huldah Gate.

[*Photo by Alex. S. Hanauer*

having been obtained, partly by recent construction as in the case of those in front of the Western facade of the Golden Gate, and partly by cleaning out and repairing ancient tanks, or by building up and cement-lining old underground vaults ; one of the three corridors leading up from the Triple Gate, for instance. At the same time a great rain collector has been made by paving with good flag-stones the whole of the Area inside the South-east corner from the Eastern wall of the city to the Eastern gate of the Mosque El Aksa, so that at the present time, fully double the amount of rain-water can be stored compared with the above-mentioned ten million gallons. Although, as we have shown, many of the places now used as cisterns were not originally intended for that purpose, as for example the rock chambers under the Beth-Moked, the great gate passage underneath Sebil Kaiet Bai [166] and another just East of the Mosque of El Burak, yet at all times the question of the water supply of the Temple Area was an important one, and even at the risk of being wearisome to the reader, I must call attention to two remarkable points.

The first is that the so-called " Great Sea " and adjoining tanks are very near the position where following the description of Middoth (*chapter v.* 4), we should look for the הגולה ביר or " well of the captivity," so called because constructed by the exiles who returned from Babylon. The second point is that the question of the Temple water-supply throws light on the conversation of Our Lord with Nicodemus (*St. John iii.*) who has been identified with Nicodemus ben Gorion, a famous contemporary of our Saviour. He was several times mentioned in Talmudic writings as having charge of the water-supply, especially of the Temple, where much was required daily. If this identification, which some do not accept, be correct, then, in the reference of Our Lord to water, we have an example of the marvellous way in which He always adapted His teaching to the needs of His hearers, illustrating it by incidents or circumstances in their daily

[169] Column in Quarry near Jerusalem.

[*Photo by Author*

lives. The following story of Nicodemus is related in the Talmud (*Taanith, fol.* 19, *col.* 2) :—

"*It happened once when all Israel went up to the feast at Jerusalem that they had no water to drink. Nicodemon ben Gorion then asked of a friendly proprietor the loan of twelve cisterns of water, promising to refill them on a certain day, or, failing this, to pay him twelve talents of silver.*

"*The day came ; it brought no rain, but a demand from the owner of the cisterns for a discharge of the obligation. Nicodemon answered that the day was not yet ended, and*

*that he was, therefore, not bound to pay. In the afternoon
the demand for either the money or the water was renewed,
Nicodemon replied that he had yet time, as the sun had not
yet set. The creditor laughed, and went to his bath in high
spirits, saying, ' There has been no rain the whole year, and
it is impossible that it should come before sunset.'*

"*Nicodemon however, went sorrowfully to the Temple*

[170]   Column inside railing near Russian Cathedral.
[*Photo by Rev. H. Stanton, D.D.*

*and prayed, saying, ' O Lord of the Universe ! Thou
knowest that I have not undertaken this obligation either for
my own glory or that of my father's house, but solely for
Thine honour, that those who keep the feast may have
water.' At once the skies were overcast with clouds, and the
rain fell in such torrents that the cisterns were filled to over-
flowing. On leaving the Temple, Nicodemon met the owner
of the cisterns, and in his turn demanded of the latter pay-*

ment for the excess of water. ' I know,' said the man, ' that the Holy One, Blessed be He! has convulsed the Universe for thy sake, but the rain came after sunset, and therefore I am still entitled to my twelve talents.' Hereupon Nicodemon again went into the Temple and prayed : ' O Ruler of the Universe! let it be manifest that Thou hast beloved ones in the world.' At once the clouds dispersed and the sun shone forth."

We continue our walk Southward. Right in front of us is the series of seven arches forming the porch of the great Mosque El Aksa. Delaying for the present our visit to this building, we descend, through the railed-off space seen just to the left of the great central arch down the staircase leading to the two great parallel dark passages or galleries conducting to the vestibule of the double or western Huldah Gate [168].

Next to the Sacred Rock this is the most interesting object to be seen in the Temple Area, being an undoubted relic of the Temple of the time of our Lord. " Huldah " means " mole," and this gate, as well as that which once stood on the site of the present " Triple " Gate were so called because of the long underground passages by which people coming through these gates approached, or else left the higher levels of the Temple Area. It was probably through this very gateway, vestibule and galleries, that yearly, at the Feast of Tabernacles, the great procession, bearing water from Siloam, swept.

Standing here, we feel that we are on holy ground, for it is almost certain that the eyes of Our Lord Himself must have rested on these very columns and ceiling adorned by Herodian carvings of the symbolic vine of Judah. The huge monolithic column shown in the foreground and middle of our picture is, besides this, interesting, because in its dimensions it exactly tallies with those described by Josephus (*Antiq. xv.* 5), as belonging to the Royal Cloister which ran along the outer Temple platform above its southern wall, and at right angles to the twin passages from the Double Gate. " The thickness of each pillar was such that three men might with their arms extended, fathom it round and join their hands again," as I have often verified by actual experiment on this pillar.

Here and there, in ancient quarries [169] on the hillsides near Jerusalem, may be seen unfinished columns still attached to the native rock. One such is now carefully preserved inside a railing just in front of the Russian Cathedral, North-west of the City [170]. Its dimensions, as Professor Clermont Ganneau shews in his " *Archaeological Researches*," exactly tally with those given by Josephus as the measurements of those belonging to the Cloister of Herod.

Besides this, there is a theory, interesting though not yet verified, that two at any rate of these columns still in quarry, were purposely cut there, and so left, in order to serve as landmarks indicating the Northern boundary-line between the territories of the tribes of Judah and Benjamin. At present all that can be said in favour of this idea, is that these two really do lie, roughly speaking, stretching Westwards, in line with the Dome of the Rock.

CHAPTER XXX.

ETRACING our steps through the long barrel-arched galleries we pass through the porch and enter the great seven-aisled Masjid El Aksa [167] built on the site and with the materials, as most authorities believe, of Justinian's great Basilica of the Theotokos (or " Mother of God "). The Crusaders turned the mosque into a church dedicated to the Presentation of the Virgin. The porch, supposed by Sir Charles Wilson to be the work of the Knights Templars, has fitted into the wall, an inscription, stating that its builder was El Melek Muadhem Isa, nephew to Saladin.

The interior of the structure is arranged like a Christian basilica, except that, as it has no apse, the plan is like the letter T. The central aisle runs between two rows of massive but stunted columns, with heavy debased Corinthian capitals of Byzantine times. One of the columns is missing and a rude octagonal white-washed pier fills its place. A great wooden architrave running above the capitals supports a row of arches, above which come two rows of windows [171].

The transept contains some magnificent columns of coloured limestone and other materials, but as they all once belonged to more ancient buildings, the pedestals differ in height and shape, and so also do the capitals, some being beautiful Corinthian marbles, and others displaying basket-work moulded in plaster. All the arches are pointed. A few of the mosaic windows are handsome, but nothing like those in the Sakkhrah. Most of the aisles are covered with whitewash, whilst the capitals are painted light brown or yellow. The interior of the dome, however, and the part just beneath it, are

[171] Nave of Mosque el Aksa.   [*Photo—C. Raad, Jerusalem*

richly adorned with mosaics and marble wainscot. The arabesques and mosaic are like, though different in design, to those in the Dome of the Rock.

At the Southern end of the central aisle is the great " mihrab," or prayer-niche, flanked by graceful marble columns and lined in its lower part with variegated

marble, and in its upper with mosaics. There is an
inscription recording its restoration by Saladin [172].
Immediately to the right is a cedar-wood " mumbar,"
or Mohammedan pulpit, with a high-peaked Saracenic

[172]   Southern end of Mosque El Aksa with Pulpit on left.

[*Photo— American Colony*

canopy over it. It is a remarkable and very beautiful piece of cabinet work, inlaid with nacre and ivory. An Arabic inscription of inlaid work running along the railing on either side of the steps and other parts of the structure, tells us that it was made in 1168 by an artist from Aleppo, Hamid Ben Dhafar, and by command of Nureddin. It was brought to Jerusalem by order of

[173] Tomb of David and site of Dormition Church.

[*Photo—Anonymous*

Saladin. Just beyond this pulpit the picture gives us a glimpse of an iron-gilt grille like that running between the columns surrounding the great Rock in the Sakkhrah. Inside it are two small " mihrabs." One is dedicated to " Isa," *i.e., Jesus*, whose reputed foot-print is shewn here, and the other to Moses. The small mediaeval marble capitals were adorned with figures of birds, now mutilated.

Just beyond the right hand edge of the picture are a couple of columns standing so near each other that it is difficult for an ordinary-sized person to pass between them. They are called the columns of ordeal, because Moslems believe that only those who can manage to slip through between them, can enter Paradise. In the year 1881, a Mohammedan, who was rather too stout attempted to win Heaven by squeezing through the gap, but died in the attempt. Since that time iron stanchions have been placed there in order to discourage this superstitious practice. There is another similar pair of columns in one of the Eastern aisles. Some other mosques, for instance that of Amr at Cairo, have pairs of columns to which the same superstitious belief attached, a poor caricature of the Gospel teaching concerning the narrow gate.

Just to the left of these columns, and between them and the above-mentioned iron-gilt grating, is seen a door-way leading out of El Aksa to the top of the pile of ruins which were once part of the Templars' quarters here. A couple of rooms here are generally inhabited by the " hareem," or womenkind of one of the mosque officials, but the prospect of baksheesh soon induces their lord and master to order them to remain behind closed doors whilst the visitor steps out to survey the really fine view extending from the Mount of Offence on the east to the Hill of Evil Counsel and Mount Zion on the south and west. In the latter direction the great new tower of the Dormition Church is very conspicuous. At its feet crouches the group of buildings known since

A.D. 1560 as the Tomb of David [173] and containing the Coenaculum [174] or chamber in which, according to tradition, our Saviour instituted the Lord's Supper; and where, later on, the Holy Spirit descended on the assembled disciples at Pentecost. Although the apartment is not really older than the Fourteenth century, yet the tradition locating the Coenaculum here is at least a

[174]   The Coenaculum, supposed chamber of the Last Supper.   *[Photo—C. Raad, Jerusalem*

thousand years older; and there is really reason to believe that the early Christians in Jerusalem had their first place of united worship somewhere close by. The flight of six stone steps seen in the background near the right hand corner leads to a room from which, through a barred door one can look into another, containing a cenotaph covered with gaudy cloths, and said by the Moslems to be situated exactly above the monument of David, in the lower basement inaccessible to Christians. The tradition is altogether worthless.

[175]   Cemetery adjoining the Tomb of David.

[*Photo—Anonymous*

The buildings, of which the Coenaculum is a part, were, from the Fourteenth to the Sixteenth century, the Convent of the Franciscan monks, who after various grievous persecutions were finally expelled about *A.D.* 1560.   In an illustration [173] taken before the building of the Dormition Church and Convent began, we see the then vacant site on which they now stand between the Neby-Daud buildings and the walled enclosure of the old American Mission cemetery [175].

The graves seen in the foreground belong to the cemeteries of the Greek, Latin and Armenian communities, and until a few years ago, were not walled in as they are now. Many of the tombstones have carved on them the working tools of the person buried beneath, for instance, the tailor's scissors, the stonecutter's chisel and mallet, the mason's trowel, and also the bishop's crozier. The circular dry-stone enclosure near the left-hand edge of the picture marks the resting-place of a Moslem saint.

We re-enter El Aksa, which during the Crusading period was, besides being as we have already mentioned a Church of the Virgin, also called the "Templum Solomonis." The buildings adjoining it East and West were at first occupied by the Latin king, but when in *A.D.* 1118, Hugh de Payens and his eight companions formed a knightly order for the purpose of escorting and guarding pilgrims visiting Palestine, King Baldwin I. gave up these buildings for their use, and the new order was henceforth known as "the order of the Brethren of the Temple of Solomon," or shorter, "Knights Templars."

The transept of El Aksa opens on the West into a great double, which was originally a triple, mediaeval hall, divided by a row of square piers which support the spandrel vaulting. This great hall, which is said by some to have been the knights' fencing school, and by others their refectory or their oratory, is entered by a small crusading porch [176] flanked on either side by four grouped marble columns.

[176] Porch to Templars' Hall.

[Photo by Miss Blyth]

The Eastern end of the great hall is separated from El Aksa proper by a railing, and from its Western portion by a wall This part is separated as a mosque for the use of women. The Eastern transept of El Aksa opens into a long vaulted and whitewashed chamber called "the Mosque of Omar." Its mihrab is remarkable, because flanked on either side with double twisted columns, the capitals of which are carved with grotesque

312

animal forms. These curious twisted columns seen here, and also at the Bab-es-Silsileh, are popularly called by Moslems the " Intestines of the Avaricious," and are believed to have been kneaded in stone by Solomon as an object-lesson to his people, in order to shew them what would happen at the last day to the entrails of the miserly and covetous, who, because they lacked " bowels of mercy " in this world would receive bowels of stone in the world to come.

Through a low door in the Northern wall of this room, which is said to have served the Templars as an arsenal, we pass successively the chapel called by Moslems " El-Arbain," and " the standing places of Zacharias and his son, John the Baptist." The larger of these has part of its apse still visible on the outside of the building. We also note a fine rose-window with six lights over the Twelfth-century portal opening from El Aksa Eastwards. At the end of the aisle further North is a cistern called the " Well of the Leaf," from a worthless legend connected with it. More worthy of notice is the spot in the pavement of the central aisle near its northern entrance, and called " The Tomb of the Sons of Aaron." It marks the last resting-place of some of the murderers of Thomas à Becket, who, as the author of " The Holy City," quoting the English Chronicler Hovenden, tells us (*vol. ii. page* 309) came on a penitential visit to Jerusalem, where they died and were buried on this spot. Hovenden relates, " that having been admitted to penance by Pope Alexander III. they went to Jerusalem." The quotation referred to ran : " *Et ex praecepto Papae in monte*

*nigro (Query, Jebel Musa), poenitentiam agentes obierunt
et sunt Jerosolymis sepulti ante ostium Templi. Quarum
superscriptio haec est. Hic jacent miseri qui martyri-
zaverunt beatum Thomam archiepiscopum Cantuariensum."
Ap. Savile's Scriptures Aug. p. 522.*

The epitaph, now totally effaced, translated into English
reads thus : "Here lie the wretches who martyred the
blessed Thomas, Archbishop of Canterbury." However,
this story of the pilgrimage of the knights, and their death
at Jerusalem, is, by some writers, believed to be a legend,
at variance with historical facts.

On leaving El Aksa visitors generally go to see Solomon's
Stables and the Triple Gate galleries. Close to and a few
yards North of the Golden Gate inside the East city wall
is a low building with two domes marking the spot
where, according to Oriental legends, Solomon used to
sit watching and controlling the evil spirits, who at his
command were raising the enormous structures whose
ruins are seen at Jerusalem, Baalbec and Palmyra.
Here, according to the same myths, his corpse remained
seated for forty years leaning on his staff of carob-
wood till the latter, eaten hollow by a worm, broke,
and when the dead body of the king fell to the ground
the Jan knew, though not before, that their master was
dead and they were free. We now traverse, proceeding
Westward, the open space North of the great platform
in the centre of the Temple-Area.

Our last illustration shews us the extremely interesting
North-west corner, rich in historical and Scriptural associations. The eight-sided domed building on the left is

" Kubbet Es Sakkhrah Es Saghira," the Dome of the Little Rock [177], so-called from the legend that when Jerusalem was destroyed by Nebuchadnezzar, and its inhabitants taken to Babylon, they carried with them into exile, a fragment of the Sacred Rock   When they returned

[177]   Dome of the Little Rock, showing staircase to Antonia.   *[Photo—Anonymous*

Seventy years later, they brought it back with them and deposited it reverently on the spot where Solomon had offered up his prayer at the consecration of the first Temple (I *Kings viii.* 23-24). Hence this building is also sometimes called Kubbet Suleiman. Exactly the same legend attaches, however, also to another small building on the great platform, and North of the dome of Mohammed's Ascension. In the background, to the right of the Dome of the Little Rock, is the minaret into which was built columns and capitals taken from the Crusading Chapel of the Presentation of Christ in the Temple, the modern Kubbet es Silsileh.

At the foot of this minaret is seen a winding staircase leading up to the Southern entrance to the former Turkish barracks on the site of the Antonia [177]. There must, at all times subsequent to the Maccabean period, have been a staircase at this point and leading up to the Castle. This staircase is, in fact, the modern representation of one which occupied the same spot, and on which we read St. Paul stood " *and beckoned with the hand unto the people. And when there was made a great silence, he spake unto them in the Hebrew tongue* " (*Acts xxi*. 40). The story of the experiences of the Apostle at Jerusalem becomes very vivid and life-like as we stand on the spot shown in the photograph.

There is something else, however, to be noticed besides the foregoing. Immediately to the right of the staircase is a carefully cut rock-hewn scarp, and at its foot the level floor of the Haram Area Westward is also seen to consist of carefully cut rock. The lower part of the houses in the background to the left of the minaret is also scarped rock. This fact takes us back in thought to the middle of the Second Century B.C. Before that time a rocky height dominated the Temple Area at its North-west corner, stretching a good deal further south than does the rock on which the former Turkish barracks now stand, and as the Roman barracks, the Antonia, stood before them. On that hill-top was situated in the days of Nehemiah, a palace, or to use the Hebrew term, " Birah " (*Nehemiah ii.* 8).

At the time of the Maccabean rising, its site was occupied by a fort called " the Baris," the Greek form of the name Birah. The Graeco-Syrian garrison of this castle molested the Jews going up to the Temple to worship, by flights of arrows. In the time of Simon Maccabaeus the garrison was forced to surrender, and then Simon, acting for his people, " thought it their best way and most to their advantage, to level the very mountain itself upon which the citadel happened to stand, so that the Temple might be higher than it. . . . And having induced the multitude to a compliance . . . they all set themselves to the work, and levelled the mountain, and in that work spent both day and night without intermission, which cost them three whole years before it was removed." (*Antiq. Bk. xiii. vi.* 7.) The scarps and levelled floor, a gigantic piece of work, are believed to be the result of those three years of constant labour. There are some authorities, however, who think, that in the passage just quoted, the Jewish historian refers to the rock-cuttings on the Akra hill, East of the Church of the Sepulchre. Others have suggested without sufficient proof, that the Birah stood South of the Temple, on the spot where Professor Macalister recently excavated on Ophel, in search of a supposed " City of David," of which no trace has been found in evidence, up to the time of writing.

We leave the Temple Area by the gate at its North-west corner, close to the above-mentioned minaret. Up a winding staircase and through a short street we emerge into the Via Dolorosa. Following it Eastward past the Chapel of the Flagellation, we turn up the first street to the left, a street of stairs ascending Bezetha. In this quarter are the remains of several ancient mediaeval

[178] Jerusalem from the roof of the C.M.S. former Girls' School. [*Photo— American Colony*

churches, especially Deir el Adas, and St. Peter's, but these need not detain us. The way leads past the great modern Moslem school El Mamunieh, interesting because recently built on the site of a once magnificent Church of St. Mary Magdalene.

From hereabouts one gets a glimpse of the low-lying houses and open spaces just North and West of St. Anne's

Church. In the time of Our Lord, this part was outside the city. In Crusading times the " Juiverie," or Jewry, was situated here. We pass the Gate called Herod's, probably because during the Middle Ages the house of Herod Antipas was shewn by tradition somewhere between it and the Via Dolorosa. The name of Deir El Adas has been supposed, without sufficient proof, however, to be derived from the name " Herodes."

A winding path between some poor Moslem buildings brings us to the door of the building formerly used as the C.M.S. Girls' School, situated on the city wall just above the so-called Solomon's Quarries. From its roof there is an excellent view of the city [176].

CHAPTER XXXI.

FROM the roof of the former Girls' School of the Church Missionary Society, whence in the previous chapter (xxx.) we surveyed the city, we descend and follow the street leading westwards downhill to the Damascus Gate [180], which is one of the most remarkable of all the city gates at present in use, and in all probability occupies the site of the Northern gate of our Lord's time. This is proved by the existence to this day of two ancient tower chambers, one on either side, and the vestiges of a massive arched side gateway just inside the entrance [182]. These remains consist of what all authorities agree in describing as ancient Roman masonry of the Herodian period.

Those who support the claims of the Church of the Sepulchre assert indeed that the tower chambers and masonry formed part of the third wall of the city erected by Herod Agrippa about eight or ten years after the Ascension of our Lord. This assertion, however, must be impossible, because, as there is overwhelming evidence to prove, there existed until the year 1870, extensive ruins of the third wall a good distance North of the present city wall. During excavations carried on in the year 1925 fresh vestiges of Agrippa's wall were discovered on a line running East and West between the English College and the new Italian Hospital. This discovery confirms the description of Josephus in all particulars. It also proves: Firstly, that the remains called "Tancred's Tower" are *not* vestiges of the Psephmus Tower and also secondly, that the present North wall of Jerusalem does not follow the line of the wall of Herod

[180] Damascus Gate. [*Photo—C. Raad, Jerusalem*

Agrippa, as advocates of the Church of the Sepulchre site hitherto have maintained.

In Roman times the gateway on the site of the Damascus Gate is said to have been known as the Porta Neapolitana, because from it the great central road led Northwards towards the city of Neapolis, now called Nablous, and in Old Testament times, Shechem. The ancient *Gate of Ephraim* (2 *Chronicles xxv.* 23; *Nehemiah xii.* 39), probably stood here, and it may have been through this gate that our Lord was led to be crucified. Roman Catholics believe that it was from this gate that Saul of Tarsus started on his memorable *journey to Damascus* (*Acts ix.*), and in order to commemorate this, a German monastic order, some years before the Great War, erected the huge building just outside the Damascus Gate and now used as " the Governorate."

By the natives the Damascus Gate is generally called " Bab el Amud," meaning " Gate of the Column," thus preserving the memory of a great pillar which, as the Medeba mosaic shows, stood, probably from the time of Adrian, just within the gate, and inside what is supposed to have been the forum of Ælia Capitolina. From this point started the colonnaded streets shown on the mosaic map.

Another name by which the Damascus Gate was known is " Bab el Nassr," meaning " the Gate of Victory," thus preserving either the tradition of a triumphal gate on the site, or else the theory that this was the proper gate for crowned heads and princes to enter by, as was the case when in 1869, the Crown Prince of Prussia, afterwards the late Emperor Frederick, and also the late Emperor Francis Joseph, of Austria, visited the Holy City with great pomp, after they had attended the opening of the Suez Canal.

As we pass out of the city by this gate we notice that the large Herodian stones forming the lower courses of the two flanking towers, show that when the engineers of Suleiman the Magnificent rebuilt it about *A.D.* 1542, they despaired of matching the huge blocks in size, and therefore, in order that their own smaller masonry should not suffer by comparison, they cut grooves across the faces of the more ancient and massive courses in the eastern gate tower. The gateway passage runs in a course of a

[181] Street scene inside the Damascus Gate.
[*Photo—C. Raad, Jerusalem*

double right angle and, as is evident from pivot sockets above and below, was intended to be furnished with several successive pairs of gate leaves, which would need to be burst open by assailants, one after the other.

From the roof of this gateway there is an excellent

view down the great central valley and along the slopes of the hills covered with buildings on either side of it.

We now again leave the city by the Damascus Gate and follow the road leading Eastwards parallel with the walls. A walk of a couple of minutes brings us to the place where the ramparts run along the edge of a great artificial precipice, the Southern side of an immense rock-hewn trench formed by quarrying through and under Bezetha during past millenniums. Lights are provided and we pass through

[182]   Herodian Tower Chamber, west of Damascus Gate.   [*Photo by Author*

the opening shown in illustration [134] of the City wall, near Solomon's Quarries (*Chapter xxiii., page* 224), and find ourselves in a huge artificial cave, the roof of which is supported by irregular pillars of different sizes and shapes, cut out of the rock itself, which here is of a creamy white colour. Being fairly soft to cut, but hardening by exposure to weather and sun, it is well adapted for building purposes. The cavern extends South-eastward for about 250 yards, and is, in some places, 120 yards wide. Here and there we notice the beds from which stones for the walls of the Temple and other edifices were hewn. Elsewhere we come across such blocks unfinished and still adhering to the rock, but with deep grooves cut all round their sides into the rock itself; these grooves were intended to receive wooden wedges which, after being thoroughly wetted when driven into position, would swell and separate each block of stone from the mass surrounding it. We also notice niches in which the ancient quarry-men placed their little smoking oil lamps whilst they marked and shaped the blocks for Solomon's Temple, and we can understand how it was that " the house, when it was in building, was built of stone made ready before it was brought thither : so that there was neither hammer nor axe nor any tool of iron heard in the house while it was in building " (I *Kings vi.* 7).

The great antiquity of the excavation, which is some-times called " the Royal Caves," and also " the Cotton Cave," from the whiteness of its stone, is attested by the discovery, during the latter half of the Nineteenth century of a " graffito," or rude picture of an Assyrian human-headed bull, cut into a rock wall, evidently by one of the exiles who returned from Babylon under Ezra or Nehemiah.

According to a local, although quite valueless, Jewish tradition, it was through a passage connecting this cavern with the Temple and Royal Palace, that about 588 *B.C.*, Zedekiah, the last king of Judah, attempted to escape from Jerusalem when the city was taken by the forces of Nebuchadnezzar. Another tradition is that in ancient times, one of the rock-chambers was used by the workmen of the quarry as a Synagogue.

CHAPTER XXXII.

JUST opposite the entrance to the cavern and about 200 yards distant, rises the counter scarp of the great trench, a sheer precipice formed by human hands and fully 60 feet high in several places. We notice that at one spot just above the entrance to another artificial cavern, generally called "Jeremiah's Grotto," there is a remarkable dislocation in the layers of rock which at this point are broken through and do not run at the same level. This dislocation or "fault" used in Crusading times to be pointed out as a result of the earthquake at the time of the death of our Lord. By a local Jewish tradition of little value, this precipice is said to have been the "Beth ha Sekelah," or Place of Stoning mentioned in the Mishna. Since the year 1842, when Otto Thenius, a German scholar, first made the suggestion, many people, including the late General Gordon, have embraced the supposition that the knoll above Jeremiah's Grotto is the true site of Calvary.

As General Gordon had very decided views on this point it is often called "Gordon's Calvary" [183]. The famous soldier had a strange and mystic idea that "the sacred Eastern hill," the greater part of which, within the city walls, is occupied by the Bezetha quarter and the Temple Area, "bore a rough resemblance to the human form," and he illustrated it by a curious drawing,

327

a reproduction of which appeared in the book of the late Sir Charles Wilson on " Golgotha and the Holy Sepulchre," page 201.

The artificial cave beneath " Skull Hill " is called " Jeremiah's Grotto," from the tradition that it was there the prophet wrote his Book of Lamentations. In Moslem tradition he is identified with Esdras, or " Ozair,"

[183] General Gordon's Calvary. [*Photo—C. Raad, Jerusalem*

and a rock ledge within the grotto is pointed out as the couch on which he slept from the time of the destruction of Jerusalem by Nebuchadnezzar, till after its restoration by the returned exiles in the days of Ezra and Nehemiah.

The " Ozair " myth is doubtless derived from the Apocryphal tale read in the Orthodox Greek Church on the 4th of November of each year, when the fall of

Jerusalem is commemorated. (*Dr. Rendel Harris " The Rest of the Words of Baruch," page 4, C.J. Clay and Sons, London.*) This Christian legend in its turn, sprung from the Talmudic one of Jechonia ha Ma'aggal, a mythical saint who, at the time of the destruction of the Holy City by Nebuchadnezzar, was greatly perplexed as to how the words of Psalm cxxvi. 1 could come to pass, and he therefore prayed for an explanation. In answer he was divinely caused to fall asleep until the Restoration was completed, and when he awoke he was astonished to find the city rebuilt and peopled. A similar legend exists in classical mythology in connection with the Cretan sage Epimenides, who lived about 594 *B.C.* and whose " Awakening " is the subject of one of Goethe's poems. Lastly, the triple legend of Jechonia, Esdras and Ozair, finding its way to the New World, has been the germ from which, in modern English literature, tales like Washington Irving's " Rip Van Winkle " have grown.

The summit of the knoll of Jeremiah's Grotto has for centuries past been used as a Mohammedan cemetery, which according to Mejr ed din (*vol. ii. page* 412), bore the name of " Es Sahirat," meaning " a place where people do not sleep, but keep awake." The adjacent small gate in the Northern city wall was in *A.D.* 1495 known as " Bab es Sahirat," but now as " Bab es Zahireh," or the " Flowery Gate." It may seem trivial to mention this, but it is a good example of similar changes of name which are important as marking historical sites. To Europeans, this gate is known as " Herod's Gate " because a street of stairs leads from it down to the " Deir el 'Ades " a former monastery, said by tradition to occupy the site of the Palace of Herod Antipas [184].

Immediately after passing Herod's Gate we cross a wide depression which is the upper part of the valley described in Chapters vi. and xxii. as opening into the Kedron at a point between St. Stephen's Gate and the Golden Gate and containing the Pool of Bethesda and the Birket Israel.

[184] Herod's Gate. [*Photo—C. Raad, Jerusalem*

On the higher ground East of this depression is a single fine old pine tree marking, according to tradition, the spot where the tent of Godfrey de Bouillion was pitched during the siege of Jerusalem by the Crusaders in *A.D.* 1099. As a matter of more recent history, it was here that King Edward VII., when Prince of Wales, encamped in 1862, during his visit to the Holy City.

The ground hereabouts is very rocky and only covered by a shallow layer of soil and rubbish brought from elsewhere, which conceals the fact that the rock surface between the great tree and the city wall is honey-combed with a number of ancient, sunken, rock-hewn tombs of uncertain date, and differing in character from other ancient tombs near Jerusalem and, more especially, from the Kokim, or oven-shaped tombs of which the traditional ones of Joseph of Arimathea and Nicodemus, mentioned in Chapter vi. and of which an illustration appears on page 384, are specimens. Illustration [185] shows the entrance to a sunken tomb. That such are very ancient is

[185] A sunken Rock Tomb. *[Photo by Author*

proved by the fact that several of them were cut through and destroyed when, in *A.D.* 1192, Saladin had the rock trench excavated through which the present carriage road runs (*Mejr ed din I. pp.* 338-9). At the North-east corner of the city wall stands a remarkable tower, called, for some unknown reason " Burj Luglug " or the " Stork

Tower." Another picture shows the city wall at this point and also the carriage road, first built in 1887, passing along Saladin's trench. A similar trench runs alongside the eastern city wall as far as St. Stephen's Gate [186]. Here and there the workmen of Saladin cut the name "Allah" into the rock as a sort of talisman to ensure a blessing on their undertaking.

[186] Northern City Wall and Trench of Saladin.
[Photo by Author

We now descend into the Kedron Valley, and notice in its widening bed, a few very old olive trees some distance below us to the left, and in front of us, to the right, the Orthodox-Greek, Armenian, Latin and Russian "Gethsemane" enclosures, with their respective olive groves and chapels. The name " Gethsemane " means " olive oil press."

In Palestine the same primitive agricultural methods that were in vogue during Biblical times are still in use. An olive oil press consisted of a massive and heavy stone roller fixed in such a way that it revolved round a central

[187] The Garden of Gethsemane. [*Photo—Anonymous*

333

pivot fixed in the middle of a great slightly concave circular stone tray or shallow basin. These rollers and their beds were often cut from the rock on the same spot where they were to be used and remained lying there for centuries after the grove which supplied the olives had been cut down. This has been the case in the upper Kedron Valley, where to this day you may see in several places the old circular stones of the ancient olive oil mills which gave its name to Gethsemane [188].

[188] A ruined Oil Press of Gethsemane.
[Photo by Capt. Hanauer, M.C.

On reaching the foot of the hill we notice on our right, and close to the road-side, some very worn rock-hewn steps, the last vestiges of a gigantic staircase which in the time of our Lord led up the Eastern slopes of Moriah towards the Temple Area. Jerusalem always has been, and still is, a city of staircases. Besides this one going upwards from the spot where, according to a very reasonable tradition, commemorated by a Greek chapel close by, St. Stephen was stoned; there were at least three others leading up to Jerusalem. One, discovered by

334

Dr. Bliss, leading up from the Pool of Siloam towards the Temple, is supposed to be the stairs mentioned by *Nehemiah, Chapters iii.* 15 *and xii.* 37. Another, starting from the same place has recently been uncovered by the Assumptionist Fathers during their excavations on the Eastern slope of Zion. It led up to the site of the traditional House of Caiaphas, where in Crusading times, there stood a Church of St. Peter and the Cock-crowing, of which many fragments and relics have been discovered. A third great rock-cut staircase, which was almost entire in the year 1862, but has since been destroyed by quarrying, led up from the bed of the Valley of Hinnom towards the Zion Gate.

Since the discovery of the remains, a little North-west of Jeremiah's Grotto, of the great church built about *A.D.* 450 by the Empress Eudocia in order to receive the supposed relics of St. Stephen, some local guides have jumped to the conclusion that the new Church, erected by the Dominicans on the site and lines of the Church of Eudocia, marks not only the tomb, but also the place of the martyrdom of Stephen. We should, however, remember that the event was not the result of an orderly legal trial, but of sudden and undisciplined mob rage (*Acts vii.* 57, 58). It is therefore not unlikely that the tradition that the first Christian martyr was stoned at the foot of the great eastern staircase is right.

Crossing the valley by a stone bridge we notice on our left a sunken court in front of the Twelfth century porch of the underground church of the so-called Assumption of the Virgin Mary, and containing one of her tombs.

The Franciscans, the Greeks, the Armenians, the Abyssinians and the Jacobite-Syrians believe in this one as marking the site of the Virgin's burial, and her Apocryphal resurrection and ascension, and the four last-named communities have " rights and altars " there. However, at the time that these words were written a paper war was being waged against them and the Franciscans by the Dominicans who, on the authority of a tradition dating back to *A.D.* 431 and the visions of a modern female, the late Katarina of Emmerich, assert that they have re-discovered the tomb of the Virgin and the house in which she lived with St. John, at Ephesus.

Proceeding on our way, the road turns Southward along the Western wall of the Latin Garden of Gethsemane containing eight ancient olive trees, concerning which the Franciscans assert that " it is historically certain that these trees have existed for over Thirteen centuries ; for they have never been subject to the tax which is levied upon all newly planted trees since the Moslem conquest " (*F. Barnabas Meistermann's Guide, page* 176).

In *A.D.* 385 a beautiful Church dedicated to the Saviour stood immediately to the South of the Franciscan Garden. During the course and vicissitudes of centuries it was destroyed, but traces of it having recently been discovered, it is being re-built.

On the hill slope just above the Latin property stands the Russian Church of Mary Magdalene, built in 1888 by the Emperor Alexander III. and remarkable for its seven gilt onion-shaped domes, as well as for some beautiful paintings within the building.

CHAPTER XXXIII.

HAVING passed the Franciscan Gethsemane garden, we leave the carriage road leading to Bethany on our left and follow the mule track down the valley. To our right, is the bed of the Kedron, and the terraced Eastern slope of Moriah beneath the city wall from the Golden Gate to the South-east angle of the Temple area. During recent years, hundreds of young olive trees have been planted, chiefly through the industry of the Franciscans. The East wall of the Temple Area, and the Moslem grave yard at its foot tower higher and higher above us the farther Southward we travel, whilst on our left, and stretching up the Western slope of Olivet is the great Jewish cemetery with its thousands of white grave stones marking the last resting-places of many generations of Israelites. Their bodies have been laid here in order to await the Judgment Day, when, according to Jewish belief, founded on *Joel iii. 2 and* 14, all Nations will be assembled for judgment in " the Valley of decision " which, according to popular ideas, is identical with the " Valley of Jehoshaphat," as this part of the Kedron is generally called. The name " Jehoshaphat " simply means " The Lord will judge " and modern Jews believe that all Israelites dwelling outside the Land of Israel, will, after death, have to roll underground until they arrive here in order to be present at the last Great Day. The only way of escaping this terrible journey is to have their eyelids, when they are dead, sprinkled with dust from Olivet. For this reason Jews resident in the Holy City often send little parcels containing " holy earth " to friends abroad.

We have now reached a spot where another road leads across the torrent bed over a bridge and thence up the steep hill side towards the Dung Gate. Connected with this bridge is the legend of the tree from which the Cross of the Saviour was made, and which was recognized by the Queen of Sheba when she visited King Solomon. For details of this legend see *Folk-lore of the Holy Land. page* 36.

On our left is a great monument popularly called " Absalom's Pillar " (2 *Samuel xviii*. 18). From the style of its architecture, which is a mixture of Egyptian and Greek and resembles that of monuments at Petra, it is evident that it is of much more recent date than that of Absalom—(who died about 1023 *B.C.*)—and that it belongs to Maccabbean times. Its lower part is a rock-hewn hollow cube ornamented outside with Ionic half and quarter columns and standing on a plinth recently discovered during the excavations of Dr. N. Slouch. Over these comes a heavy Egyptian cornice supporting a square pedestal from which rises a drum or low cylinder surmounted by a cone or tiara-like spire, springing from a cable moulding, and ending in a smaller similar moulding out of which grows an opening lotus bud [189]. The manner in which the stones of the superstructure are dressed is similar to that observed in the ruins of Arak el Emir or Palace of Hyrcanus in Transjordania (*Josephus Antiq, Book xii. chapter iv.* 11), and also at the South-

[189] Absalom's Pillar.　　　*[Photo by Author*

west corner of the ancient Temple, now the Mosque of the Ommayades, at Damascus. For these reasons the late Colonel Conder concluded that the monument is the one which was erected in memory of Alexander Jannaeus, 105-178 *B.C.*

It is only since Crusading times that this cenotaph has been called " Absalom's Pillar." Previously it was supposed to be the tomb of Hezekiah. The peasants call it " Tantoor Pharaoh," meaning " Pharaoh's Tiara," whilst two other monuments which we shall soon pass are named respectively " the Divan of Pharaoh," and the " Tomb of Pharaoh's wife."

The chamber inside Absalom's Pillar may be entered by crawling through the holes at its back, but inside there is nothing of special interest. Close to its South-east corner is a staircase leading up into the superstructure so that the inner faces of its stones can be examined. The scarped rock at the back of the rock-hewn recess in which the monument stands contains at its Northern end the carved ornaments and pediment over the door of another ancient sepulchre said to be that of Jehoshaphat. This was again exposed and excavated during 1924. It had been hidden from sight for many years behind a wall because, formerly, the sepulchre had been used as a " Genizah," or chamber where the Jews deposit worn-out Synagogue rolls and other books, and owing to this fact, had been ransacked by people searching for such curios for sale to tourists, etc. (*Rev. F. C. Ewald's Journal for* 1842, *page* 146.)

Proceeding Southward along the foot of the cliff we notice on our left, and high above us, an artificial cave distinguished by two Doric columns in its opening, and having passed it, we come upon another monument

resembling Absalom's Pillar in its lower part and surmounted not by a cone or spire, but by a pyramid, the
whole being hewn out of the rock [190]. At the present
time it is called " Zechariah's Tomb," but in *A.D.* 333
it was named after Isaiah, and also has borne the names of
Simeon and of Joseph. Its walls are scrawled over with

[190] Traditional tomb of St. James—actually the family
mausoleum of the Beni-Hezir (Nehemiah x. 20) and monument of Zechariah, with portion of Jewish cemetery in foreground.   [*Photo—C. Raad, Jerusalem*

the names of Jews who come hither to pray, more
especially when the rainy season is belated.

Through an opening in the Northern scarp of the
recess in which it stands we enter a wide rock-cut and
roofed passage which leads into the cave, or rather porch,
with the two Doric columns above mentioned, and then
on to a rock-hewn staircase conducting to the terrace

above the cliff. At the back of the porch are sepulchral chambers with niches or " locali " for dead bodies, but as these chambers are used by shepherds as sheep folds, they are haunted by hosts of fleas, and therefore are not worth exploring. The whole excavation is called " The Tomb of St. James," but a very ancient Aramaic inscription cut on the architrave outside, tells us that " This is the grave, or monument, of Eliezer, Khoniah, Joezer, Judah, Simeon, Johanan, sons of Asar . . . and of Joseph and Eliezer, Sons of Khoniah . . . . sons of Hezir." It is therefore interesting to realize that this is the mausoleum of a family mentioned in the Bible, Hezir being named in 1 *Chronicles xxiv.* 15, and also in *Nehemiah x.* 20.

An interesting New Testament association is connected with these monuments which, judging from their architectural features, must have been fairly modern in our Lord's Day. High above them to the West rose the Temple Area walls with long double colonnades along the top of their outer edges. That on the East, overhanging these tombs, was called " Solomon's Porch." In it the Saviour was wont to walk and teach. Here, a few days before His Passion, He uttered His scathing denunciations of the Pharisees. He used always to illustrate His remarks by mentioning or pointing to something in view, or else something very familiar to His hearers, such as flowers at His feet, birds passing overhead, or a fox running over the hillside. On this special occasion the sight of these monuments in full view in the valley just below Him, may well be supposed to have given point to the accusation, " *Ye build the tombs of the prophets and garnish the sepulchres of the righteous . . . wherefore ye be witnesses unto yourselves that ye are the children of them which killed the prophets,*" etc., etc. (*Matthew xxiii.* 29-35.) These ornate rock-hewn sepulchres furnished the latest instance of Jewish inconsistency in erecting monuments to the memories of those whom their ancestors had martyred.

In the *present bed* of the Kedron, just below the Tomb of Zechariah, is a heap of stones, known as the " grave of Rabbi Kolonimos," who, Two Centuries ago, ruled the Jewish Community in the Holy City. In order to prevent a massacre of his flock, one Sabbath day he was obliged to use pen, ink and paper; therefore he gave orders that, as an expiation for this sin, the only monument to his memory should be a cairn, the stones of which were to be accumulated during a Century after his decease, by casual passers by. The last stone was flung on to the heap in 1816. The spot is frequently visited by Jews who read prayers there. (*Folk-lore of the Holy Land, pages* 99-101.)

When speaking, in the preceding paragraph, of the *present bed* of the Kedron, we used italics because *the true bed,* now buried under about 39 feet of debris, lies 65 feet further West, and 240 feet to the East of the South-east angle of the Temple Area. As was pointed out in Chapter XIX., at this spot, some eighty feet of the old Sanctuary wall are buried below, whilst fully 70 feet of Herodian masonry tower above the surface, making 150 feet of ancient wall. The vertical height from its foot down to the original bed of the torrent is 107 feet below the South-east angle, so that the total height from the valley to the top of the present Herodian masonry is quite 257 feet, a most dizzy elevation (*Recovery of Jerusalem, page* 136).

About 350 yards South of Zechariah's Tomb we notice another rock-hewn monument, Egyptian in style and flat-roofed, standing in a recess cut into the edge of a terrace of the Northern slope of the Mount of Offence, so-called because tradition marks it as " the opprobrious hill," where " the wisest heart of Solomon " was led by fraud to build " foul idol shrines " right against the Temple of God upon " the hill of scandal," " by the grove of Moloch homicide, lust hard by hate " (*Paradise Lost. Book I.* 400-418).

Over the entrance to this tomb there are traces of a very ancient inscription which was destroyed when the doorway was made higher, probably in the Fourth century. At the back of the terrace above and behind this monument, is a remarkable cliff, rising about 25 feet and having its face pitted with artificial niches like those in the walls of Roman Columbaria.* This cliff referred to is probably the " Peristereon or Dovecote Rock," mentioned by Josephus (*Wars, Book V.*

---

*The Greek word "Peristereon," like the Latin "Columbarium," literally means "a dove cote." Technically, however, the word "Columbarium" means an underground sepulchre, or chamber, the sides of which are furnished with pigeon holes to receive urns holding the ashes of cremated human bodies. It is curious to find what seems to be the remains of a *columbarium* on the spot precisely defined by Josephus, as "the Dove-cote Rock, *Peristereon.*" The fact seems to prove the two terms identical.

chapter xii. 2), as one of the landmarks past which Titus'
wall of circumvallation ran [**191**].   The Peristereon
must certainly have been somewhere very near this spot,

[191] Corner of " Dove-cote Rock " or " Peristereon,"
showing pigeon holes.   *[Photo by Author*

but as far as I am aware, has not as yet been identified
by anyone.   Here begins the Northern end of the village
of Siloam which will furnish material for our next
chapter.

CHAPTER XXXIV.

HE stone houses of the village of Siloam stretch Southward along the Western rock terraces of the Mount of Offence as far as the junction of the Kedron with the " Wad er Rababi " or Valley of Hinnom, and, in the Northern part, hide from view a great number of ancient rock-hewn sepulchres and caves, some of which are now used as dwellings, stables and olive oil presses, in the same way that, from *A.D.* 300 to 636, they were used as cells for recluses and chapels in which they worshipped [192].

The older and Moslem part of the village occupies its Northern end, the Southern extension being quite modern and sheltering Jewish immigrants from Yemen in South Arabia, who first began to come to Palestine in 1882. About the centre of the Northern part of the village there is a remarkable rock terrace, the edge of which overhangs the valley and forms a steep scarp, whose foot slopes downwards until it ends a few yards opposite the so-called Virgin's Fountain. Steps rudely cut in the rock enable the villagers to climb the precipice whilst carrying water or other burdens. This precipice is named " Ez Zehwayleh " or the land-slide, and, as was first pointed out by Professor Clermont-Ganneau, this name is the modern Arabic form of the Hebrew " Zoheleth."

346

It was " by the stone of Zoheleth, which is by En Rogel," that Adonijah, the son of David, and the rival of Solomon, assembled his adherents, for he intended

[192] Village of Siloam and " Zoheleth " between stone houses, and the road along valley, in foreground.
[*Photo—C. Raad, Jerusalem*

after feasting them, to have them proclaim him king (1 *Kings i.* 9).

Just opposite the " Zoheleth," on the other side of the valley, and at the foot of the Eastern slope of Ophel, as the spur or ridge running Southwards from Moriah is called, an ancient staircase much worn and very slippery, leads downwards to a rock cave. This rock cave contains a natural spring, whence at intervals a stream of brackish water suddenly rises and rushes gurgling along a rock-cut passage or tunnel right through the hill to the Pool of Siloam at the South-west end of Ophel, and thence to the gardens further down the valley. This fountain is called by the peasants " Ain - Um -ed- Daraj," *i.e.,* " Fount of the Mother of steps," and by Christians, the " Virgin's Fount " [193], from the legend that the Virgin used to wash her child's clothes here. It is now believed by many competent authorities to be the ancient " Gihon," a name meaning the " Burster forth " or the " Gusher," and most appropriate for a spring such as this, which, by the action of a natural syphon, flows at intervals

[193] The Virgin's Fountain.
[*Photo—C. Raad, Jerusalem*

as above stated. The rock tunnel is believed to be that excavated by orders of Hezekiah, who " stopped the upper water-course of Gihon and brought it straight down Westwards to the city of David " (2 *Chronicles xxxii.* 30).

At a short distance inside the Southern end of the tunnel, which, by the way, winds considerably, the now famous " Siloam Inscription " in Hebrew-Phoenician characters, was accidentally discovered by two boys of the School of the London Jews' Society. An illustration and account of it is given on Plate v. of the Oxford " *Helps to the Study of the Bible*," a work which, I presume, every one of my readers has access to. The stone was afterwards cut away from the rock at the instigation of a Greek who hoped to sell it to advantage. He was, however, detected and punished and the inscription taken to Constantinople. (*For fuller details see Professor Rendel Harris's " Syrian and Palestinian Inscriptions," pp.* 32-35, *C. J. Clay & Sons, London.*)

The tunnel and Siloam inscription are not the only interesting things connected with the Gihon-Siloam aqueduct. A most remarkable discovery was made on October 24th, 1867, during the explorations of Sir Chas. Warren. About 50 feet from the entrance of the tunnel from the pool in the cave at the Virgin's Fount another passage coming from the North-west was discovered, and when cleared out, proved to be 17 feet long and ending in a cave. The bottom of this cave, 3 feet lower than the aqueduct, was also that of a great rock-hewn shaft or chimney rising 40 feet into the very heart of the hill and opening out into other rock-cut passages and a great chamber, a detailed account of which is given on pages 238-256 of " The Recovery of Jerusalem," (*Richard Bentley, London,* 1871).

[194] Present state of Pool of Siloam, showing south end of tunnel and columns belonging to ancient church.

[*Photo—C. Raad, Jerusalem*]

The explorations of Sir Charles Warren in Jerusalem ended in 1870, but shortly before the Great War 1914-1918, a British Syndicate re-opened and thoroughly cleared out the Gihon-Siloam tunnel and passages. By doing this they certainly benefited the people of Siloam, but, as far as is known, made no very remarkable discoveries.

Other excavations on the Ophel ridge itself, by Captain Weil, who hoped to find the tombs of David and his descendants, resulted in finding another rock-hewn aqueduct and also remains of an ancient synagogue, which, on the ground of the dedicatory inscription in Greek, is believed to have been that of " the Freed-men " or " Libertines " mentioned in Acts of the Apostles, *Chapter vi.*, 9. The length of the tunnel from the Virgin's Fount to the Pool of Siloam is 1,700 feet. Measured in a straight line the actual distance is not more than 1,200 feet. From the Virgin's Fount, a road, at present in as bad a condition and quite as unpracticable for horses, as in the days of Nehemiah (*Nehemiah ii.* 15), leads along the Eastern foot of Ophel to the junction of the Tyropœon with the Kedron Valley.

The bed of the latter, on our left, is occupied by vegetable gardens watered from the Pool of Siloam canal, and fertilized by the city sewage conveyed thither through ancient and ruinous masonry drains, open in many places, both on the slopes of Ophel and in the valley beneath. The horrible effluvia proceeding therefrom proves that the well-known lines concerning " Siloam's shady rill " and the sweetness of the lily growing there, are simply poetic licence and vain imaginations.

Where the Tyropœon joins the Kedron the road passes over an ancient dam, about 230 feet long and at present 90 feet thick. The excavations carried on by Dr. Bliss and Professor Dickie showed that on its Eastern side it is constructed of fine and embossed stones, and strengthened by seven imposing buttresses of the same character. At various times the dam was strengthened by filling the spaces between the buttresses with solid masonry.

On its Western side also it has been reinforced several times, and here a large pool was formed, the bed of which is now a vegetable garden and known as "Birket-el-Hamra," or The Red Pool. This is supposed to be that constructed by Hezekiah and called "the King's Pool" (*Nehemiah ii.* 14). ("*Recovery of Jerusalem*," *page* 238). An open rock-hewn channel running along the foot of the precipice at the Southern end of Ophel, and hanging over the pool, brings the water from the Upper Pool of Siloam eastward, to the northern end of the dam where the women of Siloam fill their jars and wash their clothes by pounding them very energetically with stones and wooden mallets. From this spot the water runs into the gardens further down.

A large artificial opening in the face of the cliff at its eastern end, is the termination of a yet more ancient aqueduct by which, previous to the reign of Hezekiah, the water of the Gihon spring was conducted down the valley.

At the opposite end of the dam is an old mulberry tree, marking the spot where, according to tradition, Isaiah was sawn asunder by order of Manasseh, son of Hezekiah, King of Judah. The legend is very ancient and supposed to be referred to in *Hebrews xi.* 37 ("*Rest of the Words of Baruch*," by *Dr. Rendel Harris*, *page* 23). At the present day, a tiny old rock-hewn chapel, now the property of the Franciscans, in the village of Siloam, contains a *modern* Greek inscription, cut in the rock about thirty years ago, for the former owner, a Moslem, by a notorious forger of antiques.

The forgery reads "This is the place of the Prophet Isaiah."

About 60 yards South-west of the old tree, the road passes the spot where in 1882, Professor Guthe and, several years later, Dr. Bliss, found the remains of the "Fountain Gate," mentioned in *Nehemiah ii*. 14. The excavations of Dr. Bliss are still open and accessible to anyone who likes to inspect the ruin.

The Fountain Gate stood at the South-east corner of the ancient Jewish city wall, which has been traced all along the slopes of the traditional Zion. It ran from the rock scarp seen in the Protestant cemetery, East of Bishop Gobat's School, which stands on the stupendous rock-hewn base of a great tower, very possibly the "Tower of the Furnaces" (*Nehemiah iii*. 11), and a long escarpment, artificially hewn, and honeycombed with cisterns for the use of a garrison.

The foot of this great scarp, which is buried 40 feet in debris, was laid bare by Mr. Maudsley in 1874, and reported on to the Palestine Exploration Fund by Colonel Conder. Professor Macalister believes this rock scarp and the tower bases to be Solomonic. If he be right, it follows that there must have been an important city needing such fortification, on the traditional Zion. (See " *A Century of Excavations in Palestine*," *pp*. 112-116.)

A quadrant-shaped pit, purposely left open in the cemetery, but protected by a masonry wall or balustrade, enables visitors to form some idea of the tremendous strength of the ancient defences of the City of Jerusalem at this point. A few of the stones of another tower at this point are still in position, and leading up to this second tower some of the steps of a rock-cut staircase. The wall exposed by Dr. Bliss ran Eastwards from this point and part of it, still exposed, can be seen in the enclosed Franciscan property just beyond the road leading from the Zion Gate down to the Valley of Hinnom.

In the several plots of land belonging respectively to the Franciscans, the Assumptionists and the Armenians, most interesting remains of ancient Jerusalem, both of Old and New Testament times, in the shape of streets, houses, mosaic pavements, tiles of the Tenth Legion, and artificial cave dwellings have been discovered as well as a series of stone weights and Jewish measures of capacity found during these excavations. A valuable article on these weights and measures appeared in the "*Jewish Chronicle*," *August* 16*th*, 1912.

To return to the Fountain Gate. The discovery that the City wall from this point onwards did not join on to the dam, which was itself a rampart, but ran Northward along the West of the greater Pool of Siloam, remarkably confirms the statement of 2 *Kings xxv.* 4, that when Jerusalem was taken by Nebuchadnezzar in *B.C.* 590,

" all the men of war fled by night by the way of the *gate between two walls* "—evidently the Fountain Gate— " which is by the king's garden."

Six hundred and sixty years later, when in *A.D.* 70 the city was taken by Titus, and further resistance was hopeless, the leaders of the insurgent Jews also tried to escape in the same direction, but failed (*Josephus, Wars, Book viii.* 5).

CHAPTER XXXV.

ROM the road close to the " Fountain Gate " excavation, we have a good view South-east looking down the lower Kedron, " Wad-en Nar," or Valley of Fire, beyond the junction of the Valley of Hinnom. In the little plain caused by the junction lies " Bir Eyub," the Well of Job, anciently called " En Rogel " [195].

Of the two buildings in the centre of the picture that to the right is an open hall furnished with a " mihrab " or prayer niche showing that it is to be used by Moslems as a place for prayer. The other structure to the left of it, marks the position of the well, the opening to and drawing-hole from which is at its back. The well is called the Well of Job because of Mohammedan legends connecting it with the afflicted patriarch of Uz. (See *Folk-lore of the Holy Land, pp.* 17-22.)

The ancient Biblical name is " En Rogel," meaning " the Fuller's Fountain." It is mentioned in *Joshua xv.* 7 *and xviii.* 16 as one of the landmarks on the Northern boundary line of Judah, and the Southern of Benjamin. Although many centuries have elapsed since the ancient fullers or washermen plied their trade there, yet the marks remain in the vats still to be seen, cut into the

surfaces of the rock terraces, on the hill slope a few yards
East of the well. More than a hundred were counted
by the late Dr. S. Merrill, United States Consul, Jerusalem,
and by myself. On May 18th, 1900, I was the first to
notice them, and afterwards to draw attention to their
existence. A photograph of these ancient and peculiar

[195] A general view of Bir Eyub, or En Rogel.

[*Photo by Author*

fullers' vats as they appeared when I first discovered
them, is shown on the next page [196]. Near the
bottom of the photograph is the cave, now silted up, in
which, according to local tradition, the Patriarch Job
lived during his affliction.

The well itself is one hundred feet deep, the surface
of the water standing at a level of from seventy to eighty

feet below that of the ground outside. After heavy winter rains, however, it rises to the opening, and over-

[196]   Ancient fullers' vats near to En Rogel.
[*Photo by C. A. Hornstein*

flowing, rushes down the valley. The news of its overflow is hailed with gladness by the population of the Holy City and its surroundings, and is considered a promising sign of a good year, and as long as the stream flows, its banks are crowded by picnickers. It is not quite certain where all the water, which in the well itself is never exhausted, comes from. The annual rains indeed augment its store, but whilst some suppose that there is a living fountain at the bottom, others think that the water comes percolating into the well through chinks and cracks in its rock walls, and that the real source is somewhere higher up the valley, possibly under the site of the Temple itself, whence will flow the stream described in *Ezekiel xlvii*.

About 500 yards South of " Bir Eyub," is a spot called Ain Lozeh, with which is connected a staircase —now buried—leading down to a tunnel opened up by Sir Charles Warren, and reaching somewhat further than " Bir Eyub." It is about 2,000 feet long, entirely rock cut and has, at intervals of about 200 feet, flights of rock-hewn stairs leading up to the surface. It ends in a large and mysterious rock chamber North-west of " Bir Eyub," but quite unconnected with it.

From notices in the works of pilgrim writers and others, we gather that during by-gone centuries the " Bir Eyub " was several times filled up in war times, and afterwards cleared out. The last occasion on which it was concealed seems to have been after the Battle of Hattin, and on the approach of Saladin in *A.D.* 1187.

Our road now leads Westwards, up the traditional Valley of Hinnom associated in Scripture with Tophet and the worship of Moloch. The rocky terraces and cliffs on our left are full of ancient sepulchres, originally Jewish, but during mediaeval times re-used as burial places, and also as dwellings for hermits and monks. Some of them are fairly large and contain chambers within chambers. This circumstance may have given rise to the Jewish tradition, mentioned in

[197] View looking Northward up the Kedron Valley.

[Photo by Author

Kimchi's Commentary on 2 *Kings xxiii.* 10, stating that " the image of Moloch was of brass and stood inside the innermost of seven chapels " (*Article on " Moloch," Smith's Bible Dictionary*).

The modern Greek-Orthodox monastery of St. Onuphrius contains several of these sepulchres, the most interesting being that with an entrance ornamented with carvings of clusters of grapes, etc. This, called by tradition " the Apostles' Retreat " from the legend that the eleven hid there when Jesus was arrested at Gethsemane, has been identified as " the monument of Ananus," the High Priest, mentioned by Josephus (*Wars, v.* 12, 2), as one of the landmarks on the line of the wall of circumvallation, raised by order of Titus, *A.D.* 70.

This particular sepulchre was used as a place of worship during Byzantine and mediaeval times. There are still remains of ancient fresco paintings on its walls and ceiling. Similar paintings may be seen on the rocks close to the convent of St. John of Chozeba in the Wady Kelt, and also at the monastery of Hajla (*Beth-Hogla of Joshua xv.* 6 *and xviii.* 19). All that I have been able to ascertain about St. Onuphrius is that he was a famous Egyptian hermit who never visited Palestine. Being badly off for clothing, he grew a beard so long that whenever he walked abroad, he was obliged to wrap part of it over his left arm, lest it should trip him up. In the monastery in the Kedron Valley, there is an old picture of him scantily attired in loin cloth and beard.

The rocky terrace, West of the Convent of Onuphrius is said by tradition to be " Aceldama," or the Potter's Field, " the field of blood " purchased by the Jewish priests, as a cemetery for strangers, with the thirty pieces of silver flung down by Judas in the Temple (*Matthew xxvii.* 3-10).

The ruin seen to the right of the convent enclosure is the " Chaudemar," or great burial vault where pilgrims who died in the Hospital of the Knights of St. John used to be interred in a deep rock-hewn pit. It was generally believed during the Dark Ages, that the earth hereabouts possessed the peculiar property of accelerating decomposition, and that it was also endowed with the strange gift of discerning the different national-ities of human bodies buried in it, and was wont to reject

[198] Entrance to rock tombs at Aceldama. [*Photo by Author*

the corpses of Romans.   Shiploads of this earth used to be conveyed to Europe to various cemeteries, such as the Campo Santo at Pisa, and at Rome (*Monroe, as quoted by Barclay, " City of the Great King," page* 208).

Several of the sepulchral caverns hereabouts have Greek inscriptions, generally + τιζ αγιαζ ζιων cut over their entrances.   A few have names such as Pachomios, or Thecla.   The longer inscription indicates

362

that from the Fourth to the Seventh centuries, Greek monks from the convent on Mount Zion, were buried here [198].

Up to the year 1908, two of these sepulchres were used as dwellings by Moslem peasants from Siloam, and about 1856, an explorer, visiting what he supposed to be a quite deserted tomb here, on entering an inner chamber, found, to his great surprise, that it was a magazine filled with copper cooking utensils, rolls of cloth and calico, saddlery, etc., which had evidently been stocked there by some local " Ali Baba " and his gang of robbers.

The road from " Aceldama " now leads Westwards up the valley to the " Birket es Sultan " and its surroundings, shown in the illustrations at the commencement of this work.

CHAPTER XXXVI.

EAVING the Jaffa Gate we pass the great pile of grey buildings which form the modern citadel of Jerusalem, on our left [199] and then immediately drive down the road along the Eastern side of the traditional valley of Gihon. We have on our left the steep declivity of the traditional Zion, crowned with the Southern extension of the Western walls of the modern city, the towers of which, at this point, for some reason or legend as yet unascertained, are known as the towers of Ghazza. Just beyond these towers, which end at the South-west corner of the city, are various Christian cemeteries and Bishop Gobat's school, the latter built upon the great rock-cut bases of ancient towers and the rock scarp of the city of Jebusite times. These remains have been described in Chapter xxxv.

On the other side of the road one passes the Jewish settlement of Jorat el Anab [200], so called from a small grove of zizyphus or ju-jube trees on the spot ; next, the old aqueduct from Solomon's pools, restored, as attested by a now buried and undated Arabic inscription, by the Sultan Mohammed Ibn Kelaun, one of the Baharite dynasty of Egypt, who reigned between 693 and 741 of the Hejra (*A.D.* 1293-1340).

The arches, now buried but clearly visible until a few years ago, over which this aqueduct crosses the valley, are, however, mentioned six centuries earlier by Arculphus, who visited Palestine in *A.D.* 697. This aqueduct, which is known as the "lower level one," to distinguish it from the great Roman work, traces of which we pass later on, and which was probably originally constructed by Pilate (*Josephus, Antiq. xviii. iii.* 2), was still in use until about the year 1880, and conducted water to the Temple-area. The aqueduct is now a ruin, and a scanty supply of water reaches the fountain lower down the valley, and also the Temple-area, through four-inch iron pipes laid down several years ago.

The Jewish settlements stretch up the hillside on the Western slope of the valley as far as the olive groves—amongst which is the recently discovered mausoleum of the Herodian family—and the Montefiore almshouses, with a ruined windmill at the back; whilst in the bed of the valley one passes a huge enclosure, nearly six hundred feet long, and called "Birket Es Sultan" by the natives, although local guides point it out to tourists as the lower pool of Gihon, a name which is wrongly applied.

Though first mentioned about *A.D.* 1170, as the German lake, probably because the great open cistern in its lower or Southern end is supposed to have been constructed by the German knights, it is doubtless a work of very great antiquity. The cistern is used to collect the rain-water from the adjacent rock terraces, and the waste from the above-mentioned iron pipes. Horses are washed, and Arab boys bathe in it, and then the stagnant, evil-smelling liquid is pumped into water-carts and used to water the roads. Though the dust is laid, yet the benefit is counterbalanced by the sickening smells, and by the mosquitoes, which doubtless cause much of the fever prevalent at Jerusalem during the summer months.

In the upper part of the Birket, a cattle market, or fair, is held every Friday [201], whilst on other days,

[199]   The Citadel of Jerusalem.   [Photo by Author

the terraces seen in the foreground of the picture are occupied by picturesque groups of people hard at work crushing potsherds, by rolling heavy rounded stones to and fro over them in order to make " hamra," with which rain-water cisterns are cemented. The carriage·

366

road runs round the Southern end of the pool, over the dam and past the Sixteenth century fountain built upon its centre. Here at certain hours of the day, poor people are allowed in summer to fill their vessels from taps fed by the iron pipes, whilst a pompous Arabic inscription informs us that " this blessed ' sebil ' was built by orders of our lord the great Sultan and magnificent Khakan,

[200] Jorat el Anab and the Citadel of Jerusalem.

[*Photo by Author*

the Sultan of the Arabs and Persians and Roum—the Graeco-Romans—the Sultan Suleiman Khan, son of the Sultan Selim Khan, at the date of the year four and forty and nine hundred." The date agrees with those on the present city gates and walls built by the same Suleiman the Magnificent, *A.D.* 1536-1542 [202].

[201] Birket es Sultan, shewing Cattle Market, Cistern, Dam and
Fountain, and British Ophthalmic Hospital.

[Photo—American Colony

As we turn round to the Western side of the valley, we look down Eastward into the valley of Hinnom, catching a glimpse of the Yemenite settlement at Siloam.

A winding ramp, or ascent, on the right leads to the road cut, probably by the engineers of Justinian, through the solid rock in order to enable the great columns of rose-coloured limestone for the buildings of that Emperor in the Temple-area, to be conveyed by oxen-drawn carts to their destination. Directly afterwards, we pass on the left that most valuable institution, the British Ophthalmic Hospital of the Knights of St. John, where thousands of patients, including many Jews, find relief.

A few minutes later finds us rapidly passing the Railway Station and German colony on our right, and on our left, the Hill of Evil Counsel, with the traditional tree on which Judas hanged himself [203], into the traditional plain of Rephaim, which of late years has been parcelled out into plots, where houses are being now rapidly built, and trees and vines planted everywhere. Thirty years ago, here was a great open plain, bare except when the summer crops were growing, and where any day you might see herds of gazelles racing along out of gun-shot range, and then stopping to timidly look at the passer-by. Now, owing to the railway and enclosure walls, they are no longer to be met with hereabouts.

About a mile away, on a hill-top to the West, we notice Katamon, the country seat of the Orthodox Greek Patriarch, where a chapel has been built over what the Greeks believe to be the grave of the aged Simeon (*St. Luke ii. 25, etc.*).

On the higher range behind, and a couple of miles from where one stands, one sees the Moslem village of Malha perched on its hill-top. The sheikh of this village has, it is said, a room fitted up with European

[202] Mural Inscription of Suleiman the Magnificent.

[*Photo by Author*

furniture and a piano, the gift of the railway company as a token of appreciation for help received from him during the construction of the line from Jaffa. No one in the village can play the piano, or ever uses the furniture, still, to have a room fitted up in European style is considered a mark of distinction.

Away to the South-west one notices the bare hill-tops of the mountains of Bether (*Canticles ii.* 17), and nearer at hand, about half a mile distant, the white stone houses and blue smoke of Beit-Sufafa, which once was a hospice of the Knights Hospitallers. One writer on Palestine (*Williams' " Holy City," vol. i. p.* 69) also identifies it, rightly or wrongly, with " the Sapha of Josephus, where Alexander the Great on his march from Gaza to Jerusalem, with the avowed purpose of destroying the latter city, encountered a host arrayed in other arms than those that he was accustomed to meet ; the whole multi-tude of the Jewish people, clothed in white, with garlands in their hands—the priests in their sacred vestments of fine linen, headed by the high priest, arrayed in his robes of purple and scarlet, and the mitre with the golden plate emblazoned with the incommuni-cable Name of the God of Israel. On beholding them, the humbled monarch, to the amazement of all his retinue, approached alone, prostrated himself before that Name, saluted the representative of the Most High, and promised protection to the Holy City, where His Presence dwelt."

Thus, everywhere, as we proceed on our journey, we find interesting associations, some historical and others legendary or traditional, or specially invented for credulous pilgrims. Here, on the right, is an enclosed olive-grove, surrounding a large house, on the spot where, according to the Greeks, Benjamin was born

(*Genesis xxxv.* 16-18), and therefore called " Kast Benjamin "—whilst an ancient cistern on the left, its mouth enclosed within the circle of a stone pipe from the aqueduct of Pilate, is pointed out as the Well of the Wise Men, because it is said to mark the spot where, after leaving Herod, they to their " exceeding great joy " recognised, by its reflection in the water, the guiding star which they had lost sight of, when they turned aside to Jerusalem to seek direction at the Temple-gate and in the Palace-hall.

[203]   Tree of Judas.   [*Photo by Author*

To allow our horses to take breath, we halt at the convent of St. Elias, where, under the united shadows

372

of an ancient olive tree and a modern telegraph pole, pilgrims are shown the depression made in the surface of the rock by the weight of the weary Tishbite, when he rested under a juniper tree in the wilderness of Beer-Sheba, three days' journey to the south of us. By

[204] The Tomb of Rachel.   *[Photo—American Colony*

the road-side, is a stone seat, lately built by his widow in memory of the famous artist, Holman Hunt.

A fresh start is now made, and almost immediately afterwards we get the first glimpse of the truncated cone of the Frank Mountain, or the Herodium, where Herod the Great was buried, and where his grave may probably yet be discovered ; and also of Bethlehem.

After passing Et Tantoor, where a Roman Catholic order supported a hospital before the Great War, but now only a hospice ; and the field of peas which were turned into stone because the owners refused some to the Virgin ; and where, about 1857, the last fierce fight occurred between some Turkish troops and the Ta'amireh Bedouin, one halts at the Tomb of Rachel [204], the appearance of which is changed since the Bedouin graveyard adjoining it was walled in.

In former years at this place, before the present good carriage road was made, it was customary for Jews to come out and stay overnight, and the missionaries of the London Jews' Society were wont to pitch tents close by, where they received Jews and other visitors, with whom they often had most profitable intercourse. Nowadays, however, it is no longer worth while doing this, as the Jews come here for an hour or so, only just long enough to perform their devotions, and then hasten back to Jerusalem.

The Tomb of Rachel consists of a whitewashed " ewan " or hall, used as a mosque, and therefore furnished with a " mihrab," or prayer-niche, to show Moslems the direction of Mecca, and, connected with the hall by a door, an inner and dome-covered chamber, in the centre of which a great block of masonry plastered over and whitewashed, is the cenotaph covering what is supposed to be the actual Tomb of Rachel. Here

Hebrew prayers are gabbled over, not in unison, but every one according to his or her own time and liking.

The visitor can often see Jews passing long threads of divers coloured wool round the cenotaph, and reeling off others which have already been passed round it, and which, having been thus hallowed, are then considered as most efficacious for use as amulets

[205] Dislocated stone pipes of Roman syphon.
[*Photo—A. S. Hanauer*

to protect sick persons, especially women, from danger. There are a great many oil lamps burning in the room, and the general atmosphere is often so bad that one is glad to escape into the open again.

Just beyond the Tomb of Rachel, the road divides, a branch turning off to the left towards Bethlehem, and in the fork thus formed there have been found traces of the aqueduct of Pilate already mentioned. Just at this point the road crosses the valley by a syphon formed of huge blocks of perforated stone, or stone pipes [205]. Some of these have been broken out of their places and smashed up, whilst on others which have been spared,

[206] Lower Pools of Solomon.   [Photo—C. Raad, Jerusalem

I have had the satisfaction of detecting traces of ancient Latin inscriptions, which, when examined by competent authorities, turned out to be the names of centurions who had command of the different bands of workmen who constructed the aqueduct. Similar Latin inscriptions have been found in England on the ruins of Roman fortifications.

Proceeding on our journey we pass the extensive olive-groves that lie between Bethlehem and Beit Jala, a large Christian village which is identified by various authorities with the Zelah or Zelzah of the books of Joshua and Samuel (*Joshua xviii.* 28 ; I *Samuel x.* 2), and also the

[207] Upper Pool of Solomon and Castle.　　　　[*Photo by the Author*

Giloh of Ahithopel's story (2 *Samuel xv., xvi., xvii.*). The population, mostly Christians, and originally of the Greek Church, are notorious, like those of many other Palestinian and Syrian Christian villages, for the readiness with which not only individuals but whole families exchange one form of Christianity for another whenever circumstances, such as the likelihood of obtaining the protection of some foreign consulate, or getting their military taxes paid, seem to render such a change advisable.

As far back as the early days of the first missionaries of the London Jews' Society in Palestine, we read in the journals of Dr. Joseph Wolff as follows :—" The people of Beit Shallah offered to me to embrace the faith of the Inglees if I would pay 1,500 piastres, less than £15 sterling, tribute to the Pasha of Damascus " ; and " soon after the arrival of the Anglican Bishop (Alexander) in Jerusalem, they offered themselves, through their sheikh, as Protestant converts ; but as no negotiation was entered upon, the sum required for this transaction—or transition—must remain unknown " (*Williams*' " *Holy City*," *vol. ii., page 572, text and footnote*).

Under such circumstances it is not a matter of surprise that in our day both Latin and other missions should have been most successful in proselytizing from amongst the ranks of the Orthodox Greeks at Beit Jala, and that more than one imposing " mission " school and church are conspicuous amongst its stone buildings.

The country around Bethlehem [208] and Beit Jala is very remarkable for its productiveness, and, during recent years, many of the once bare hillsides have been reclaimed, terraced, and planted with olives, figs and vines, the verdure of which makes the landscape very beautiful.

Leaving behind us the former Protestant German Orphanage, now used as a lunatic asylum, one soon comes in sight of the village of El Khudr or Mar Jirius (St.

George) to the left. The great building conspicuously towering above the fellah dwellings is a church and

[208]   Bethlehem.   [*Photo—C. Raad, Jerusalem*

convent of the saint of that name and people from the whole countryside used to bring such of their relatives as were insane to this place to be cured. A few minutes later one passes the well-known Pools of Solomon [206 and 207].

Concerning this remarkable place, it can only be written that the old Saracenic castle guarding the pools and springs is, I believe, the direct lineal representative, in all probability, firstly, of the tower of Edar, or the flocks (*Genesis xxxv.* 21) ; and secondly, and at a much later date, of the habitation of Chimham (*Jeremiah xli.* 17).

In the Ain Atan, one of the four springs rising in its proximity, we may easily recognise the name Etam, which was that of the fountain whose waters supplied the Temple at Jerusalem, and also of the city Etam of Judah. This city, mentioned as a town which, lying apparently between Bethlehem and Tekoa, Rehoboam, fortified together with them and others (2 *Chronicles xi.* 6), is probably identical with the ruin " Khirbet el Khoch."

We pass this on the way from the pools to the village and beautiful valley of Artass, with its peach, pear and other fruit orchards and vegetable gardens winding away Eastward, like a river of verdure between high and barren limestone hills toward the now desolate and utterly ruined site of Herodium. This place received its water supply through the rock-hewn aqueducts, the traces of which may easily be followed along either side of the valley.

The name Artass, or Urtass, is said to be a derivative or a corruption from the Latin " Hortus," and was given to the place in mediaeval times, because it is supposed to be identical with that where Solomon had his famous gardens at Etham (*Josephus, Antiquities viii. ch. vii.* § 3 :

[209] Church and Convent of the "Hortus Conclusus"
at Artass.

[*Photo—American Colony*

and Ecclesiastes ii. 5, 6). During the Crusading period it probably belonged, at least in part, to the Knights Hospitallers.

At the head of a valley coming in from the South-west there exists to this day, the ruin of a great building, on one of the stones of which can be noticed a well-carved cross of the famous military brotherhood. As this ruin is called Deir el Benat, *i.e.,* " Convent of the Maidens," it is conjectured that it may have been a nunnery belonging to the sisterhood which is known to have been connected with the order.

Just where the valley above mentioned joins the Wady Artass, a nunnery and church have been recently built inside an enclosure. The nuns, who hail from South America, call themselves " the Sisters of the Hortus Conclusus," *i.e.,* the Enclosed Garden, the reference being to the passage in the Song of Solomon, iv. 12, in which he compares his beloved to such a garden.

The institution is ostensibly an orphanage for Roman Catholic girls ; besides which, the sisters do some dispensing and nursing amongst the fellahin [209].

If the unwritten, or traditionary history of this part of the country is to be credited, the Moslem village of Artass was an important place during the latter part of the Sixteenth century and for a long time after. When Suleiman the Magnificent constructed or restored the lower-level aqueduct from the pools to Jerusalem, he is said, by the peasantry, to have exempted the Artasihs, or Artassites, from the payment of any taxes, on the condition that they were to guard the aqueduct and pools and keep them in repair.

Many who are interested in the modern Jewish agricultural colonies in Palestine, may perhaps not be aware of the fact that the first germ of these was undoubtedly " The Agricultural Manual Labour School," a work of faith started in Artass about 1849 by a band of American enthusiasts, led by a lady named Mrs. Minor, and in co-operation with Mr. Meshullam, a Hebrew Christian, some of whose descendants still own gardens and houses in the beautiful valley. The first report of the institution was printed in America. It was entitled " Tidings from Jerusalem," and passed through several editions.

[210] Tombs of Joseph of Arimathaea and Nicodemus.

[Photo—American Colony

[See Chapter vi. pp. 62-63.   Chapter xxxii. p. 331.]

CHAPTER XXXVII.

A S a fitting conclusion to our "Walks," I now proceed to briefly explain the historical evolution of the City, illustrated by a series of specially drawn plans which I have prepared. On well-known Egyptian monuments and documents dating back to the Fifteenth century *B.C.*, Jerusalem is mentioned by the name of Uru-Salima, which means "the strong, sound, impregnable city," or "the city of peace, or security." Of peace, because of its strength, which ensured security to the citizens. It was a hill fortress garrisoned by Egyptian troops, and probably occupied much the same position as that of the present citadel between the head of the "Maktesh" valley, where the pool of Hezekiah now is, and the upper valley of Hinnom.

The City was also known as "Jebus," or rather "Yebus." This name, as is shewn by Colonel Conder (" *The First Bible*," *pp*. 34, 35), is derived from the ancient Akkadian, and signifies "town of safety," or "of rest." "Hence it appears that the two names of the city, which were used simultaneously, were of the same signification, ' Jerusalem ' being Amorite or Semitic, and ' Jebus ' the Hittite or Mongolic title of the town." This leads us to suspect that the inhabitants, not counting the Egyptian garrison, were a mixed race, a suspicion which is confirmed by Scripture. We are told respecting the population, in *Ezekiel xvi.* 3, 45, " Thy father was an Amorite, and thy mother a Hittite." " Your mother was an Hittite, and your father an Amorite."

It was probably an agricultural community, cultivating the surrounding hill-terraces and also the well-watered " King's dale," where Melchizedek met and blessed Abraham, and dwelling, like many of the modern fellahin of Siloam, in rock-dwellings on the slopes of Moriah, south of the present Temple-area and also on the declivities of Zion, west of the Tyropoeon. In times of danger they would retreat to and find shelter in, the fortified acropolis, or castle on the Western hill.

When the Israelites took possession of Palestine, the children of Judah ravaged these low-lying settlements with fire and sword (*Judges i.* 7, 8), although they belonged to the territory of Benjamin, and the population was afterward increased by a colony from that tribe. "And the children of Benjamin did not drive out the Jebusites that inhabited Jerusalem : but the Jebusites dwell with the children of Benjamin in Jerusalem unto this day " (1425 *B.C.* circa. *Judges i.* 21).

Forty years later, " Jebus, which is Jerusalem " was still " the city of a stranger " (*Judges xix.* 10-12). The Jebusites were not subdued till the time of David, who took the lower part of the city by force (*Josephus, Antiquities vii.* 3, 1-2). The fortified town on the heights holding out, was at last taken by

Joab and his men, who got into it through the Tsinnor, translated " gutter " (2 *Samuel v.* 8), probably an underground passage or drain. In the year 1837, their exploit was successfully imitated by the Fellahin, who obtained possession of modern Jerusalem in a similar manner.

Having taken the City, David and Joab united the upper part to the lower by building walls, North, West and South. When David died, 1016 *B.C.*, the whole circumvallation was incomplete, there being [*Plan* 212] a gap or " breach " on the South-eastern side, or " Millo Quarter." This was filled up by Solomon, who executed the plans of his father, and having built the Temple on the summit of Moriah, and a palace, just South of the Temple, rounded off the work by building Millo, and repairing " the breaches of the city of David his father " (1 *Kings xi.* 27).

The use of the term " Zion," and " Daughter of Zion," as an appellation for the whole city of Jerusalem, comprising the city of David, the Millo quarter, Temple and palace-buildings, probably began at this time, and is adopted by Prophets, Psalmists and Evangelists when speaking of the earthly Jerusalem and the Jewish nation as types of the Heavenly City and the Church of God. For instances see *Psalms lxv.* 1 ; *lxxxiv.* 7 ; *xcvii.* 8 ; *Hebrews xii.* 22 ; *Revelation xiv.* 1.

As the city increased in extent both Northward and Southward during the reigns of the successors of Solomon, fresh fortifications were added. We are specially told of such towers, gates and walls having been erected by Uzziah, Jotham, Hezekiah and Manasseh (2 *Chronicles xxvi.* 9 ; *xxvii.* 3 ; *xxxii.* 5 ; *xxxiii.* 14). Remains of these walls, South of the Temple were first discovered by Sir Charles Warren. Another portion was, later on, found by Professor Guthe about 1882, and this portion has quite recently been again exposed and more thoroughly examined by Professor Macalister and Rev. Garrow Duncan. It has been reported on in the Press as *a new discovery*, though, as a matter of fact, it is shown on the plan at the end of *Benzinger's "Hebraische Archaologie," Tubingen,* 1907. By order of the British Department of Antiquities, a tower and bastion of this wall have been left exposed as " a national monument."

In the reign of Josiah 634-610 *B.C.*, there was a special quarter, called the " Maktesh," or " mortar hollow," which was frequented by foreign merchants, silversmiths, and jewellers (*Zephaniah i.* 11). This has been identified, in great probability, with the deep hollow now occupied by the Pool of Hezekiah, the Muristan, and the three bazaars, and in all periods subsequent to that of the Jewish kings was, as it is still, the chief centre of commerce and traffic inside the city walls. [*Plan* 214] shews the probable extent of the city at the time of the Babylonian Captivity (588 *B.C.*), when the Temple, palaces and city walls were destroyed. When, at the close of the Seventy years' captivity, the children and some of the older people amongst the exiles, returned, the Temple first, and later on the outer walls, were re-built on the old foundations, *but not the palace.* Hence the extent of the city was much the same as it had been at the time of its destruction by Nebuchadnezzar.

[*Plan* 215] shews the site of the city in 429 *B.C.*, as restored by Nehemiah. It was practically the same in the time of our Lord (*A.D.* 33).

[*Plan* 216] shews the Temple-area enlarged by Herod, who included in its quadrangle the space to the south, where the palace had stood South-east of the Temple ; and part of the Millo Quarter south of the Sanctuary; in fact, the space which we have several times mentioned as extending from Wilson's Arch southward to the South-west angle, and thence as far as the Double Gate. Along and inside this, West to East, stretched his great Stoa, or Hall, with its three cathedral-like aisles supported on a hundred and sixty-two mighty columns. Herod's palace, castle and gardens were on the Western hill. Fig. 1 on this diagram shews the possible position of the High Priest Annas' palace ; Fig. 2, that of the Asmonean palace and Herod Agrippa's house ; Fig. 3, the council-chamber, close to the gate Shallechet ; Fig. 4, the Xystus ; and towards the lower left hand corner the site of Caiaphas' palace, in mediæval times occupied by the Church of St. Peter and the Cock-crowing.

At the destruction of Jerusalem by Titus, *A.D.* 70, the whole city was destroyed with the exception of the West wall of the Upper City, which was preserved that it might serve for the protection of the Legionary Camp [*Plan* 217], established on the hill top. This portion of the City is now occupied by the Citadel, the compound of the London Jews' Society and the Armenian and Jewish quarters, and the three towers, Phasaelus, Hippicus and Mariamne.

For an interesting account of this Legionary Camp I must refer the reader to the valuable article of the late Sir C. Wilson in the Palestine Exploration Fund " Quarterly Statement " (*April*, 1905), and also to his book " Golgotha and the Holy Sepulchre " (*pages* 142-148).

Roman and foreign merchants and such Jews as had taken no part in the war, would settle down amidst the ruins of the ancient city for purposes of trade. It is not likely that Jewish or Christian settlers would have elected to take up their abode in close proximity to the pagan squatters. It seems, therefore, that the very ancient tradition is extremely credible, that the early Christians, who returned from Pella, settled to the South of the city, where in the Thirteenth year of the reign of Hadrian, *A.D.* 130, a Christian church and seven Jewish synagogues existed (*Williams'* " *Holy City*," *vol. I. page* 206 *and footnote*). As a matter of course, both Jews and Christians would settle as far as possible from the pagans, who, as seems very likely, lived just north of the camp close to a temple of Venus erected on the spot where the Church of the Sepulchre now stands. After the insurrection headed by Bar Cochba, had been quelled, Hadrian rebuilt Jerusalem and called it Ælia Capitolina. A temple to Jupiter was erected on the site of the Jewish Temple on Moriah, and the city was adorned with colonnades and various fine edifices. Its walls ran, in all probability, on exactly the same lines as do those of the modern city.

The plans shewing the courses of the different torrent-beds traversing the rock-site of Jerusalem, and also the extent of the city walls during various periods of its history, were drawn over photographically reduced copies of a plan shewing the position of the walls of the modern city; and given to me several years ago by the late Dr. Merrill, United States Consul, Jerusalem.

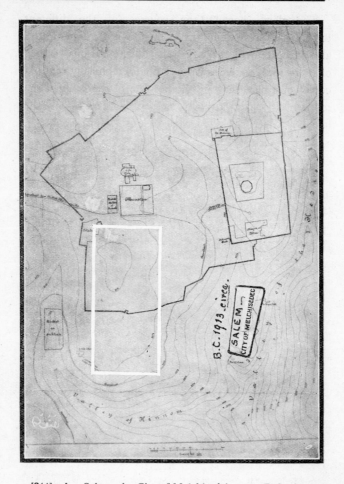

[211] **A.** Salem, the City of Melchisedek, 1913 *B.C* circa.

NOTE.—*The space in the white frame represents approximately the ground occupied by later pre-Davidic settlements.*

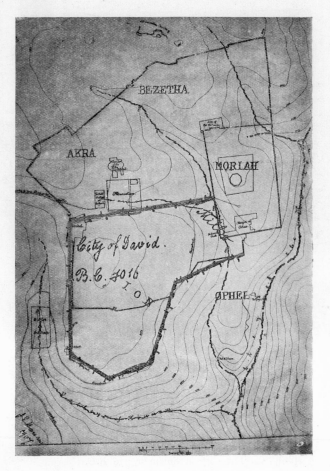

[212] **B.** City of David, 1,016 *B.C.*

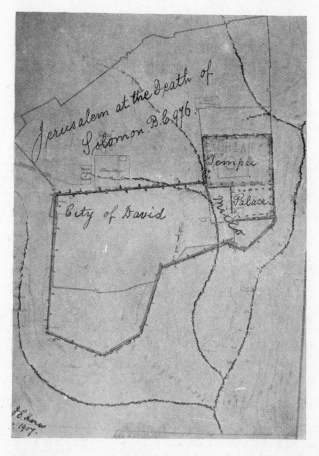

[213] C. The City of Solomon, 976 *B.C.*

394

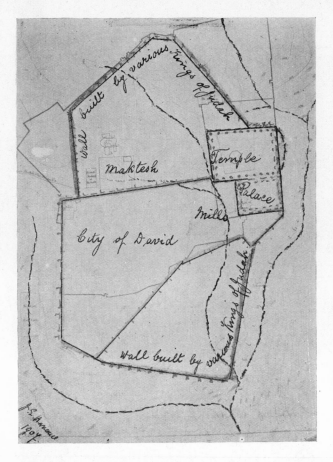

[214] **D.** Jerusalem at time of destruction by Nebuchadnezzar, 588 *B.C.* (City of Zedekiah).

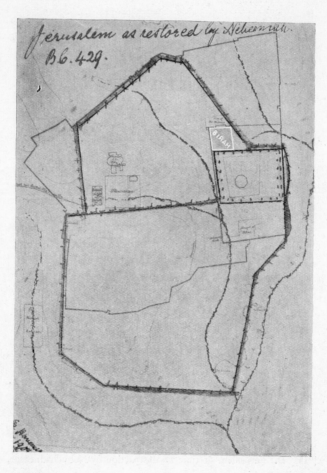

[215] E. Jerusalem as restored by Nehemiah, 426 *B.C.*

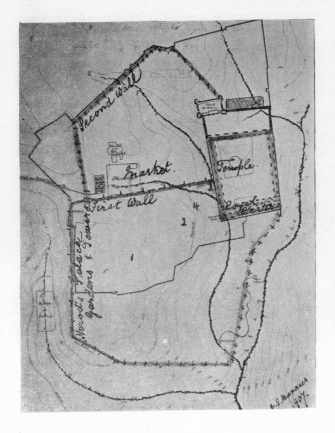

[216] F. Jerusalem in the time of Our Lord.

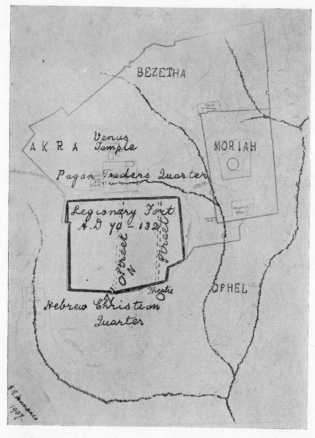

[217] G. Legionary Camp at Jerusalem, *A.D.* 70-132.

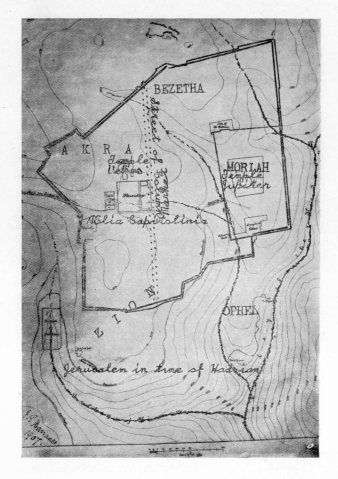

[218] H. Aelia Capitolina—which practically followed the lines of modern Jerusalem.

399

CHAPTER XXXVIII.

The Vessels and Furniture of the Temple of Jerusalem.

HE question as to the present location of the Holy vessels belonging to the Temple of God at Jerusalem is one that still awaits answer. It is known that the Ark of the Covenant was not carried to Babylon by Nebuchadnezzar, about *B.C.* 600, but so far as we possess any record, it has never since been seen.

According to 2 Maccabes ii. 4-7, the Tabernacle, the Ark, and the Altar of Incense, were, by Divine command, hidden by Jeremiah the prophet in a cave on Mount Nebo, and " *as for that place, it shall be unknown until the time that God gather His people again together, and receive them unto mercy*." Influenced by this statement, about the year 1859 the leader of a small German sect, having settled his followers in the Holy City, started off alone on a pedestrian tour to Moab, in search of the Ark, and has not been heard of since.

There are those who believe the Ark to be buried somewhere in Jerusalem, and some years ago, I had submitted to me for perusal, a very learned essay, written in German, to prove that it will be found buried under the ruined charnel-house of the Knights of St. John at the traditional Aceldama. In order to demonstrate the correctness of his theory, the erudite author, a Swede, came here in person, armed with a spade, in order to dig for the relic ! As he only stayed a short time, and no more has been heard of him, it is presumed that he was not particularly successful.

As to the rest of the Temple furniture, everybody knows that the consecrated vessels that were saved from the conflagration of the second Temple, *A.D.* 70, were carried by Titus to Rome as trophies, and displayed in his triumphal procession, after which they were portrayed on the monumental Arch in Rome still bearing the name of the conqueror, and the preservation of which witnesses to the truthfulness of Josephus, and teaches the danger of slighting and mis-using religious privileges.

The subsequent history of the furniture thus taken to Rome is very interesting. The golden vessels and implements were laid up in the Temple of Concord of Vespasian, whilst the scrolls of the law and the purple veils were deposited in the Imperial palace. In the reign of Hadrian, the golden plate engraved with the Name of the Eternal, which had adorned the forehead of the high priest, was seen at Rome by Rabbi Eleazar, the son of Joses, a contemporary of Rabbi Akiba, *A.D.* 135.

In the Twelfth year of Commodus, *A.D.* 191, both the Temple of Concord and the Imperial palace were, it is said, destroyed by fire, and many varied and costly treasures perished in the flames. It appears, however, that the sacred vessels of the House of God were rescued, as in the Fifth century we find them often and unhesitatingly mentioned (*Williams' " Holy City," vol. i. page 191, and footnotes*).

[219]   Ancient Bronze Vessel found in Cyprus.

[Photo by Author

We may conclude that they had been saved from destruction, and securely laid up in the public treasury at Rome, where they were found when Alaric, king of the Goths, plundered Rome, *A.D.* 410. He does not seem to have removed them all; for when, Forty-five years later, Genseric, king of the Vandals, sacked the Eternal City, among the other spoils he carried to Africa, were the holy vessels of the Jewish worship, which remained in Carthage nearly Eighty years, till the victory of Belisarius restored them again to the Romans, *A.D.* 455. That portion of them, however, which had been, as above related, taken by Alaric, was carried to Carcassonne in Languedoc.

Many of them are said to have been adorned with green stone, and their fame exposed the place to a vigorous siege by the army of Clovis. It was, however, unsuccessful, and when the town was relieved by Theodoric the Goth, the rescued treasures were, apparently, carried to Ravenna, and nothing more is known about them. Those which were recovered from Carthage by Belisarius, were exhibited in a triumphal procession at Constantinople; just as, Four and a half centuries earlier, they had been at Rome itself.

This fact of their having been thus displayed at Constantinople is attested by Procopius (*De Bello Vandalico, lib. ii. ch.* 9, *vol. i., page* 255), who was secretary to the Emperor Justinian, and an eye-witness. He relates, circumstantially, that a certain Jew, having noticed the sacred vessels amongst the spoils, told one of the officers of the Emperor that they could not be brought into the palace without grave danger, nor be safely kept anywhere but at the place where Solomon had originally dedicated them. He represented that it was for this reason that Genseric had been allowed to take Rome, and that in turn the Vandals had been conquered by the Romans.

Frightened by this statement, Justinian immediately sent them to Jerusalem, where he had built two churches— those of the Divine Wisdom and of St. Mary—within the area of the ancient Temple, as well as others elsewhere.

There is some reason for thinking that they may have been carried off again, this time by the Persians, who in A.D. 614, took and plundered the Holy City ; but there is not sufficient proof for this opinion. Two different local traditions point to their still being hidden in the Holy City. In the first place we have the fact that no orthodox Jew resident in Jerusalem will dare to set foot inside the ancient Temple-precincts, because he believes that the sacred vessels are still buried there, and if he be so unfortunate as to tread over the spot his death will ensue during the course of the year.

In the second place, we have the popular local Christian statement that somewhere under the pile of buildings connected with the Church of the Sepulchre, there is a secret vault containing, beside the holy vessels, untold treasures. In conversation with the late Dr. Schick, who was a most competent authority, I was informed that such a vault really exists. It was described as being provided with a heavy iron door, which is hidden behind some painted work, and is provided with three locks, each of which is closed by a special and different key. Each of these three keys is in the charge of a different bishop of the orthodox Greek Church, and the vault cannot be opened until these three dignitaries agree to meet together for the purpose, each producing his own key. This reminds us of an incident that occurred in Crusading times. ' (*Besant and Palmer's " History of Jerusalem,"* *chapter xiv. page* 384.)

Whether these popular ideas be correct or not, it is unfortunate for the authenticity of these interesting relics, which, as we have seen, have travelled from Asia to Europe and Africa, and back again to Asia, that the author of the book of Maccabees clearly describes the complete spoliation of the sacred treasury at Jerusalem by Antiochus Epiphanes about 170 *B.C.*, and that he carried the spoils to Antioch. Amongst them, special mention is made of the golden candlestick, the table of shew-bread, the golden altar of incense, the vials and flagons, the golden censers and precious vessels, as well as the veils of scarlet and fine linen.

Nor is there any doubt that such sacred vessels as were returned from Babylon, and those that had been dedicated by Ptolemy Philadelphus, *B.C.* 285, fell into his hands; for we are expressly told that " he emptied the Temple of its secret treasures, and left nothing at all remaining," and we nowhere find any evidence that these vessels were subsequently restored. On the contrary, we learn from 1 *Maccabees v.* 48-51, *and Josephus, Antiquities xii. vii.* 6, that Judas Maccabaeus, on the purification of the Temple, after its desecration, provided it with *new* vessels and altars and veils, and these therefore, must have been those which were taken into Rome by Titus, the fortunes of which we have told.

Whether these, or indeed any of Solomon's or Herod's vessels for the service of the Sanctuary still exist, is a matter of serious doubt, but a fairly recent discovery in

Cyprus aroused great interest amongst antiquarians, as it proves that in other places, furniture and vessels of analogous pattern to those of the Jewish Temple were in use and may yet be discovered, especially if made of bronze or copper.

Bible students will remember that in Solomon's Temple, besides the great brazen sea, there were ten round lavers of brass, placed on square and wheeled bases (1 *Kings vii.* 27-39). Five of these were ranged on the Northern and five along the Southern side of the court of the priests, and used for washing the sacrifices (2 *Chronicles iv.* 6; *Josephus Ant. VIII. iii.* 6). The bases themselves, or at least what remained of them, were mutilated by Ahaz, and carried away as plunder by Nebuzaradan, after the capture of Jerusalem (2 *Kings xvi.* 17; *xxv.* 13). No mention is made of their existence in the Second Temple, and therefore we may assume that they never were restored.

During the excavations in Cyprus, three curious bronze vessels were discovered, two of them exactly answering in their general features to those above described. The third differed in its having a triangular instead of a square base. Of the two first, one is said to be now in the British Museum. It is described as being in a defective condition, the wheels being destroyed as well as part of the structure. Its side-ornamentation shews female figures looking out of casements.

The other vessel is splendidly preserved, though covered with green patina or copper rust, proving its antiquity. It was till lately, perhaps is still, in the possession of

Mr. Caremfilaki, of Larnaka. Though in its dimensions, it is much smaller than those described in Scripture, in shape and ornamentation, as shewn in illustration [219], it is practically identical, except that the four birds at the corners do not seem to be mentioned in Scripture.

The reproduction is from the drawing in Professor Furtwangler's official report in the Transactions of the Royal Bavarian Academy of Science at Munich. (*Ueber ein auf Cypern gefundenes Bronze-gerat. Ein Beitrag zur Erklärung der Kultgerate des Salomonichen Tempels. Von A. Furtwangler. Vorgetragen in der Philos-Philol. Klasse der K. Bayer. Akad. d. Wiss. Munchen.*)

In Conclusion.

MY task has come to a close, for here our "Walks" through the streets, and around the walls of modern Jerusalem, must end. Our observations on things noteworthy have been by no means exhaustive. In the vicinity, though further afield, there are many places and monuments, such as Bethlehem, Bethany, the traditional Tombs of the Kings, Judges and Prophets, and the Convent of the Cross, etc., of which full descriptions may be found in every Palestinian guide-book, or in the journal of every tourist in Syria.

We have sketched the changes by which the City attained its present area within the walls, and noted most of the still extant relics of different periods in its chequered history. Jerusalem, as we have seen, has been for four thousand years past undergoing a process of evolution and development. The transition is still in progress, and has by no means reached its last stage.

When I first entered it as a child, the Holy City was a torpid little Eastern town, consisting chiefly of ruinous, mainly one-storied old vaulted buildings occupying parts only of the space enclosed within the mouldering grey and brown Sixteenth-century walls; whilst the other portions were bare and waste fields of ruins, and the outside desert stretched up to the jealously guarded City-gates. Now all this is changed, and is still changing. Stately stone buildings, churches, convents, hospitals, schools, hotels and dwelling-houses fill up not only the area within the walls, but a great extent of country all around, for Jerusalem has become a large bustling and still growing City, whose gates are now " open continually," and " not shut day nor night."

If this were all, we might think that it is merely passing again through one of those prosperous periods or phases of its history, which have been more than once repeated during Roman, Byzantine, and even Saracenic pre-Turkish times. But there is one feature of its present condition by which it is specially distinguished from former ones. This is the predominantly, and steadily growing Jewish element in its population, and also in that of the country in general.

No Jews were allowed to reside within the walls of Ælia Capitolina, nor even in the Holy City of the time of Constantine. The favour shewn them by Julian the Apostate, who (*A.D.* 362), suggested and encouraged an abortive attempt to re-build the Temple, was not continued under his successors. The Moslems were more tolerant than they, but the Crusaders, always glad of an opportunity or a pretext for ill-treating the Jews and " sacrificing them to their father, the devil, for the honour of the Cross and the Church," discouraged their residence in Palestine.

In *A.D.* 1163, when Rabbi Benjamin, of Tudela, visited the country, its whole Jewish population amounted only to 1,900, all counted, and everyone poor, as compared with the large and prosperous communities in neighbouring Moslem States, for instance, 3,000 " many of whom were rich and learned men " at Damascus ; " 2,000 warlike and independent Jews " at Palmyra ; and 3,000 in the important mercantile town of Alexandria.

At this time there were only 200 Jews, dyers, in Jerusalem itself, and they lived " under the tower of David," close to the present Jewish quarter within the walls. They were considered inferior to the Moslems, and by the laws of the Latin Kingdom were not allowed to hold any land (*Rey,* " *Colonies Franques,*" *page* 104 ; *Conder,* " *Latin Kingdom of Jerusalem,*" *page* 242).

In *A.D.* 1187, that is twenty years after Rabbi Benjamin's visit, we find the Jewish community restricted to the out-of-the-way "Juiverie" or Ghetto in the Northeast corner of Jerusalem, behind and north of St. Anne's Abbey. With the expulsion of the Crusaders from the City, their condition seems to have improved greatly, so that in *A.D.* 1227, *i.e.,* forty years later, we find Nachmanides acquiring the well-preserved ruins of the Church of St. Martin, on the site of the present Great Perushim synagogue, for his people, and restoring it as a Jewish place of worship, owing to the Hebrews of the Holy Land having been strengthened by the arrival of numerous immigrants, headed, in *A.D.* 1201, by a party of some 300 rabbis from France and England (*Luncz's* " *Jerusalem,*" 1881, *Chronological table, page* 2).

This purchase of St. Martin took place just two years before Frederic II. obtained possession of Jerusalem by friendly treaty with the Moslems, in spite of violent opposition of the Pope and his clergy and the Templars and Hospitallers. This liberal-minded Emperor defied the interdict of the Pope and even did not scruple to have the monks of Acre flogged through the streets during Holy Week. The conditions made by the Emperor were such as must have seemed most pleasant to the Jewish community, accustomed to incessant insult and outrage at the hands of Papist Christians.

In *A.D.* 1492, the Jewish colony at Jerusalem was further strengthened by the arrival of refugees from Spain, and in 1846, when Rabbi Schwarz wrote his account of the Holy Land, he tells us on page 23 that there were then 8,000 Jews in Jerusalem, out of a total Jewish population of 28,000 in the whole of Palestine.

Now the Jewish element in Jerusalem is about ten times what it was then. The city is, to a great extent, Jewish. This is especially noticeable on Saturday, the Jewish Sabbath, when Hebrew shops are closed ; and as the peasantry do not find it worth their while to bring their farm produce to market on that day, the public thoroughfares generally regain the quiet Sabbath-air brought about originally by the influence of Nehemiah (*Chap. xiii.* 20-21) 445 *B.C.*

This remarkable re-gathering of the Jews to their ancient capital is very suggestive and cannot fail to rouse the attention of every thoughtful student of the Bible. It undoubtedly seems to indicate that the prophetic utterances concerning the final return of the Jews to their own land are being fulfilled literally, in our own days, and under our very eyes. They are returning— in unbelief, it is true—but actually re-peopling " the old wastes, the desolations of many generations."

These things should incite us not only to take an interest in the history and relics of the Jerusalem of the past, but eagerly to work with all our powers and talents for the welfare of the Jerusalem and its people of the present day, in full confidence that the Jerusalem of the future will be great and glorious, and the time fast approaching when, according to His gracious and faithful promise, the Lord will " arise, and have mercy upon Zion ; for the time to favour her, yea, the set time is come."

> " Already earth begins to hear
>   Old prophet-tones with int'rest new,
> And long foretold events appear
>   Swiftly unfolding to the view ;
> And Zion's hope, so long deferred,
>   Hastes to its glad fulfilment when
> According to His faithful word,
>   God will remember her again."
>
> *(Writer unknown).*

J. E. HANAUER.

Jerusalem, 1926.

WORKS OF REFERENCE QUOTED FROM
OR MENTIONED IN THE TEXT.

The Holy Bible.

Josephus' Works.

Ali Bey's Travels.

Antonnius Martyr—Pilgrim Text Society's version.

Archaeological Researches—Prof. Clermont Ganneau (Palestine Exploration Fund).

"Beit el Makdas," Dr. Schick.

R. Benjamin of Tudela—Bohn's Edition.

Bible Dictionary, Hastings.

Do.   Smith's.

Biblical Researches, Robinson.

"Century of Excavations in Palestine," Prof. Macalister.

"City of the Great King," Dr. Barclay.

Colonies Franques, Rey.

Contrasts and Teachings of the Catacombs, Benjamin Scott.

Crusader's Almanac for 1906.

Early Travels in Palestine, Bohn.

"Eutychii Annales," Pilgrim Text Society's version.

"Felix Fabri," Pilgrim Text Society's version.

"First Bible," Colonel Conder.

Folk-Lore of the Holy Land, Hanauer.

Glimpses of Bible Lands, Dr. Munro Gibson.

"Golgotha," Mommert.

Do.   Sir C. Wilson.

"Hebraische Archæologie," Dr. Benzinger.

"Heilige Land," Rabbi Schwarz.

History of the War in Syria, Hunter.

"Holy City, Jerusalem," Dr. Russell Forbes.

"Holy City," Williams.

"Horae Hebraeice," Lightfoot.

Isaiah and Zephaniah, Jerome.

Jerusalem, 1881, Luncz.

Jerusalem, Ancient, Dr. Merrill.

Do.   Thrupp.

Jerusalem, Ancient and Modern, Tenz.

Jerusalem, History of, Besant and Palmer.

Jerusalem, Latin Kingdom of, Colonel Conder.

Jerusalem, Recovery of (Palestine Exploration Fund).

Jerusalem, Siege of, Lewin.

Jewish Intelligence (L.J.S.).

Jewish Missionary Intelligence (L.J.S.).

Koran, The, Sale—Chandos Classics Edition.

Letters to the Seven Churches, Sir W. M. Ramsay.

Life of Jesus the Messiah, Dr. Edersheim.

Meistermann's "Father Barnabe Guide."

Modern Egyptians, Lane.

"Nach Jerusalem," Ludw. Aug. Frankl. 2nd vol.

Norman Chronicle.

Ordnance Survey Map of Jerusalem (1864-5).

Palestine Exploration Fund's Memoirs—

Jerusalem Volume.

Quarterly Statements.

Paris, Matthew (W. Watt's edition), Hodgkinson, London, 1640.

"Prospect of the Temple, &c.," Lightfoot.

"Psalms in Human Life," Protheroe.

"Ratisbonne, Father, Conversion of"—Granville Popular Library.

Saewulf—Pilgrim Society's version.

"Scriptores Angl."—Ap. Savile's—Hovenden's Chronicle.

Tales told in Palestine, Hanauer.

Talmudic Treatises "Middoth" and "Taanith" (P.E.F. Quarterly Statements).

Temple Services, &c., Dr. Edersheim.

"Uns el Jelil," Majr-ed-din's—(Arabic). Cairo Edition.

Zuallardo's Travels.

SPECIAL SCRIPTURE REFERENCES.

GENERAL INDEX.

GENERAL INDEX.

Meaning of some Arabic Names used in the Index.

Ain— Fountain.
Bab— Gate.
Birket — Pool.
Harat— Street or Quarter.
Khalif— Successor of Mahommed.
Kubbet—Dome.
Neby— Prophet.
Suk— Market.
Tarik— Way or Road.
Wad— Valley.

To Visitors to Jerusalem.

It is well worth your while to visit the Mission Centre of Church Missions to Jews (London Jews Society) close to the Jaffa Gate and opposite to the entrance to the Citadel.

This Society commenced work in the Holy City in the year 1820 and erected **Christ Church,** which was the first consecrated Church of England Place of Worship to be erected in Palestine and also in the Turkish Dominions, and the Church where Bishop Michael Solomon Alexander, the first Anglican Bishop in Jerusalem and a former missionary of the Society, first officiated.

Services are held regularly and a warm welcome is given to all visitors. Doubtless, many will be glad to worship in the Church actually within the City walls.

Adjoining Christ Church are the **Industrial Mission** premises where Printing work and Wood and Carpentry work is carried on. A fine selection of books, wood work, articles made from the really well-seasoned Palestinian Olive wood, curios and other articles are always on sale at reasonable prices.

In addition, in the compound is the **Girls' Day School** for the education especially of younger Jewish children.

The magnificent fully equipped **Hospital** maintained by the Society and which has been described by the Lord Bishop of London as **"probably the finest mission hospital in the World"** is situated about half a mile outside the city, close to the Jaffa road. The Hospital administers to about 1,200 In-patients and 15,000 Out-patients each year and is the wonderful outcome of the first attempt made by the Society in the year 1824. **This was the forerunner of all other Medical Missions.**

Very near to the Hospital is the **Boys' Boarding School** where a number of Jewish pupils are housed and educated under Christian influences.

The Society which is carrying on these Institutions in Jerusalem commenced with one station in London, in the year 1809, and the work has spread in these days to other Stations in England, Ireland, Germany, Holland, Roumania, Poland, Palestine, Persia, Egypt, Abyssinia, Morocco, Tunisia and Algeria.

Amongst its other helps to the Mission Field, the Society published the first **Hebrew New Testament** in 1817 and the **English Liturgy in Hebrew** in 1837.

Means alone limit the possibilities of the work.

_____

CHURCH MISSIONS TO JEWS.

The London Society for Promoting Christianity amongst the Jews.

Patron.
HIS GRACE THE ARCHBISHOP OF CANTERBURY.

Vice=Patrons.
Over 140 **ARCHBISHOPS** and **BISHOPS** of the **ANGLICAN COMMUNION.**

Headquarters of the Society :
16, Lincoln's Inn Fields, London, W.C. 2, England.

_____

See next page.

Some other Books on The Holy Land.

EVERYDAY LIFE IN THE HOLY LAND. By the late Rev. James Neil, M.A.   10s. 6d., postage 9d.

PALESTINE AND THE BIBLE. By the Rev. Samuel Schor, who was born in Jerusalem.   17th Edition. 85th Thousand.   1s., postage 1½d. ; Cloth Covers 2s., postage 2d.

PEEPS INTO THE HOLY LAND. By John Finnemore.   With twelve full-page illustrations in colour, by John Fulleylove, R.I.   2s. 6d., postage 5d.

HOW AND WHERE THEY LIVED IN BIBLE TIMES. With numerous illustrations.   By E. B. Trist.   2s. 6d., postage 4½d.

THE LAND WHERE JESUS LIVED. For Young People.   With 22 Illustrations.   By Gertrude Hollis.   3s. 6d., postage 4½d.

PEEPS INTO PALESTINE. By the Rev. James Neil, M.A.   Strange Scenes in the Unchanging Land, illustrative of the Ever-Living Book. 1s. 6d.   Cloth Covers 2s. 6d., postage 3d.

Also beautifully coloured Postcards of Palestine Views,   1s. packet of 10.

Book of Palestine Snapshots, 12 principal views, 3½ in. by 2½ in., bound in Suede,   1s.

Olive and other Wood articles made in Industrial Mission, Jerusalem.

Mother of Pearl from Bethlehem.

Olive Oil Soap from Mount Carmel, also Curios.

May be obtained from Headquarters—
16, Lincoln's Inn Fields, W.C. 2. London.